PHOTO DISPLAY

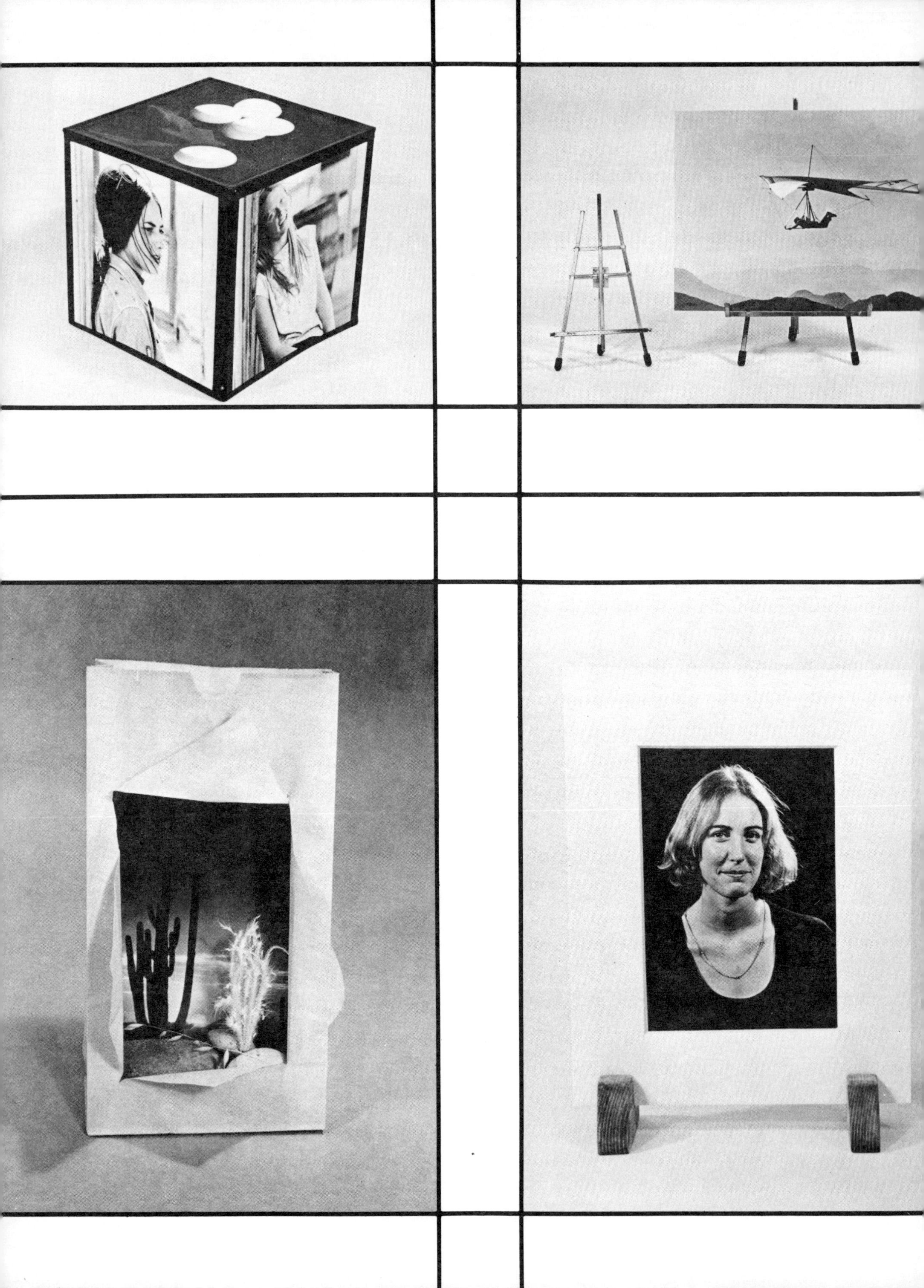

PHOTO DISPLAY

Bruce H. Mitton

Foreword by Tom C. Cooper

DOLPHIN BOOKS
Doubleday & Company, Inc., Garden City, New York
1980

Library of Congress Cataloging in Publication Data

Mitton, Bruce H. 1950–
Photo Display.

Bibliography: p. 125.
1. Photographs—Trimming, Mounting, etc.
2. Photographs—Conservation and Restoration.
3. Photographs—Albums. I. Title.
TR340.M57 770'.284
ISBN: 0-385-15538-7
Library of Congress Catalog Card Number 79–7874

Printed in the United States of America

First Edition

ACKNOWLEDGMENTS

I would like to thank my editorial assistants
G. Kay Casey and Kathryn E. Guenther
for all the help they gave me
in organizing this book.

FOREWORD

We are a visual generation. During our waking hours, we are literally bombarded with images: signs, papers, pictures, diagrams—and television. It has been estimated that the eyes of an "average" person focus on more than a hundred thousand images a day! Perhaps the word *bombarded* is especially appropriate, because for sure not all these images are pleasant or desirable.

It has also been stated that we are rapidly becoming visually illiterate. This statement is usually used by critics of television in issuing a warning that too much time is spent in front of the "boob tube."

I will not attempt to defend the viewing habits of today's society. But I will quickly and adamantly state that there is a growing segment of our population that is visually sophisticated. As editor of *Arizona Highways* magazine, a publication that relies heavily on photography, and as a photographic-gallery owner, I was in touch with many people who demonstrate a highly developed ability to enjoy, create, use, and display dynamic, interesting, and lasting imagery. These people vary in age and degree of education and are not just photographic artists. They are also mothers who wish to record and preserve a visual record of their children's lives, an executive who wishes to capture lighter moments of a sales meeting, a youngster who wants school pictures of his or her classmates. The range of visually aware people seems limitless.

We need only look at the growth of the photographic industry since that day in 1826 when the first photographic image was recorded to realize how much impact photography has on our daily lives. Americans alone spend billions on cameras, film, and processing and displaying their pictures.

Stand on the rim of the Grand Canyon and look around at the people hidden behind every type of camera imaginable. Or go to a high school graduation exercise and you'll observe that the event concludes with a free-for-all of posing, crowding, pushing, and bursts of light from electronic flash. So photography has become an integral part of our life-style, so much so that the total impact of photography in America can be best described as "explosive."

This brings us to the matter of using photographic imagery in our life-style. There are literally hundreds of books on how to improve picture taking, but most usually stop short of discussing how to use or enjoy the photographs. That's where this book begins.

Author Bruce Mitton has made an exhaustive study of the many techniques for displaying photographs. I believe this is the most comprehensive publication of its kind. When you have finished reading *Photo Display,* you will learn that there are seemingly endless methods of displaying and enjoying photographs. You'll also learn that many of these methods require little money and technical skills. The results can be very rewarding aesthetically, and perhaps give one a whole new appreciation of the visual world.

Finally, the question inevitably comes up: What makes a good photograph? The answer, of course, depends on the purpose for which the photograph is to be used. If that purpose is to provide a piece of decor for your own home, or to display treasured moments, then my answer is that a good photograph is one that *you* enjoy and appreciate today—and tomorrow, and the day after that.

TOM C. COOPER

CONTENTS

AUTHOR'S NOTE

Displaying photographs is not something new. What is, is the acceptance of photography as a source of decorative art for the home or office. I'm not quite sure why we have this sudden approval of photographic art for home and office decor, other than it is readily available and pleasing to look at.

Certainly the Eastman Kodak Company's advertising campaigns and book *Photo Decor* haven't been detrimental to the idea. Television and print advertising by Olympus, Canon, Polaroid, Minolta, and Kodak help emphasize picture taking. Trendwise, taking pictures is the thing to do.

Photography workshops and courses have been developed all over the country. People of every age are trying to learn how to take better photographic images.

Good pictures require a great deal of photographic knowledge, knowledge that isn't attained overnight, nor in a week or two of schooling. It takes repeated experience with some sort of camera—a lot of picture taking and picture analysis. What could you have done to make a particular picture better? Change the composition? the lighting? the type of film? the lens? exposure? or maybe the focus?

For the individual who is truly looking for photographic understanding, displaying one's own work will help make the photographic knowledge visible. In return, one should ask repeatedly, "Can the image be improved?" If not, you've reached the picture perfect. But how many perfect pictures do you have? Certainly not as many as each photographer would like to think.

On rare occasions, a photographic image will stimulate a human emotion. The heart may skip a beat; loneliness, joy, and even sorrow might be felt. Those are the photos I consider picture perfect. Fortunately such images are few and far between. If every photograph taken and shown were that stimulating, I'm afraid the world might be full of photographic indifference, as we all would become conditioned to the emotion a photograph might produce.

For now, we must be satisfied with the rare photo that produces human response, even when it's not our own work. We can be educated by our mistakes and learn from the pictures captured by others.

You, as an individual and as a photographer, can learn every time you click the shutter within your camera. As your picture-taking abilities improve, you can then take as much pride in showing your photographs as you do in taking good pictures.

Take as much pride in showing your photographs as you do in taking good pictures. . . .

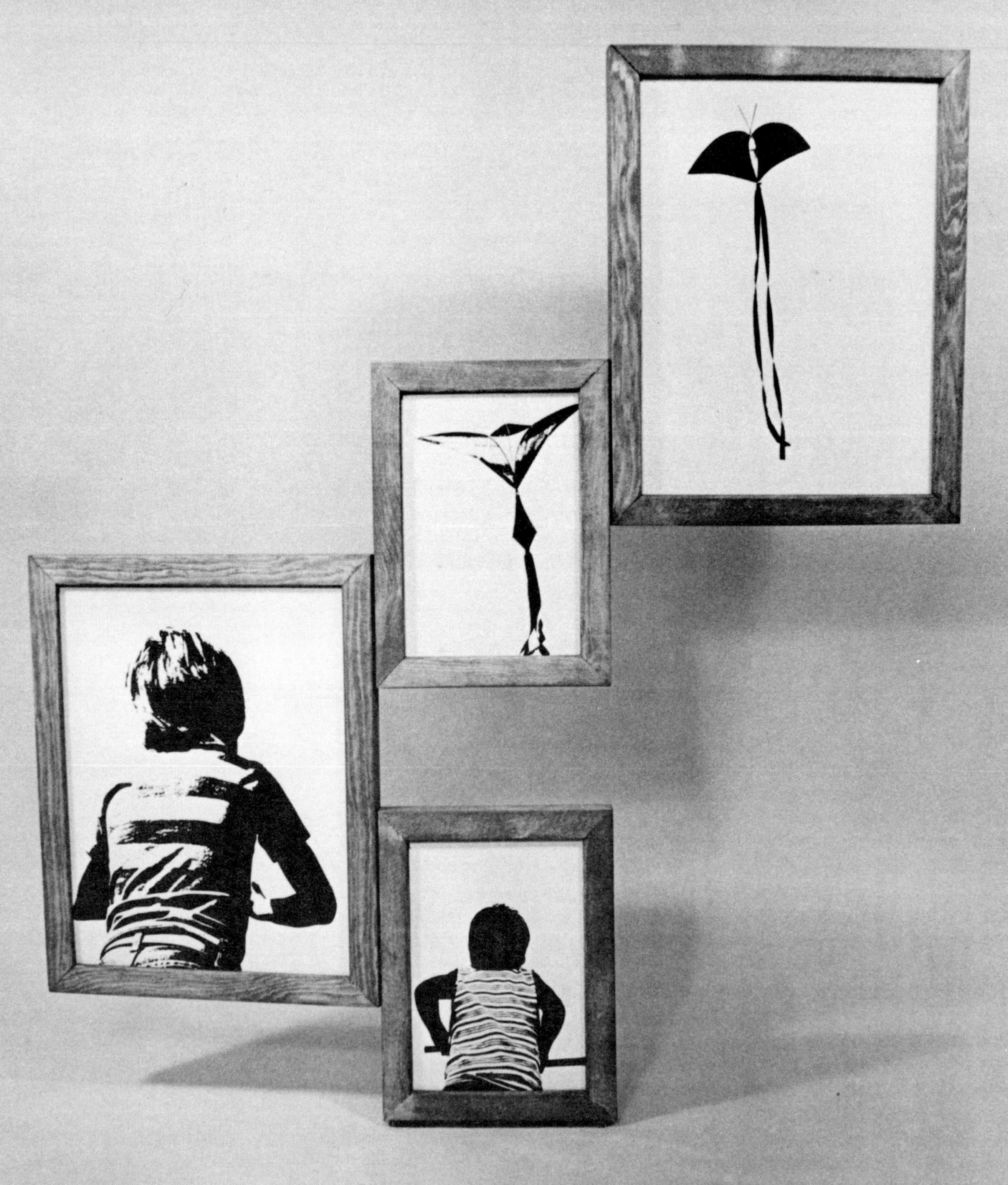

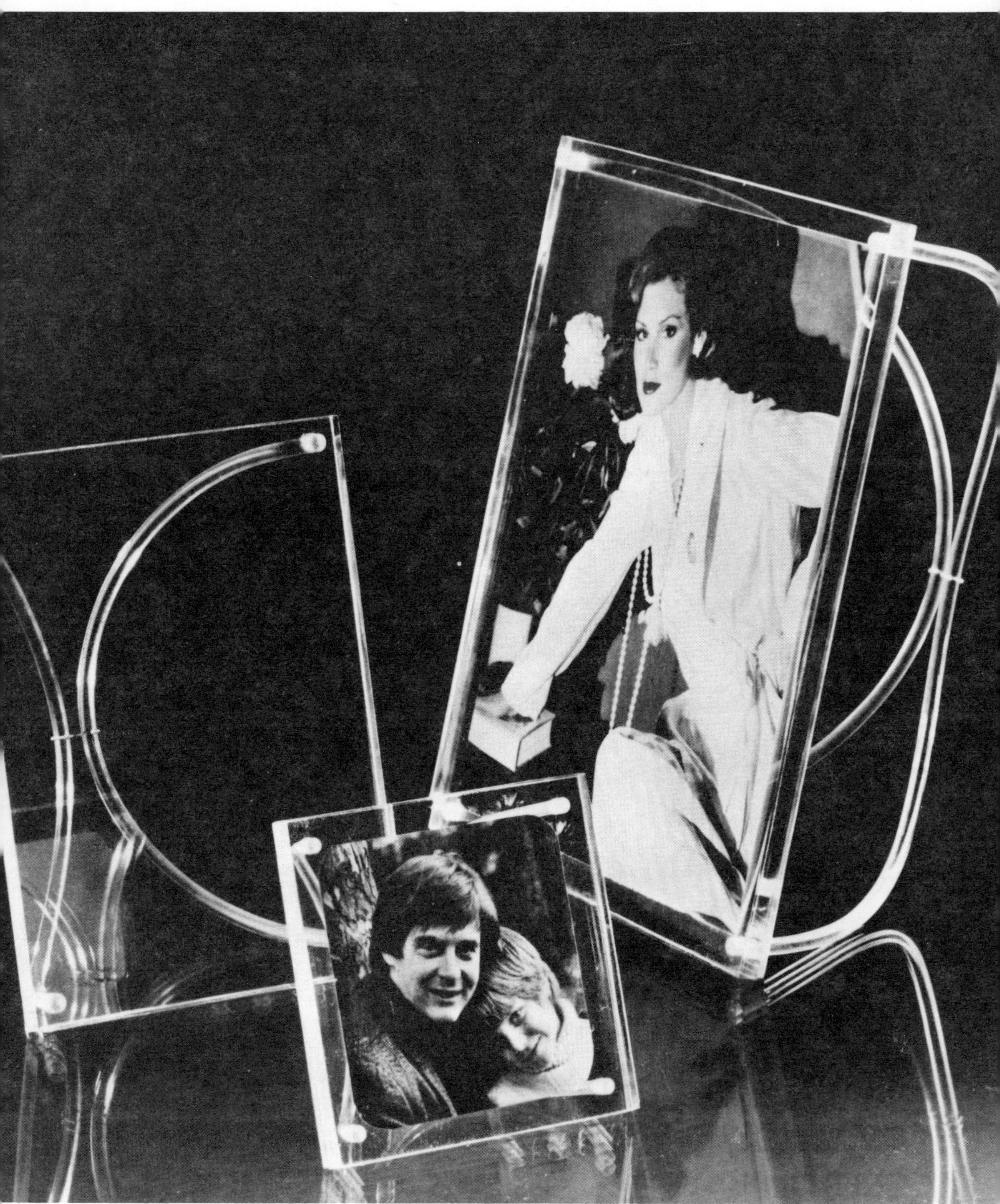

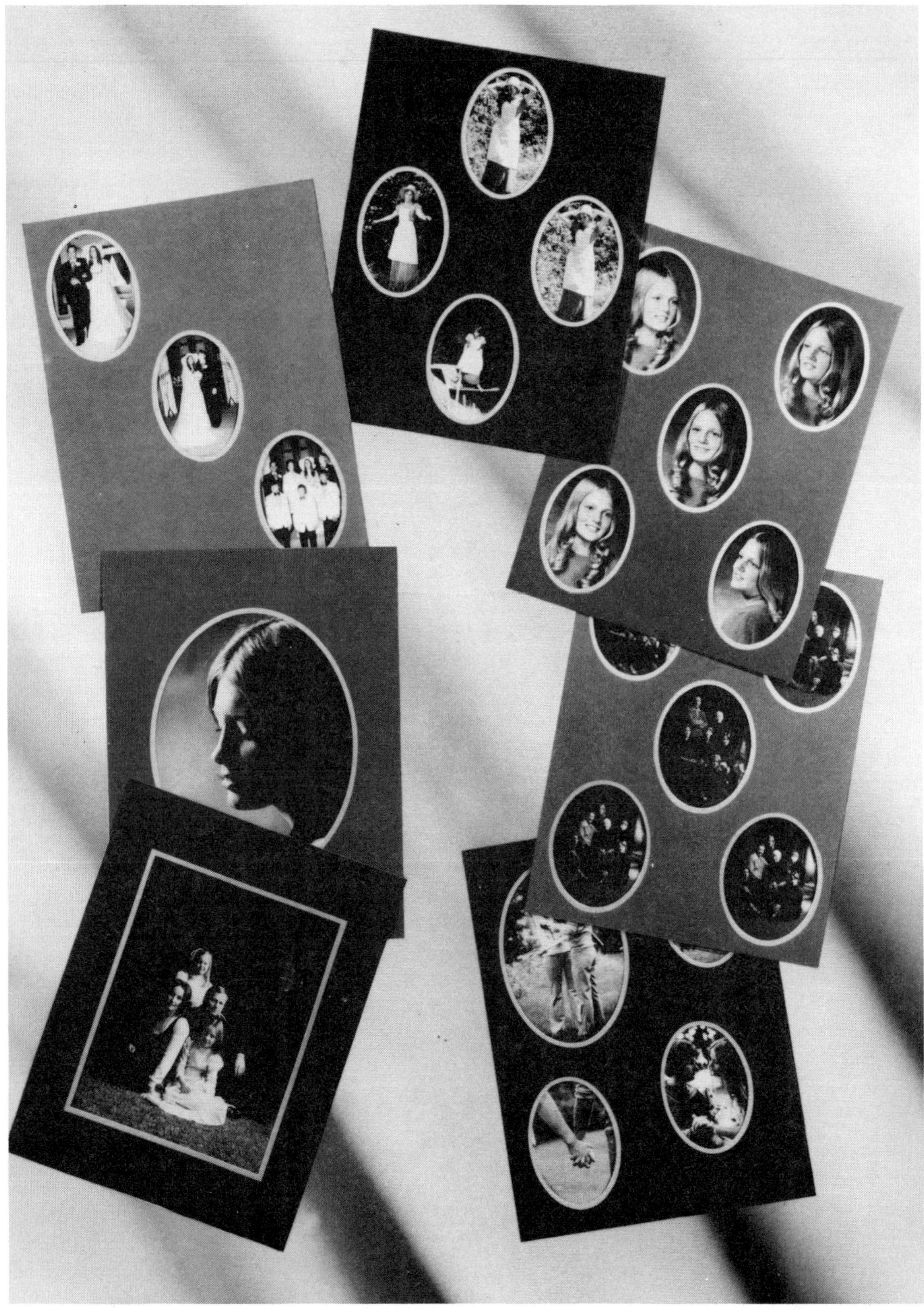

PHOTO DISPLAY

1

PICTURE PRUDENT

Photography has been clicking with popularity, reaching for a level of saturation. Taking pictures oneself and collecting prints by recognized photographers have been the thing to do. Now prints of all sizes and content are finding their way into interior design whether it be for home or office.

No longer do pictures have to be taken by the trained professional. Instead, anyone who has a desire to take quality pictures can do so. Cameras are readily available, from the inexpensive to systems costing thousands of dollars. Names like Kodak, Polaroid, Olympus, Nikon, Minolta, and Vivitar have become household words. They are just a few of the camera and photo-equipment manufacturers located around the world.

Pictures are everywhere. They capture very special moments. As soon as the picture is taken, the image becomes history. Like written or spoken words, a picture can describe detail, provide documentation, preserve, and explain. In short, pictures communicate to those seeing the image.

The ability of a picture to communicate and capture very special moments is what makes photography so important. Time only goes forward, but there are people, places, and events everyone would like to remember at one time or another. Those special instances, captured on film, make one's life what it is. You can't go back. But memory can be brought back into focus by seeing a fragment of the past caught by a picture.

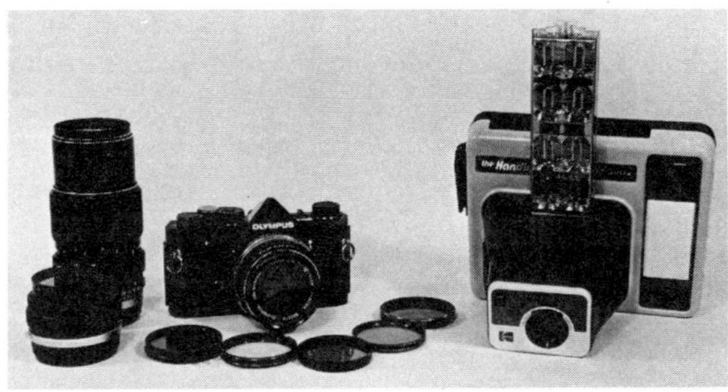

Cameras come in all sizes and shapes, including the interchangeable-lens 35mm and the aim-and-shoot Kodak Handle.

Capturing those special moments isn't expensive if you shoot one or two rolls of film a year. If you are like most people who enjoy photography, you take pictures every chance you get. The cost of film and processing gradually grows. The more pictures you take, the more money you spend on film and processing.

Your time and money are spent on photographic supplies; therefore your pictures should be considered an investment. Your returns on your investment are memories, smiles, or, simply, attractive pictures. Make the most of those returns and display and protect your photographs. Your favorite pictures should be shared with your friends, family, and, most important, yourself—the photographer.

Unfortunately, once a picture is taken, developed, and printed, only a very few people get to see the finished product. The picture is stuffed in a drawer, closet, cookie jar, or who knows where.

This book deals with various ways to display and, when necessary, store photographs—all types of photographs: large, small, black-and-white, color, and even slides. The object of this book is to help you get the most out of your photographs and negatives, providing you feel that your pictures are a visual pleasure that can be shared only if they are seen.

The majority of printed pictures returned to you from your photo dealer are not very large. They may be only three inches by five inches. The instant pictures some cameras produce are even smaller. But no matter what size the picture, it can be displayed effectively and provide visual enjoyment.

Displaying photographs is for the imaginative. There are no limits to how you can display your best photos, as you will see from some of the illustrations in this book.

Your very best photos can be made much larger than those you are accustomed to seeing. If you have the money and desire to have a large print made, it can be done just as easily as shooting the picture. What may be bothersome is finding a quality lab that will convert your print, negative, or slide into the results you want. The photo dealers and labs are in the business of helping you with your photographic needs, so don't be afraid of demanding the finest quality they can produce. If the first photo lab doesn't provide quality work, try another.

No matter how good your camera, not all the pictures you take will be good. They may appear to be good to you, but we will have to assume the majority of people looking at that same picture might feel it could be better. Even professionals, who earn their living from taking pictures, do not get perfect images every time they point a camera. However, they do eliminate their mistakes and exhibit only their best work. That's how they manage to succeed in a highly competitive business.

Unlike professional photographers, many of us find it difficult to part with the pictures we take. Unwillingness to discard bad photos is one of the pitfalls of anyone who takes pictures. There's a fear of discarding a special instant that is seldom, if ever, captured again. It's easier to stick both good and bad photos in a drawer, closet, or shoe box. You'll have to decide which is the lesser of two evils: holding on to bad pictures that will probably never be seen again or throwing those pictures away and promising yourself to do better the next time you use your camera.

Obviously, you can't display every photo you've ever taken. There just isn't that much room in your home. You can store the better-than-average photos, and you can certainly display your very best.

Before you start reaching for your favorite pictures for display, you need to know a few things about picture quality, appeal, and problems that might occur if not guarded against. Let's start with answering a most difficult question.

WHAT IS A GOOD PICTURE?

Photographic judgment is based on what appeals to the viewer. Either you like the picture or you don't. If a picture appeals to you and most of the people who look at it, it must have some good qualities.

To help judge the quality of pictures, we can categorize them to some extent. First, good pictures are generally technically superior. This means the exposure, composition, focus, and quality of the negative, print, or slide is as good as it can be with whatever camera and processing facilities you have available.

Next, a picture's content can be classified. Most pictures you take will fall into the category of being either visually pleasing, historical, documentary, having artistic appeal, or maybe a combination of the categories.

The majority of pictures the amateur takes fall into the historical or documentary category. This means photographs of family members and possi-

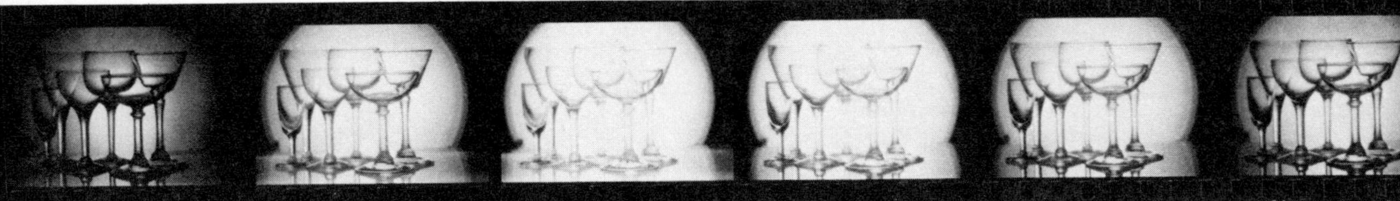

By bracketing at least one or two exposures, one picture should be the best you can take.

bly travel shots. As a photographer, the amateur is trying to catch moments he wishes to remember later on in life. Many of the pictures you see hanging on the walls of various homes are of family members. Billy on his first birthday, Billy at five, Billy graduating from high school, Billy graduating from college, Billy getting married, Billy's wife and the new baby, and so on.

A picture's content shouldn't make one picture better than another, providing the technical quality is the same. Unfortunately everyone has his own subject preferences. These inherent prejudices often sway one's judgment of a photograph.

The most important thing to remember is that pictures are good as long as you like them. You may have to tolerate criticism that can be both constructive and destructive. But if you learn from the criticism, your picture taking should get better.

The subject of a photograph is not nearly as important as the technical quality. Any subject can be good as long as the focus, exposure, and composition are as correct as they can be. Good technical quality is most difficult to obtain. There are numerous books written on the subject explaining how to obtain the best quality with the camera equipment you have available.

Professional photographers—not all, but most—help eliminate their chances for technical error by "bracketing" their pictures. Bracketing is nothing more than varying the exposure, or amount of light striking the camera's film. Pros will shoot a great number of pictures of the same subject but change the shutter, or aperture, of their camera for each shot. They may also change their angle of view, hoping to get the best possible picture by the time they are finished.

Let me give you an example. I have done photography for various publications and have seen staff photographers in action. On one occasion, a photographer had just received an assortment of slides from processing. There were fifteen rolls of 36-exposure slide film in the shipment. I asked if I might watch the editing of the photos, a rare privilege. Professional photographers dislike acknowledging the fact they don't get good pictures all the time. By watching the editing, I would get to see the good with the bad.

The photographer laid out the first roll of slides. There were thirty-six pictures, all of the same thing, but various exposures, lenses, and angles of view were used in the picture taking. There were technically and visually good images on that particular roll of film.

The remaining fourteen rolls of film were photographed the same way. Each roll of film was of one subject, with various exposures and lenses used.

What the photographer had was fifteen very good pictures, which could be used for publication. He had shot 540 pictures to get fifteen good ones. Success seemed inevitable.

As far as I could see, it was a costly photo assignment. The magazine's management didn't care, as long as the photographer captured the pictures needed to fill some of the pages of the publication.

You or I couldn't do what the staff photographer did for the assignment. It's just too costly. I do bracket my photographs, but not to that extreme. Two or three pictures per subject should be adequate, providing the camera is in proper working condition.

The photographer was going to have to edit his collection of slides to decide which fifteen pictures were the very best. He would edit his photos, just as you should edit yours.

PHOTO EDITING

Editing photographs is nothing more than getting rid of the ones that are far from good. The first step is to pick out the ones with the wrong exposure. Exposure is the amount of light striking the film. Prints as well as slides or negatives can be either too dark or too light.

The easiest way to judge exposure is to compare photos or slides. Some will be too dark, showing very little of the image. Others will be too light, looking washed out.

The incorrectly exposed pictures are either too dark or too light. Don't fool yourself by saying you were trying to set a mood by making a noonshot photo look like night. Toss the incorrectly exposed photographs unhesitatingly into the nearest wastebasket.

Next, you can look for photos that are not focused correctly. Any photograph that looks a little fuzzy is out of focus. A seasoned photographer likes to use the term "soft focus." This is a nice way to say the picture is not as sharp as it could be. Once in a while, you may have a photograph that is good even though the focus is not as sharp as it could be. Keep that one, and throw the rest of the out-of-focus pictures away.

Finally, look for the pictures that have poor composition. The composition of a photo is the arrangement of the elements or subject matter. Composition varies greatly. A general rule you might want to use in judging photo composition is the "rule of thirds." It's not a law of photography that has to be used, but it does work for many pictures.

The tendency for beginning photographers is to put everything in the center of the film or the camera's viewfinder. This works, but often results in dull, unimaginative photographs. The dead-center syndrome can be alleviated by using the "rule of thirds."

To illustrate, take a pencil and divide a piece of paper into three equal parts, both horizontally and vertically (see diagram at right). The intersection of these lines gives you a choice of four focal points for placing the strongest and most interesting portion of the material being photographed. The rule can be applied to horizontal, vertical, and square pictures.

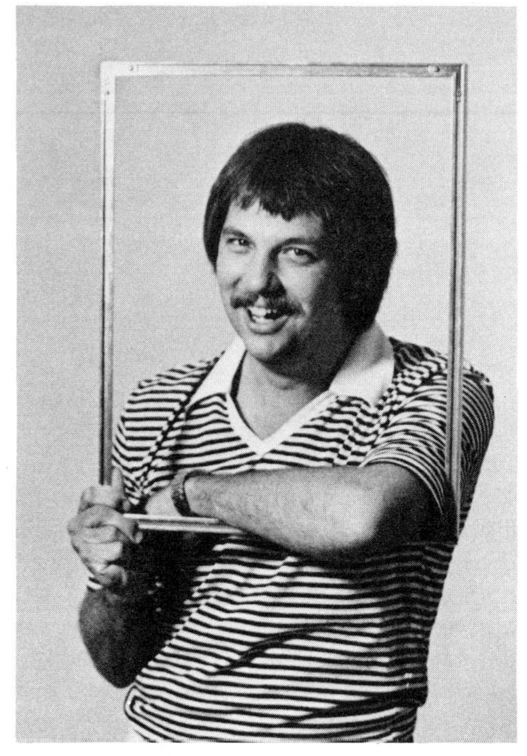

Some pictures may be slightly out of focus, but if it's a one-time shot you might want to keep it.

RULE OF THIRDS

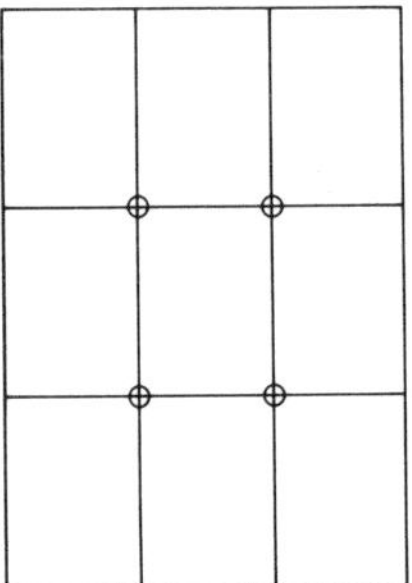

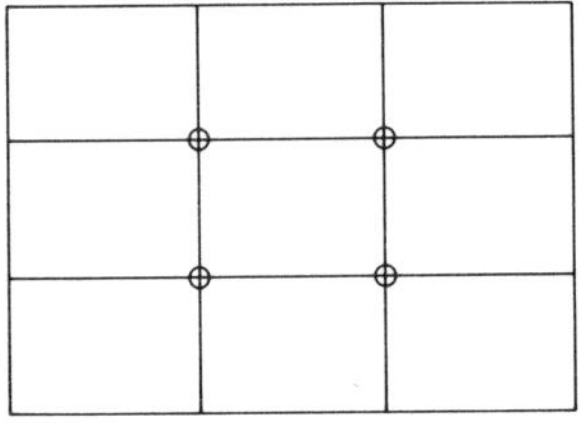

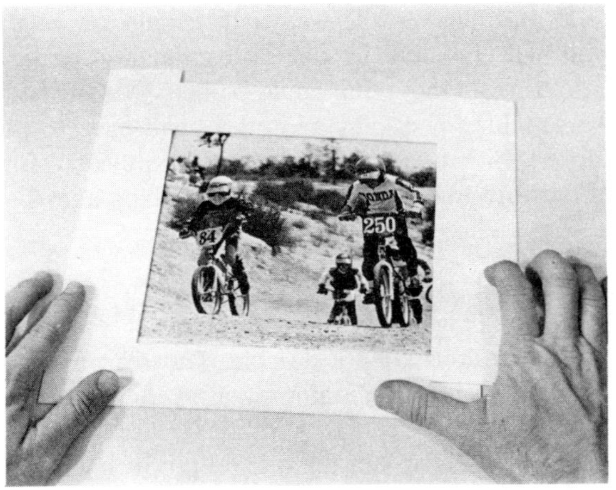

Cropping squares cut from cardboard will help you to decide a print's best composition.

Look at the whole picture when editing for composition, especially the background. Are there trees and telephone poles growing out of the heads of people in the picture? Are there distracting shadows? Are people cut in two, so they look funny? These are just some of the things to look for when judging the photo's composition. Good composition is definitely a matter of judgment. You'll have to be ruthless with yourself concerning what's good and what's bad composition.

Fortunately, you don't have to throw all the badly composed pictures away; some can be salvaged by proper cropping.

CROPPING PHOTOS

Cropping is the act of eliminating a part of the photo that detracts from the appearance of the picture. Cropping does have its limitations. You can't remove objects from the center of the photo, so constructive cropping is limited to the perimeter of the photograph.

You can construct a small set of cropping squares by cutting two wide L's from pieces of cardboard or construction paper. Then, by placing the cropping squares over the photo, you can move them around to see how the picture's appearance can be improved.

There's an easy way to crop many of the pictures you already own. A paper cutter or scissors will remove what is not needed in the photos. Of course, the photo will no longer be the size it used to be and may not fit as well in albums or frames as normal-size photos. (Do not cut pictures made with instant cameras. The film has a sealed backing that contains developers. If you cut this type of picture, the developers will leak out.)

Custom processing can also be used to crop photos. Take the picture and/or negative to a photo store and explain how you want the photo cropped. They will make a new print and crop the photo as best they can.

When editing, be sure to consider cropping photos before you throw your pictures away. What looks awful at first glance can be improved greatly by cropping. Slides can also be cropped to some extent (see Chapter 6).

As a general rule, to improve your picture taking, try to crop your photo when you take the picture. As you look through the viewfinder of your camera, consider what's going to be captured on the finished photograph. If there is a way to eliminate distracting objects, do so before you take the picture. Either move unnecessary objects, relocate the subject to be photographed, or move yourself and the camera to find a better angle of view, before clicking the shutter.

What you are doing is cropping with the camera. Nowadays, what you see through the viewfinder is what you get on film and the finished photograph.

By now you should have an idea of what makes a good photograph. The most important element of a quality photograph is the viewer. Either he likes it or he doesn't. You can improve the chances of the viewer's approval by considering the following.

1. Subject—Is it interesting, common, exciting, or prone to viewer's prejudice?
2. Composition—Are only the needed visual elements in the picture, or is it cluttered with unrelated objects?
3. Exposure—Are the tones or colors as close to reality as possible?
4. Focus—Is the focal point of interest in the picture as sharp as it could be?
5. Photographer approval—Do you really like the picture?

If you answer the above questions honestly, you will be able to distinguish quality photographs from those that could be better. Many will be suitable for display and others will have to be stored. Either way, the pictures must be cared for if they are to be enjoyed during the years ahead.

PICTURE CARE

Photographs are not durable. They can be easily damaged if care is not taken in their storage, handling, and display. Additional care must be taken with slides and the picture-producing negatives. Their small size makes them very susceptible to often irreparable damage.

Pictures themselves can be damaged in a number of ways. One of the most common methods is by improper handling. The results can be smudges, scratches, and tattered corners. Spilled beverages can cause unsightly stains on many prints.

Another source of picture harm is through chemical contamination. This can occur through poor processing of the finished prints. If all the chemicals used in development are not removed, stains, fading, or yellowing can occur. If you don't process your own prints, you'll have to rely on the know-how of the photographic lab you use. If you do your own darkroom work, you must take the time to process your prints according to chemical and photographic-paper instructions supplied by the manufacturer.

Another problem with photos is the paper they are printed on. Resin-coated instead of fiber-based paper is often used by processors because of its short drying time and ability to lie flat. However, the resin-coated papers have angered gallery owners who sell photographic prints at high cost. They worry about the buyer who may feel cheated when the resin-coated paper deteriorates from improper care. This paper, which is basically a plastic, may crack on the surface and destroy the image. On occasion, the actual image may peal from the backing used in the paper's manufacture.

Photo-paper manufacturers feel they can overcome any problems with added research, so resin-coated papers may eventually be the standard for print reproduction.

Unfortunately, prints (no matter on what type of paper) are susceptible to many chemicals found in the environment. Mounting boards and some adhesives can hasten a print's decline.

Even though a proper mount and adhesive are used, caution must be taken when handling the mounted photo, to prevent yellowing and ragged-looking edges.

Quality or historical photographs, like other fine art, need special handling to assure full return on the investment. Prints that are to be mounted and matted should be done with 100 percent cotton rag boards, to eliminate any contamination from residual acid compounds that can be absorbed from low-grade mounting boards and adhesives.

PRINT STORAGE

It's not possible to display all your photographs. If you are an avid picture taker, there isn't enough room on walls, shelves, albums, and so forth. Some pictures will have to be stored.

Special acid-free storage boxes and envelopes are probably the least expensive and most practical way of storing all sizes of mounted and unmounted prints. A storage system combining both envelopes and boxes will make for easy labeling and later retrieval of desired prints.

For the photographer who wants to store prints with the best possible protection, the metal, epoxy-covered Saxe print box is the answer. It comes in various sizes from 8×10 inches to 16×20 inches. An added ¼ inch on both the length and width makes for easy removal of mounted prints.

Another storage method for small prints is the use of photo albums. These booklike holders can be used for shelf storage and also offer limited display (see Chapter 2).

All types of vinyl or polyethylene holders are available for print storage and protection. They come in various sizes up to 8×10. Most of the plastic holders are prepunched for placing into three-ring notebooks and binders.

File cabinets, shoe boxes, and anything else you can think of will hold prints for storage. Successful storage depends not only on the protection offered but also on accessibility. Will the prints be easy to recover, once they are stored?

Depending on how many photos you plan on storing, a simple or elaborate indexing system will need to be developed. Alphabetical order,

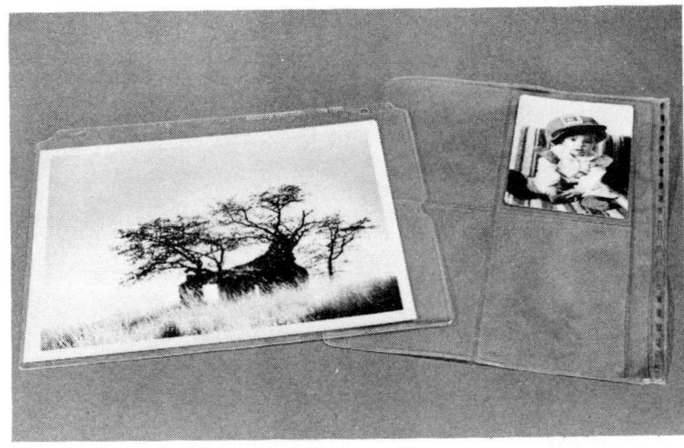

Vinyl pages come in all sizes for storing photographs.

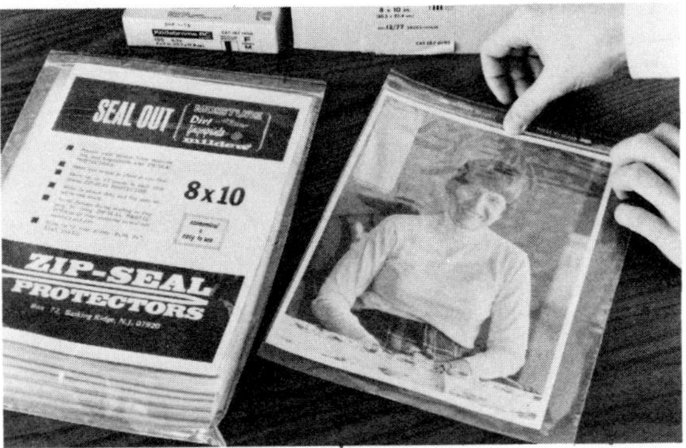

Plastic storage bags protect your favorite prints from moisture, dirt, and fingerprints. Photos courtesy Zip-Seal Protectors.

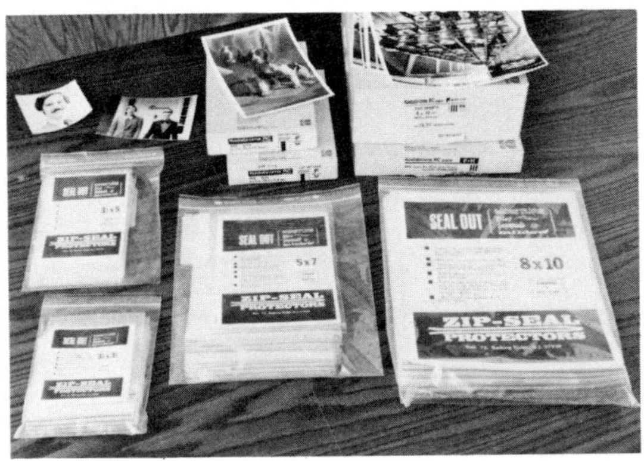

arrangement in categories, or even a simple numbering system will work. Indexing is time-consuming, but time-*saving* when it comes to print retrieval.

During storage, prints can be damaged if precaution is not taken to prevent envelopes containing prints from getting crushed or forced out of shape. Acid-free tissue can be placed between prints to prevent them from sticking together and to avoid damage to the prints' surface.

Once you decide on a storage and protection method that offers easy retrieval, you can concentrate on displaying your favorite photographs, knowing the rest are well protected.

NEGATIVE FILING AND STORAGE

Negatives are as important as your prints. If you are using negative-producing film, without the negative there wouldn't be a print. Negatives are usually small and very susceptible to dirt and scratches, so extreme care must be taken in their handling.

How you store your negatives is up to you. But keep in mind that you may need to retrieve a certain negative if you plan on having an enlarged or duplicate print made. You want to store your negatives so you can find them when you need to.

Within these pages, there are illustrations of various methods for storing and preserving your negatives. They'll give you an idea of what's available. A trip to a local photo supply dealer will give you additional ideas and help you to decide what method will fit your budget. The more negatives you have processed, the more sophisticated your storage and retrieval system will have to be.

One very economical method of negative storage is the envelope they and the prints are returned in from processing. You don't have to touch the negatives, but you do have to put some type of content label on the envelope. The envelope and negatives can then be placed in a file or box for storage.

A number of manufacturers offer notebooks with removable pages designed for holding negatives. Some have corresponding blank pages for subject identification.

Protective glassine or plastic filing envelopes are available for every size of negative. Once the negatives are placed in the protective envelopes, file holders can be used for organizing and labeling their content.

Small negatives are returned cut into strips of four, five, or more. Don't get file-happy and cut your negatives into individual subjects. You'll just be adding to the handling problem and increase chances for damage. Negative strips are small enough without making them even smaller.

The less handling of negatives the less damage

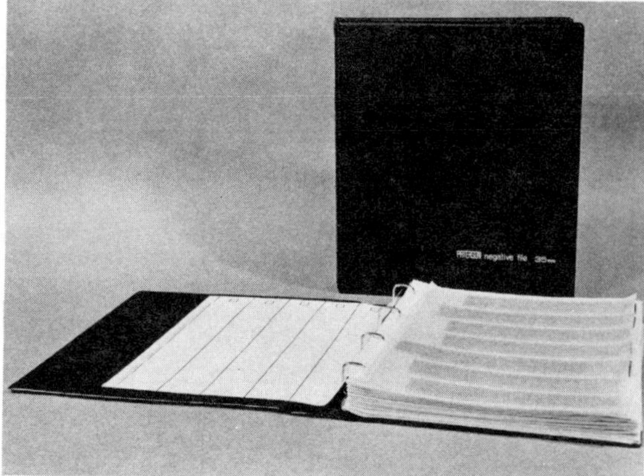

Specifically designed binders and negative-storage systems are available from photo supply dealers.

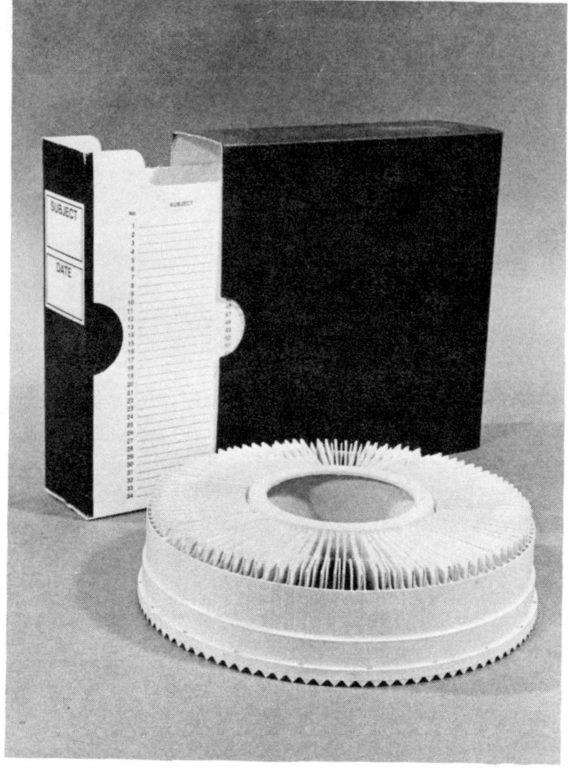

Slide trays with protective boxes work as storage systems.

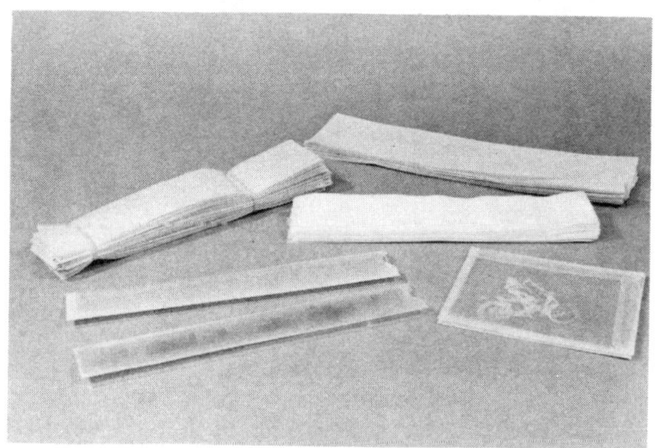

Glassine or plastic holders help protect negatives.

done. Choose or develop a system to fit your needs and, once started, keep it up to date by proper filing and labeling.

SLIDE STORAGE

Slides (transparencies) are almost as small as negatives, but they come with a protective mount for handling, and instead of a negative image, they offer a positive one.

Slides are generally used for projection on a screen, and they have to be inserted into some sort of tray or cube. Loading and unloading slides can be time-consuming. Once the slides are organized, you may want to store them in the projection tray or cube, so unnecessary removal and reloading is prevented. (Slide projection and organization are discussed in Chapter 6.)

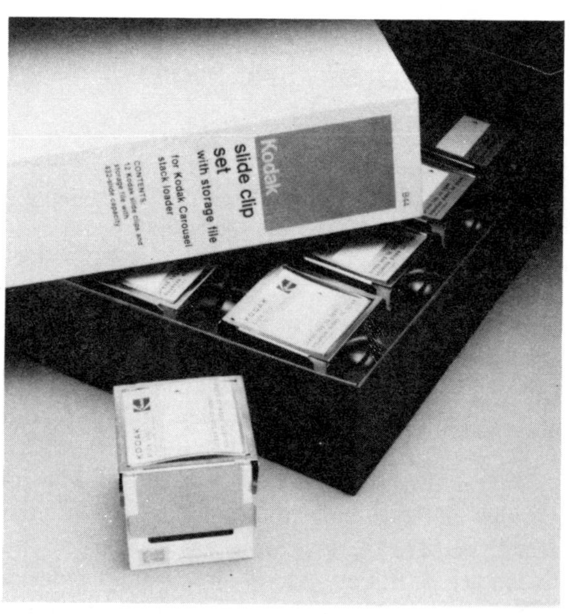

Kodak slide clips and storage file protect slides until ready to be projected. Photo courtesy the Eastman Kodak Company.

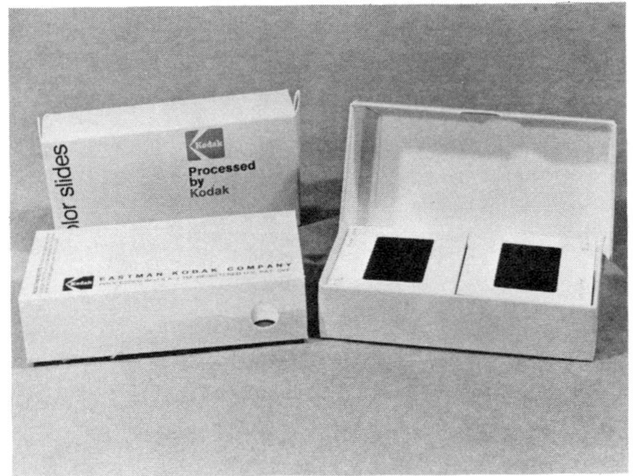

An economical way to store slides is in the box they are returned in from the processing lab.

For duplicate and not-so-good slides, the boxes of plastic or paper supplied by the processing lab for their return can be used as an economical means of storage. It will be necessary to use some sort of coding, labeling, or indexing system so you know what is in the box without having to open each one when you are looking for a particular slide.

Special slide-storage boxes are available from your photo supply dealers. They hold a great number of slides and allow for identification on the top of the box.

Vinyl, polyethylene, plastic, and glassine envelopes and pages are made for slide holding. Some are rigid; others are flexible. There are those that offer top loading and those that are loaded from the side. Slide pages can hold four, six, or twenty slides, depending on the size of the film. They can be stored in boxes or in three-ring notebooks.

Elaborate, custom-made slide-storage systems are manufactured for those who have thousands and thousands of slides. The units are large and expensive. For the hobbyist, they are impractical, but for those who rely on slides for programs and sales, there's nothing better for convenience and organization.

As with prints and negatives, the storage and filing system you use will depend on your needs. Indexing and labeling are the key to success for quick retrieval.

Light, moisture, and heat can be damaging to slides and negatives. Too much moisture can cause fungus to grow on transparencies. Ultraviolet radiation from the sun can cause the dyes to

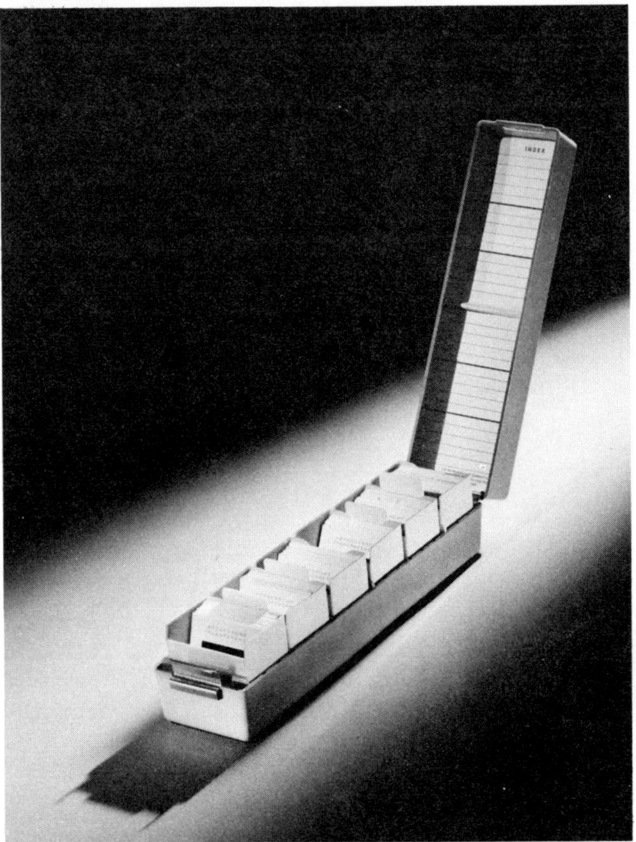

Boxes designed for holding slides allow for indexing on the inside of the cover. Photographs courtesy the Eastman Kodak Company.

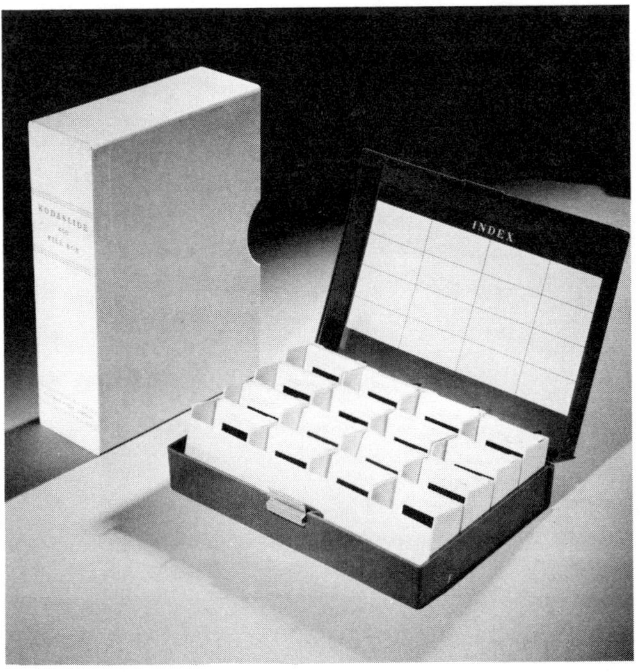

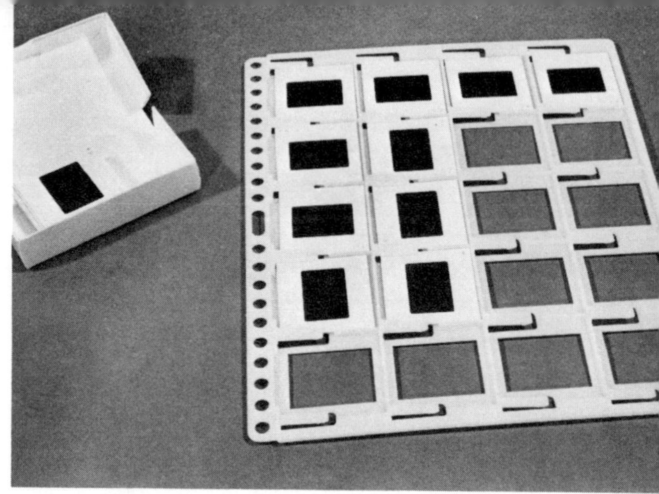

Three-ring binders make good storage units for slides held in vinyl or rigid plastic pages.

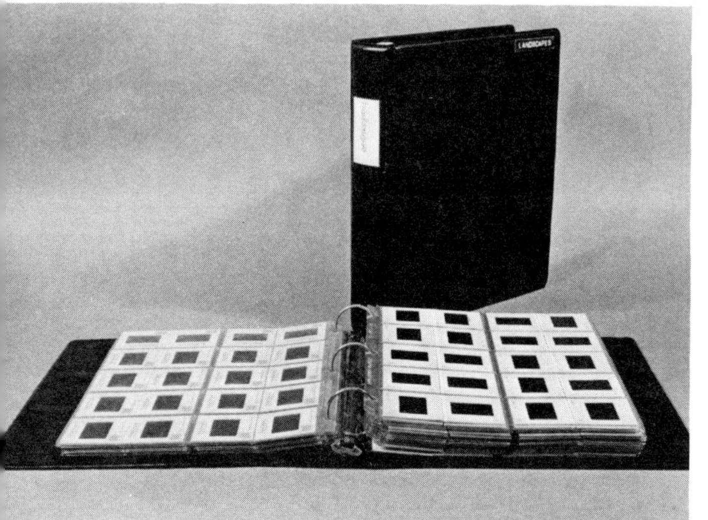

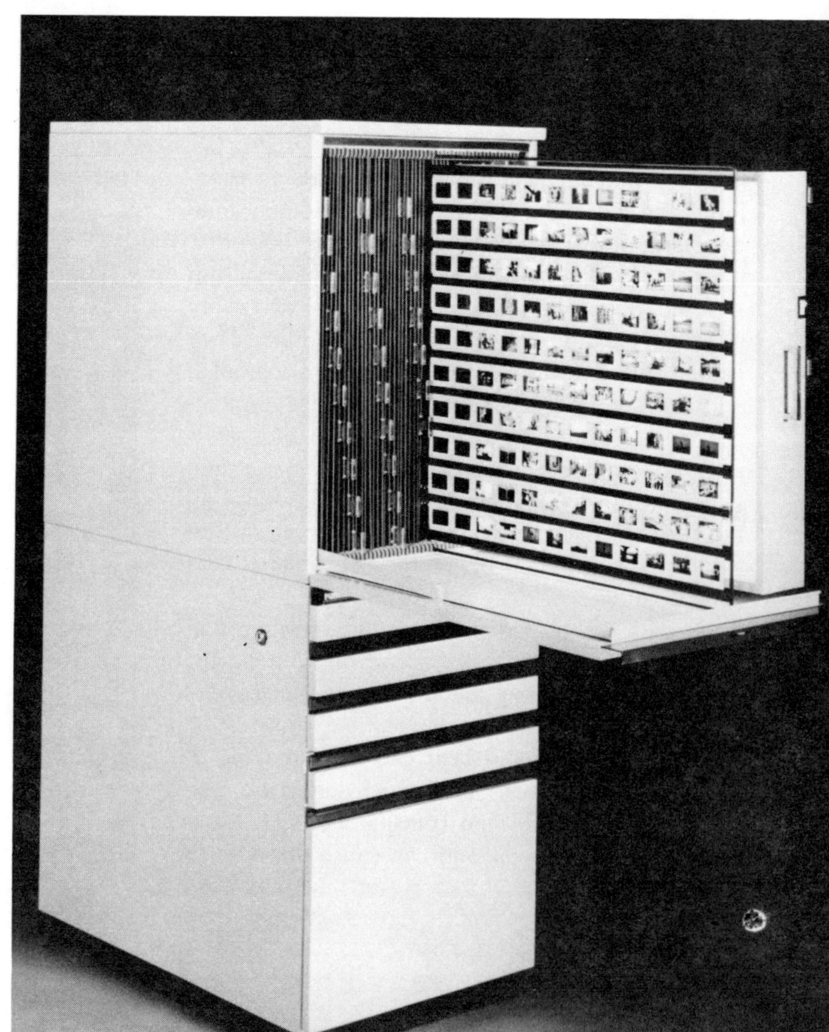

An elaborate slide storage unit with built-in light source. Photo courtesy Multiplex Display Fixture Company.

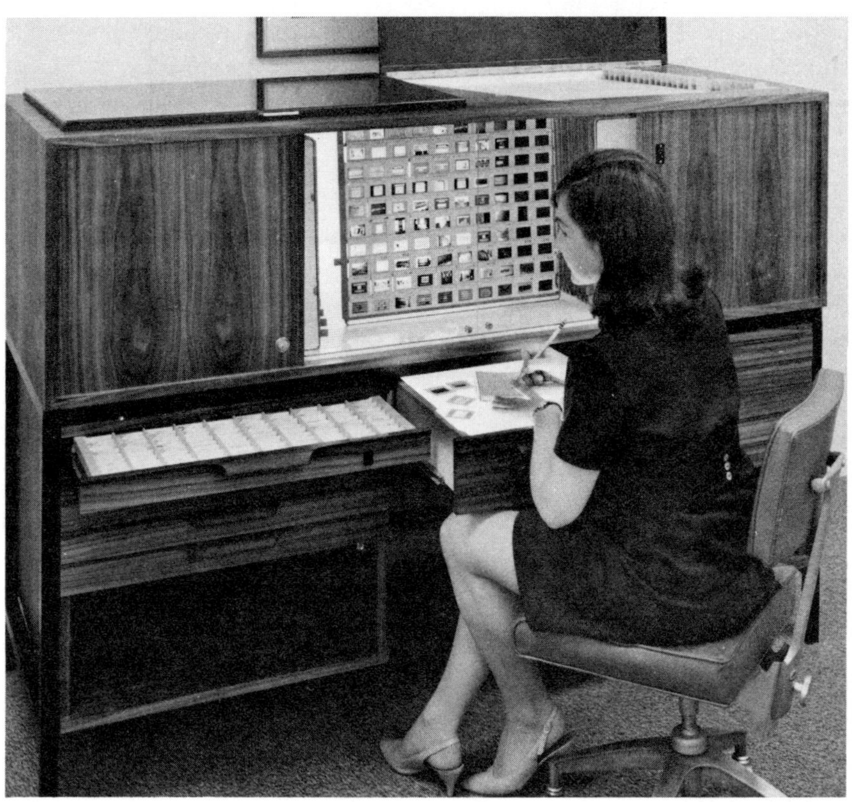

This storage system offers a work center for sorting and viewing slides. Photo courtesy Elden Enterprises, Inc.

fade in color slides. Too much heat can cause the softening of a negative's emulsion.

Dark closets, drawers, and closed containers will avoid the damage caused by ultraviolet. Humidity can be controlled by keeping the air circulating in the storage area. The addition of silica gel to closed storage containers will help keep moisture down. Heat and cold are the easiest to control as long as you don't store your slides and negatives in closed areas that have no heating or cooling systems.

For the most part, slides, negatives, and prints do not deteriorate so quickly that you can't get years of enjoyment from your photographic efforts. A little prevention will keep most catastrophes from occurring.

How well you take care of your negatives, slides, and printed photographs depends on what you think your photographic efforts are worth. Professional photographers make their living from their pictures, so you can be assured that the utmost care is taken by them in all storage.

For the amateur, little expense is needed to safeguard against major picture and negative destruction. Your pictures may be important only to you today. Your friends and family may find your photos of value tomorrow, when the memories that pictures can capture will want to be enjoyed again.

2

PHOTO ALBUMS

Photo albums are as plentiful as photographs themselves, simply because they are readily available and offer two returns for the investment. First, a photo album is capable of holding a great number of small prints. Second, the photo album acts as a storage system; once filled with photos, it can be neatly placed on a bookshelf.

The shortcomings of photo albums are the limited viewing they offer and the unorganized hodgepodge people place in them. The limited viewing offered by albums cannot be changed; only one or two people can comfortably look at the pictures in an album, but the content can be organized and presented in a pleasing manner.

PLANNING A PHOTO ALBUM

Often, a picture taker will accumulate an abundance of unrelated pictures, stuffing them in boxes and drawers until there is no more room. At that time, the picture taker will decide a photo album is needed.

Too often, an album is purchased and the next step is to place as many photos as possible into the blank pages. It's done. The photo album is positioned on a shelf and forgotten until a new album is placed on the shelf next to the old one.

In a sense, the method works. The prints are stored and the album offers limited viewing at a later date. The content, however, is undocumented, unrelated, and not very pleasing to look at. There's nothing wrong with gathering a collection of photographs before purchasing an album. But, before the album is bought, the photos should be edited and sorted to see how many are related in subject matter. After sorting, one may find that two or three albums are needed. For instance, one album may be needed for travel pictures, another for family members or even a party, and so on.

The specific content of a photo album is almost unlimited. It can contain a great variety of related pictures. Albums come in a wide range of sizes, and once you know how many pictures go where, you can purchase the albums that match your needs.

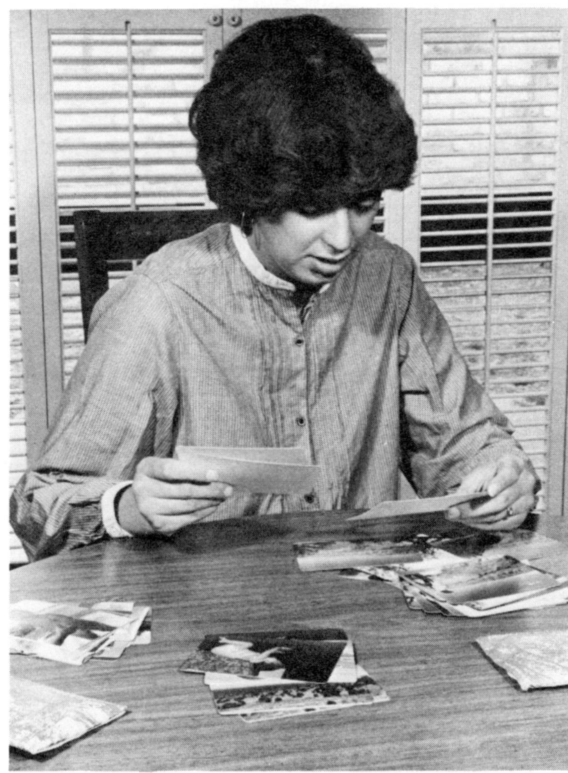

Before purchasing a photo album, sort your prints to determine how many albums you really need.

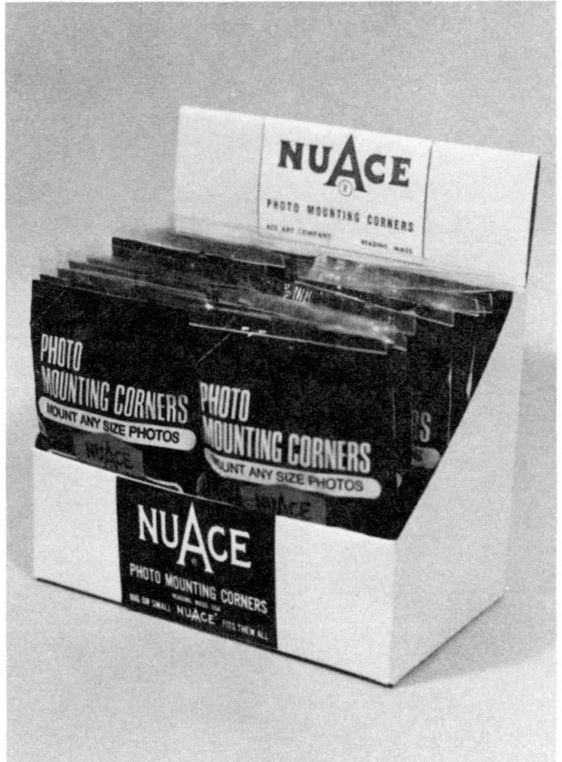

Photo mounting corners are useful for attaching prints to album pages. Photo courtesy the Ace Art Company.

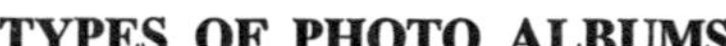

TYPES OF PHOTO ALBUMS

All commercial photo albums are basically the same. They offer a protective covering, and inside they hold some sort of pages that pictures can be attached to. The size of the album and the actual pages are what vary. Before purchasing a photo album, consider whether the album pages can be added or removed. You may wish to expand or reduce the size of the album.

Some albums come with blank pages of heavy paper. The photographs put on the pages need to be held in place by glue, adhesive strips, or commercial photo-mounting corners. The arrangement of the photographs is left to you.

Other album pages offer a protective plastic covering that holds the inserted photographs in place. Again, photo placement on the page is left to the individual preparing the album.

Some album pages are designed for a specific size of photos. The pages have cutout windows that hold three, four, or even six photographs.

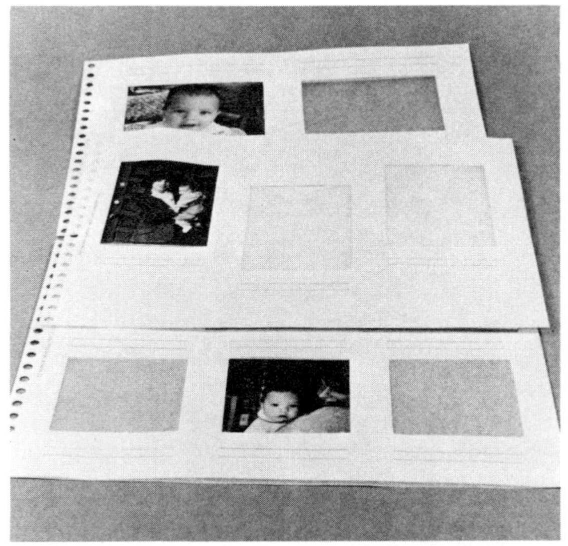

Some album pages are designed for a specific size of photos. Make sure you know the print's dimensions and whether you need horizontal or vertical holders.

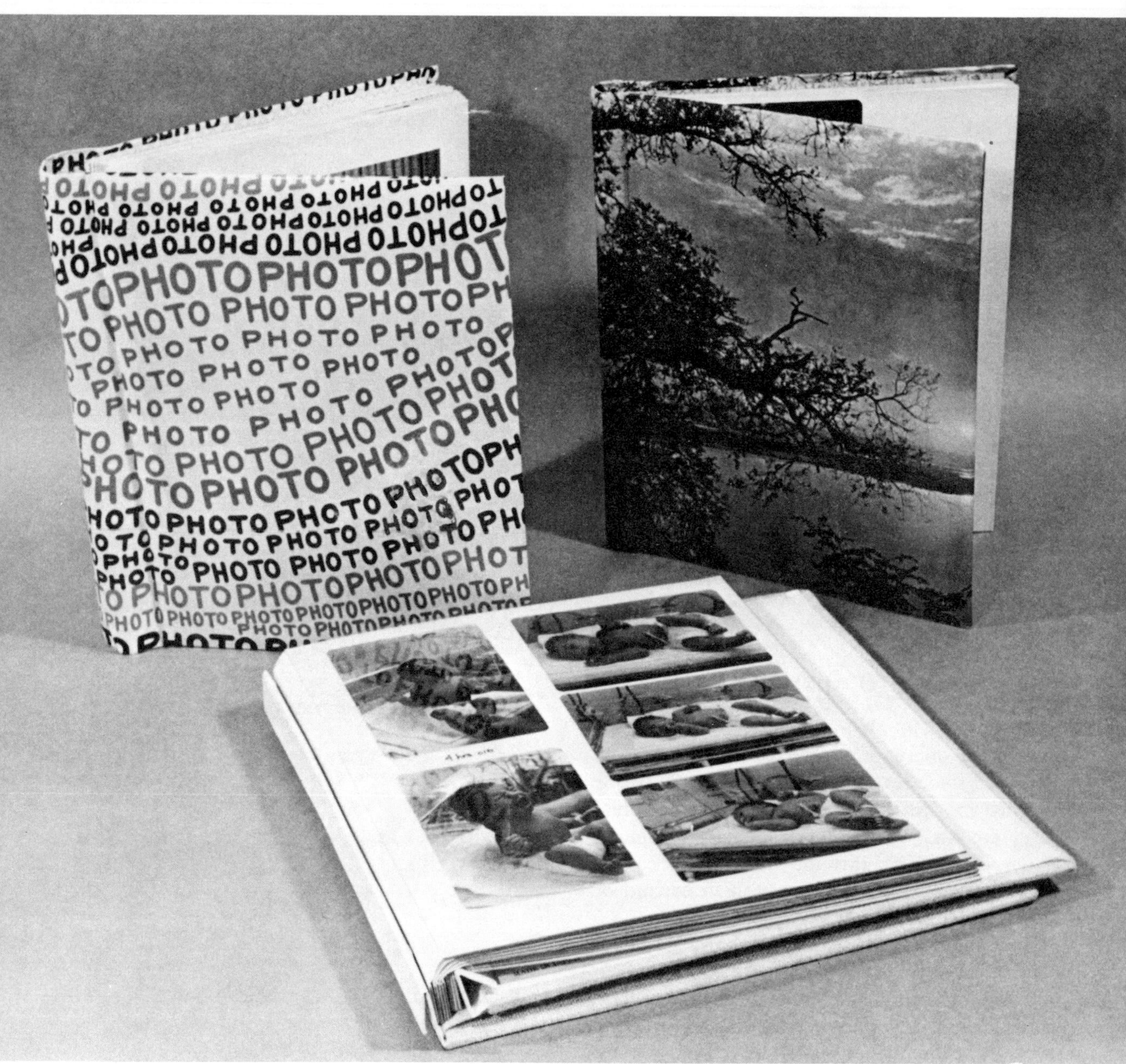

Albums come in a variety of sizes and covers. Some offer plastic-covered pages for easy insertion of prints.

Keep your album pages consistent so the viewer does not have to turn the book sideways to view prints.

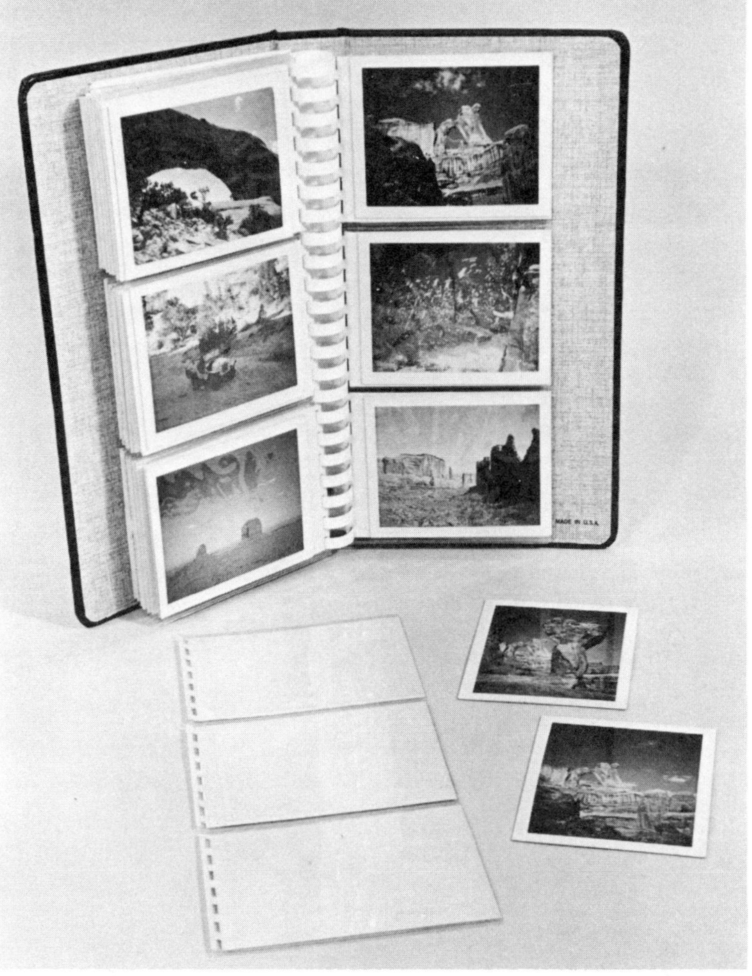

The cutouts are for horizontal or vertical pictures, for prints of rectangular shape. Before purchasing this type of album page, you should consider the number of horizontal and vertical prints you have.

Finally, there are vinyl pages that hold photographs. The pages are very similar to the holders for negatives and slides discussed in Chapter 1.

ALBUM ORGANIZATION

Once your albums have been purchased, don't start placing photographs on the pages as quickly as you can. Take the time to edit and crop your photographs so that only your best possible pictures will be seen. When that's completed, the next step is organizing the photos in a logical or enticing arrangement.

If a photo album is devoted to a family member, the pictures should be in a chronological order, showing increase in age from infancy on. Theoretically, this type of album should keep expanding in size as more and more appropriate photographs are added.

There are a number of ways to develop some sort of order to your photo albums. Pictures can be dated, events can be sequenced, or a broader approach can be taken such as family members, a trip, or specific events.

Usually, pictures should be self-explanatory, but to help keep records and refresh one's memory, words can be added. When descriptive phrases are added, the viewer won't have to sit next to the album's owner to get a verbal, often boring, background for each photo. A picture is a visual pleasure that supposedly offers a thousand unspoken words.

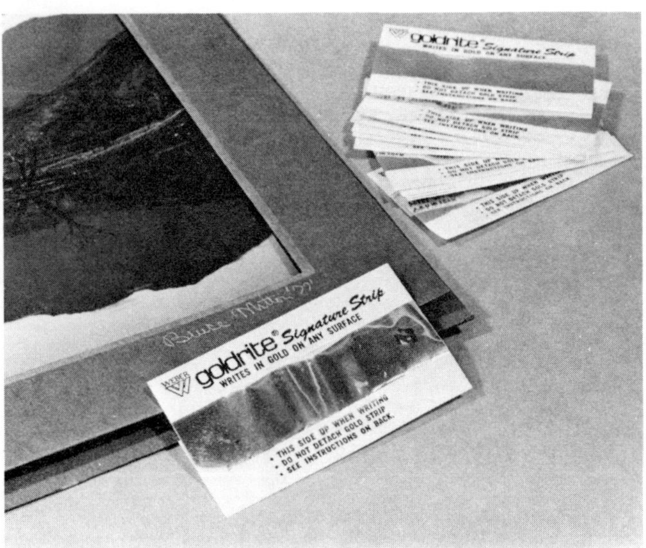

These small strips enable you to write in gold for labeling photos in an album or folder.

The method and exact number of descriptive words you add to your albums is up to you. If your penmanship is above average, you may write directly on the album page below each picture, using a felt-tipped or ball-point pen.

For the typist, various-sized self-adhesive labels can be used. The labels are convenient if you wish to change the photo in the album at a later date. The label can be covered or removed.

For limited wordage, such as a date, you may want to use transfer type, which gives a professional look but requires time and patience in applying. Transfer type should be used only if it will be protected from heat and undue pressure, if it is to stay in place.

Small strips are available that offer limited writing in gold. The strips are placed over the print or album page and you can write the photographer's name or a date to help with identification. The strips are small and should be limited to just one or two words for the best effect.

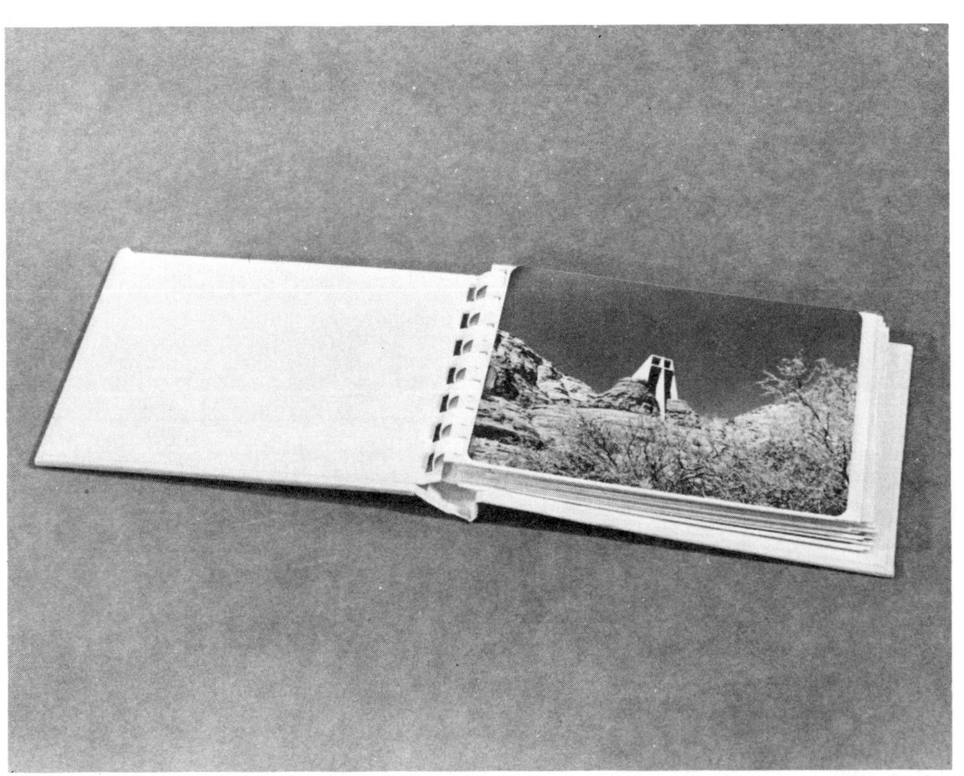

Small albums are useful for related photos.

For the individual who wants a photo album that looks more like a published book, you may want to invest in typesetting by a printshop. The printed type can then be placed beneath or next to the photo, using an adhesive. Typesetting can be somewhat costly, but the results are truly professional.

SMALL ALBUMS CAN BE EFFECTIVE

Not all photo albums are as large as three-ring binders. Small commercial albums not much larger than a 3½×5-inch photograph are available. These small books will sit nicely on a coffee table.

Visitors in your home will pick them up out of curiosity. They are small, holding only a few photographs, so you need to fill the pages with very pleasing images. Think of the little books as a portfolio—the finest work you can produce—like a portfolio used by a photographer looking for work.

The content may be organized, or it may be an accumulation of important events related to the album owners.

Small or large, there should be a commercially available album that will fill your photographic needs. If not, you might want to design and construct your own, unique photo albums.

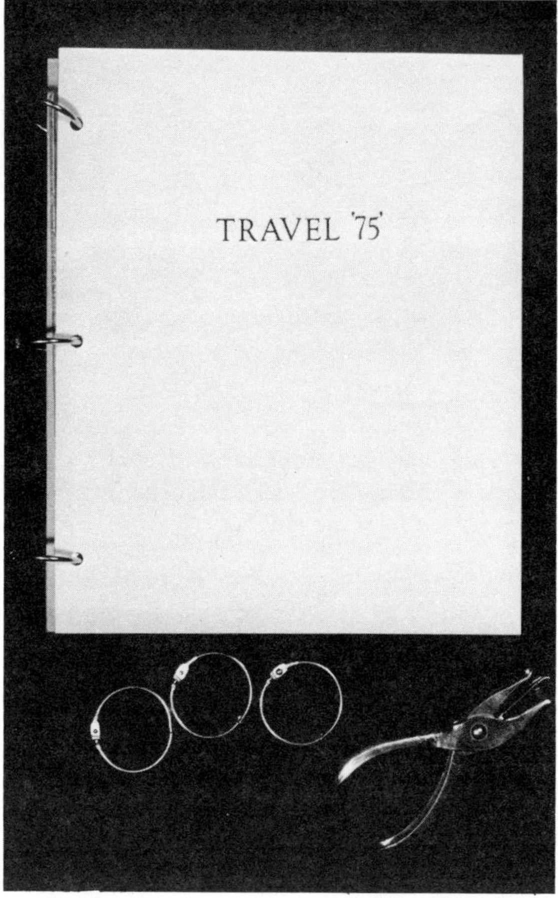

Your own albums can be made from cardboard and binding rings.

MAKING YOUR OWN PHOTO ALBUMS

Undoubtedly the simplest way to obtain a photo album is by purchasing one at any of the many stores that deal in such merchandise. The photographs you place on the album's pages will make it unique. However, you may find your bookshelves are beginning to look like a wide assortment of album covers, whereas instead you would prefer a little continuity in appearance.

The continuity problem can be remedied by purchasing only one type of album, from a specific manufacturer. Another solution is to put together your own album covers and pages. There are a number of ways to construct your own albums. The difficult task will be designing a cover or developing a page-binding system.

THREE-RING NOTEBOOK

A simple, three-ring notebook is the easiest of album covers and binding systems to obtain. There's a wide selection available in various colors and widths. Also, the system offers quick addition and removal of pages.

Various-size picture-holding vinyl pages can be purchased from your local photo dealer and some office supply houses. The vinyl pages are prepunched for three-ring binders.

If the clear vinyl pages do not appeal to your taste, you might want to use heavy construction paper of one or several colors. Once the paper is cut to the proper size, holes can be punched for the three rings. Proper adhesives or photomounting corners can be used to hold the pictures in place. Reinforcement circles should be used around the punched-out holes to help pre-

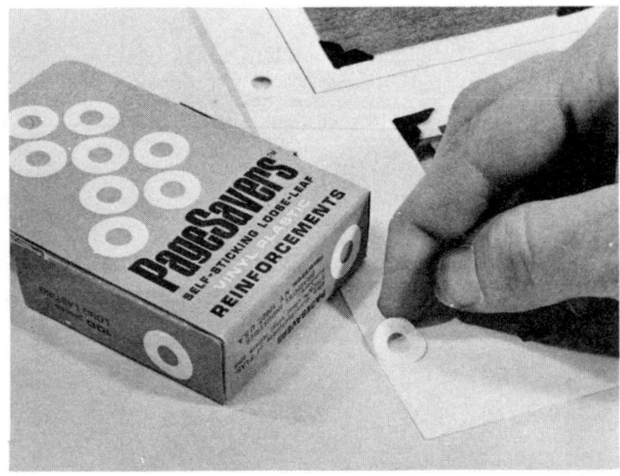

For added strength, reinforcement circles should be added to pages to lessen the chances of their being ripped from the album.

vent the pages from ripping. Using your imagination and available resources, you can add descriptive or identifying words to the albums by typing on self-adhesive labels or relying on good penmanship.

Before the album is completed, you may wish to put some sort of reference information on the cover or down the side for easy identification of content. Self-adhesive labels can be used, or if you plan to make a great number of similar albums in the future, you might want to try color coding with a separate index. Good identification makes it easy to pull the correct album from the shelf, without having to thumb through your total album collection.

MOUNTING-BOARD ALBUM

Another album you can make is done by using mounting board, mounting adhesive, and a binding system supplied by a printshop.

The first step is to select a proper mounting board. White or any color that does not conflict with the actual photo image can be used.

A size needs to be determined, allowing an extra inch or more for the binding. You may want to use one of the standardized dimensions of 8×10 or 11×14 inches, which are readily available. Then you won't have to worry about trimming the boards to the same size.

The mounting boards need to be taken to a printshop that does binding. They'll punch out the holes for either three-ring or spiral binding. Use your telephone to find which shop can supply the service you need.

Anything handled, especially by youngsters, is going to become soiled by dirt and grease. You may want to go to a little added expense and have the cover of your album laminated with plastic. If you plan to decorate the cover for

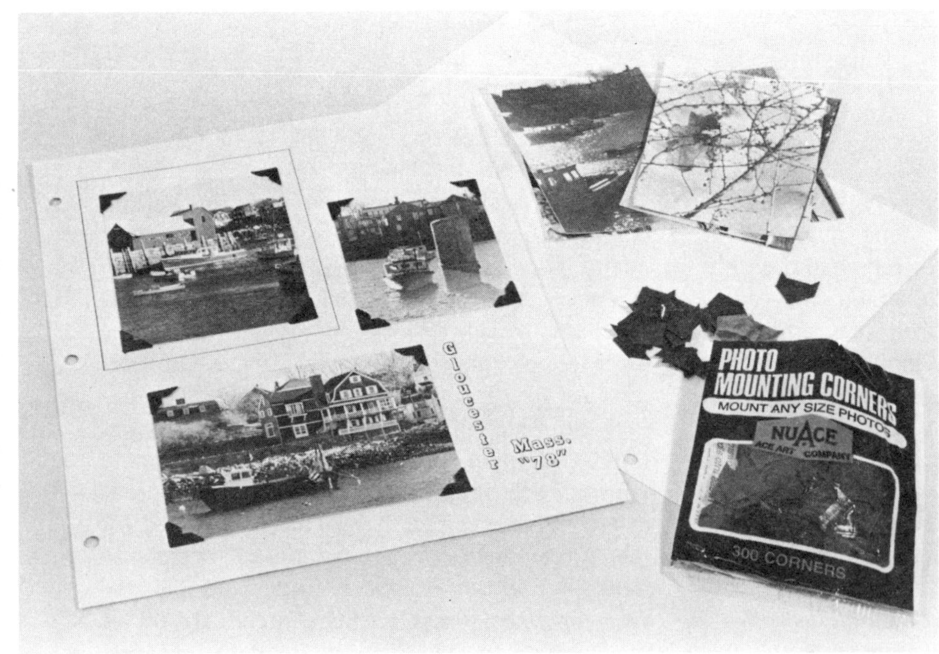

A little creativity and constructive cropping make an interesting album page.

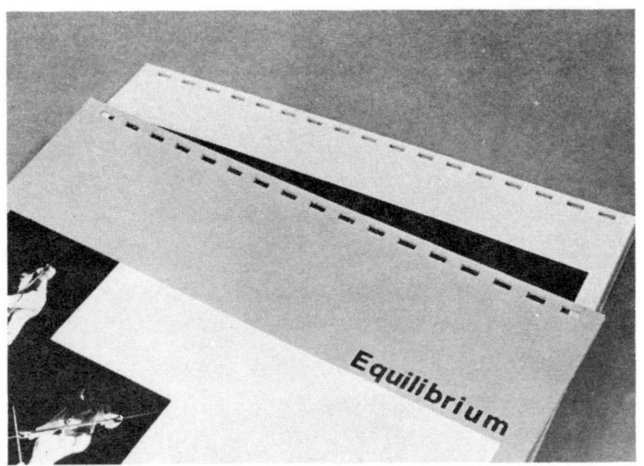

Heavy mounting board can be punched at a binding shop for a sturdy album.

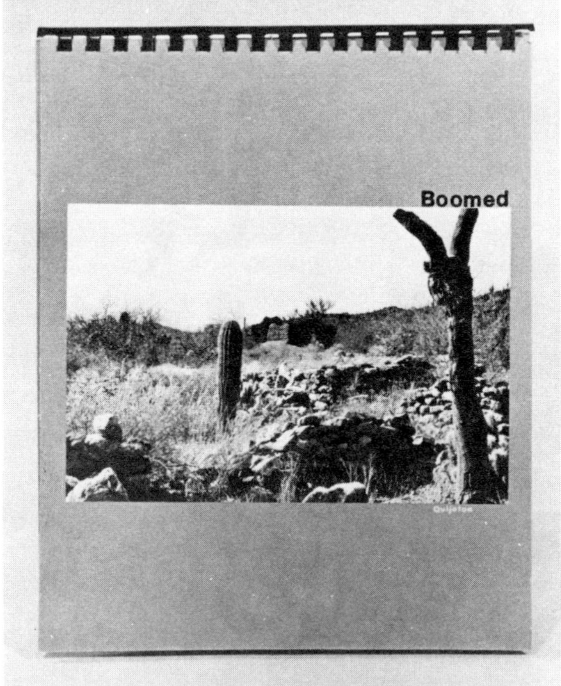

This album can stand on its own for noticeability.

identification with words or the addition of a special photograph, do so before the lamination.

Lamination is done under high heat, melting the plastic over the object being covered. The process is permanent and has to be done by a printshop or bindery that has the necessary equipment. (Individual photographs can be laminated for a hard protective covering. But remember that the process is permanent, and cannot be undone. Save photo lamination for special prints that get more than routine handling.)

Once the mounting boards are bound or at least punched for the binder, you can attach your desired photos to the pages. Attachment can be done using any of the mounting adhesives. (A complete discussion on mounting techniques can be found in Chapter 3.)

If only a few pages have been inserted between the mounting board's covers, you can stand the handcrafted album on a coffee table so that it is noticeable and available for perusal.

BOX ALBUM

We can debate whether a box full of mounted prints is an album, portfolio, or a print storage system. Call it what you will. The main issue is whether the system will help you to display and store many of your favorite pictures.

People are generally curious, and a plain or decorative box sitting on a coffee table or shelf with the words "Take a look inside" or "Open me" on top is bound to raise interest now and again. Inside should be individually mounted prints of the finest quality you can produce. You can make your own box of mounted prints. Bedford Creations, Ltd., manufactures the Photo Box, which "stows and shows up to 200, $3\frac{1}{2} \times 5$-inch photos in protective sleeves."

The content of box albums should be organized. One trick is to use photos that are sequenced. This is nothing more than a series of pictures that are related and have a beginning and an end. You may want to call it a photo story.

For example: you might want to use a series of photographs that show the new baby in the family going through a bath. Start with the subject undressing, then playing with soap or a toy in the tub, splashing water, getting wrapped in a fluffy towel, and then getting dressed for a stroll through the park. The ideas for sequencing photos are unlimited. The secret is presenting the photos so they build to a climax or logical finish, like a good novel.

Instead of a photo story, you might want a photo essay in the box. This is a series of unrelated photos that have a central theme. The photos should be of such quality that the viewer will understand the theme or statement without your having to tell what it is. If you pick easy

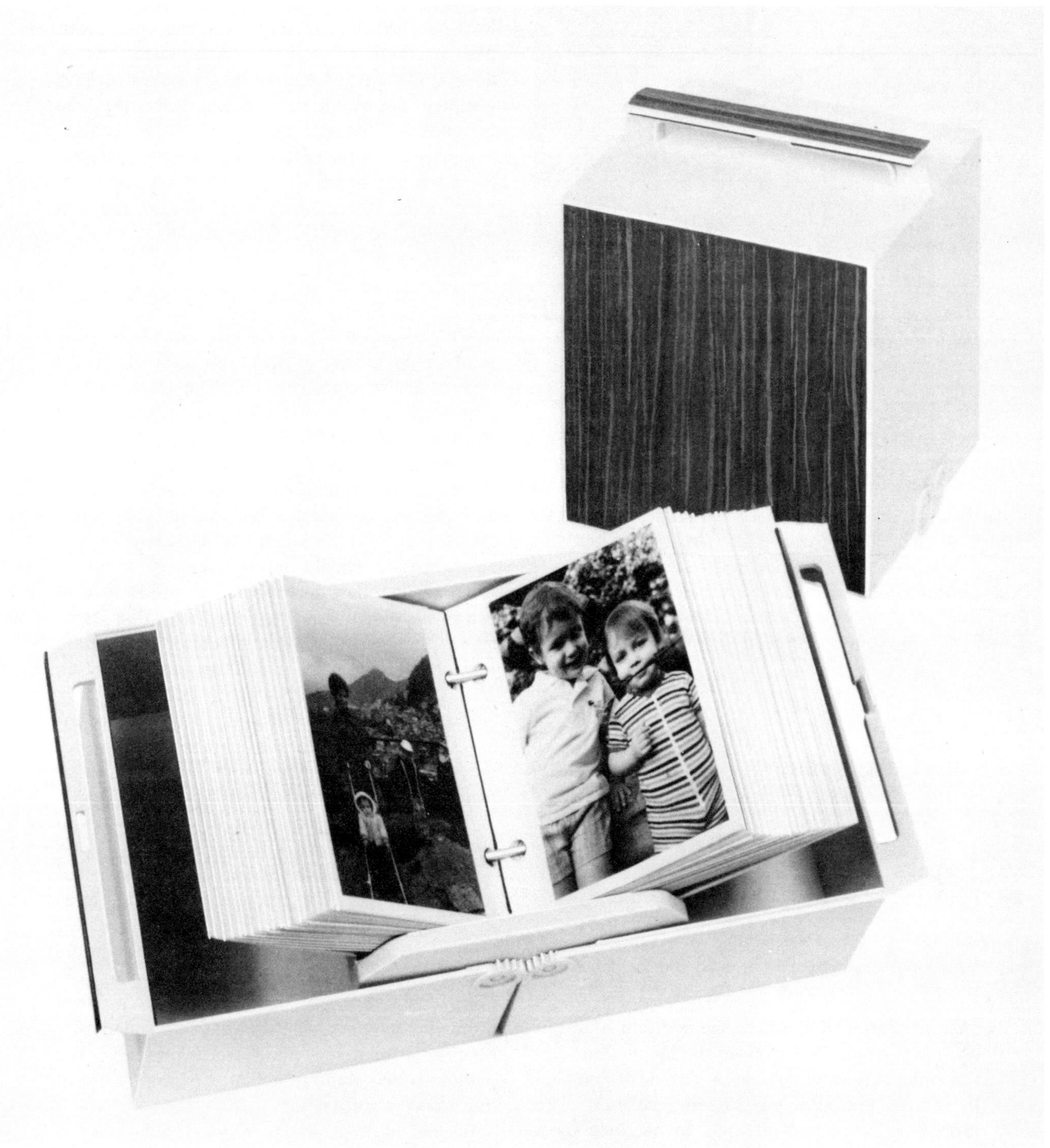

Photos in a box make an interesting tabletop album. Photo courtesy Bedford Creations, Ltd.

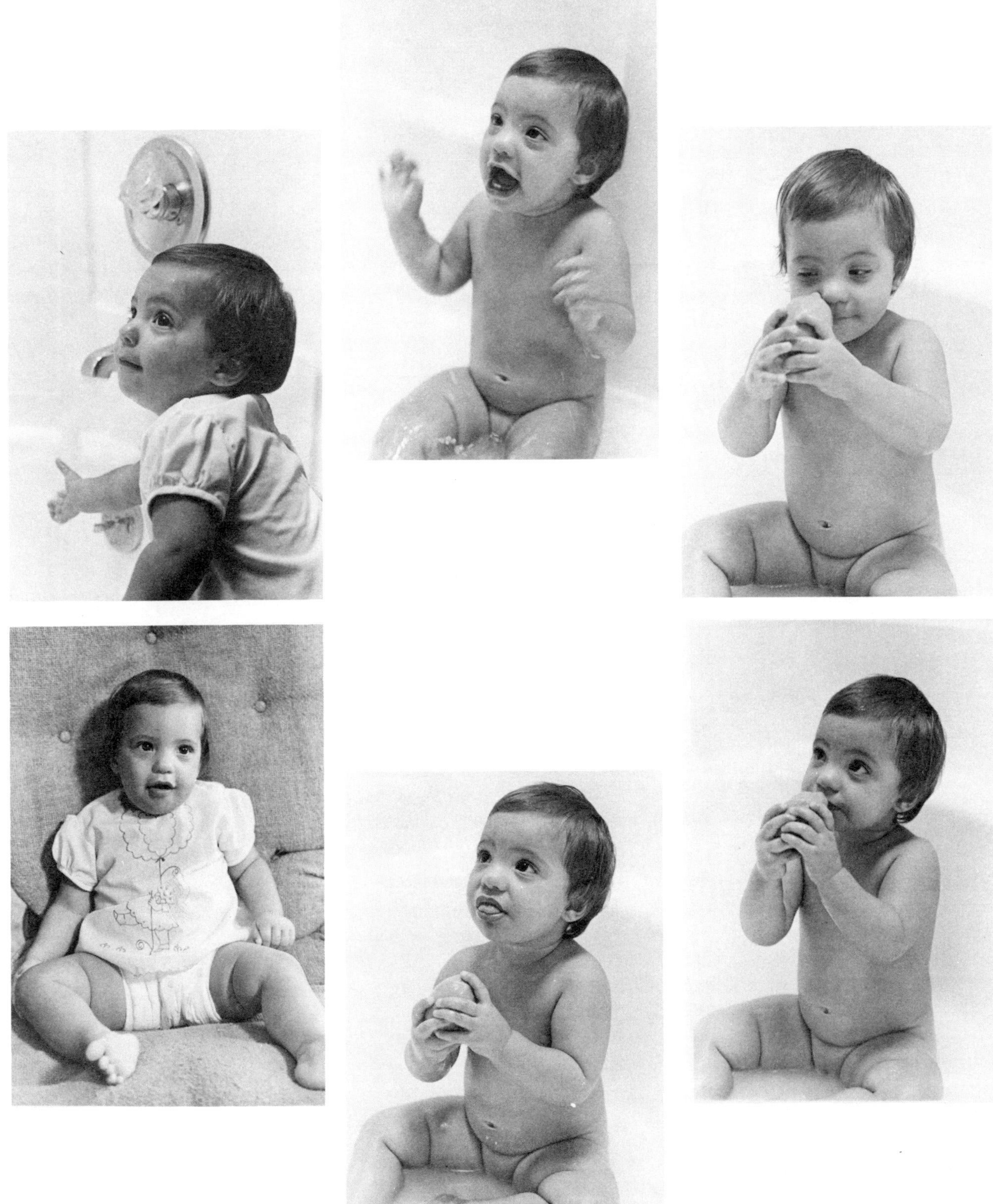

A photo essay or story adds continuity to your albums and display methods.

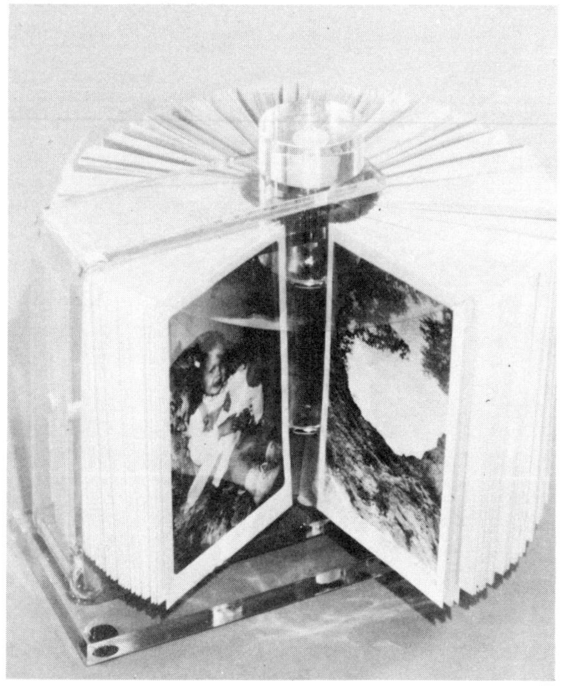

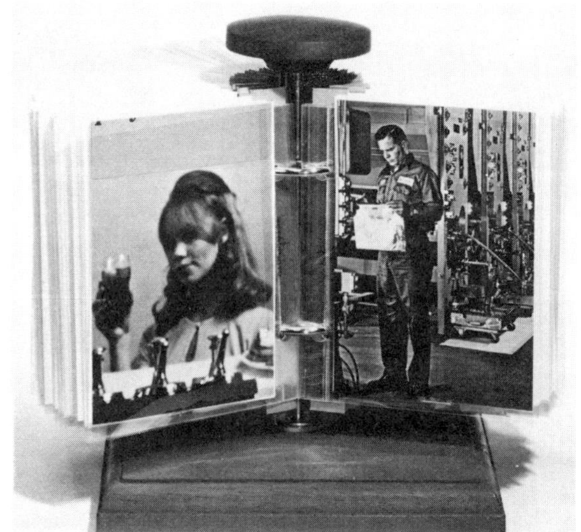

The Roto-Photo Company produces a variety of rotary photo-display systems. Photos courtesy the Roto-Photo Company.

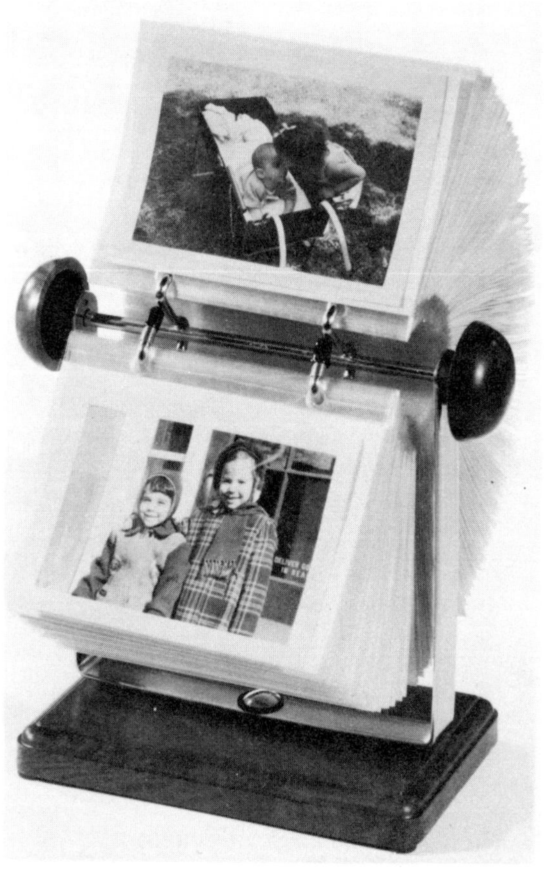

subjects like shadows, laughing children, rain, etc., you shouldn't have any problem with a viewer's distinguishing the theme.

THE ROTO-PHOTO SYSTEM

Anyone who has worked in an office with the need to keep a large number of addresses has seen a rotary file system. The same principle has been adapted for photographs.

The Roto-Photo Company manufactures a complete line of horizontal and vertical rotating systems. With the spin of a knob, you can go through a tremendous number of pictures. Plastic sleeves that hold the photos can be added and removed for editing and sorting. Depending on the model number, the rotary file can hold as many as five hundred pictures of either 3½×5- or 3½×3½-inch size.

Since the systems are capable of holding many pictures, it would be impossible to organize or relate the total photographic content. The systems will have to be used as a grab bag for miscellaneous photographs gathered through the years.

If the photos you have are not square, you'll need to use one file for horizontal and another for vertical photos, to make viewing as easy as possible. If someone is willing to look at as many as five hundred pictures, he shouldn't have to be troubled by twisting his neck to view vertical and horizontal pictures.

Photo albums are popular, but they shouldn't be left on the shelf to gather dust. Pictures are to be seen, and the only way they can be viewed is to make them available to anyone who is willing to look at them.

Keep in mind that an organized album is much better than one that is just a melting pot of unrelated pictures. Written but brief statements about a photo are better than your verbal description. Let the photos speak for themselves.

Pictures in an album don't have to be all the same size. If you are an avid reader who enjoys the photos found in magazines and books, you'll notice their size varies from page to page. Your album pages can look the same way.

If you arrange and vary the size of the photos, mixing horizontals with verticals, you are controlling the layout and design, just like art directors that put together books and magazines.

If you make your photo albums visually pleasing, people will be more than willing to look at the pictures and you'll be getting a good return on your photographic investment.

3

MOUNTING BOARDS, MATS, AND ADHESIVES

Small photographs lie flat and manage to stay that way. Larger prints have a tendency to curl, losing their shape. This can be annoying, making the prints difficult to view and store.

To solve the problem, a print or grouping of prints can be mounted to a variety of rigid materials. Heavy cardboard, wallboard, plywood, Fome-Cor, and even aluminum sheeting can be used. Depending on the size and how the print is to be displayed, the thickness of the mount can be fairly thin or from one to two inches thick.

All the materials, except for 100 percent rag mounting board, contain substances that can reduce the life of a print. However, for the most part, the deterioration is so slow you'll get many years of enjoyment from any of the mounting materials mentioned.

MOUNT SIZE

The actual size of the print's mount can vary. Ready-cut mounting boards are standardized in 8×10-, 11×14-, and 16×20-inch formats. They should be obtainable at art and photo supply dealers.

The standardized mounts allow room for wide borders if small prints are attached to them. If the extra border is undesirable, it can be trimmed with a paper cutter or a straightedge and cutting tool. If you want the added border a mount can provide, you'll have to trim the print's white or black border before attachment.

Whenever a print is to be placed on a mount, the size should be carefully considered. The combination of print and mount should be aesthetically pleasing. You don't want the mount to be so large that it overpowers the print.

If your mount size is standardized, the prints can be neatly stacked. Mounts of the same size will fit the same frames, so pictures can be interchanged without the necessity of purchasing a variety of frames. Mounts can be standardized, while the size and shape of the print can be altered by constructive cropping through trimming.

Mounts should not be confused with the term *mat*. A mat goes over the print and mount. At times, a mount acts as a mat when it is oversize, adding border to the attached print.

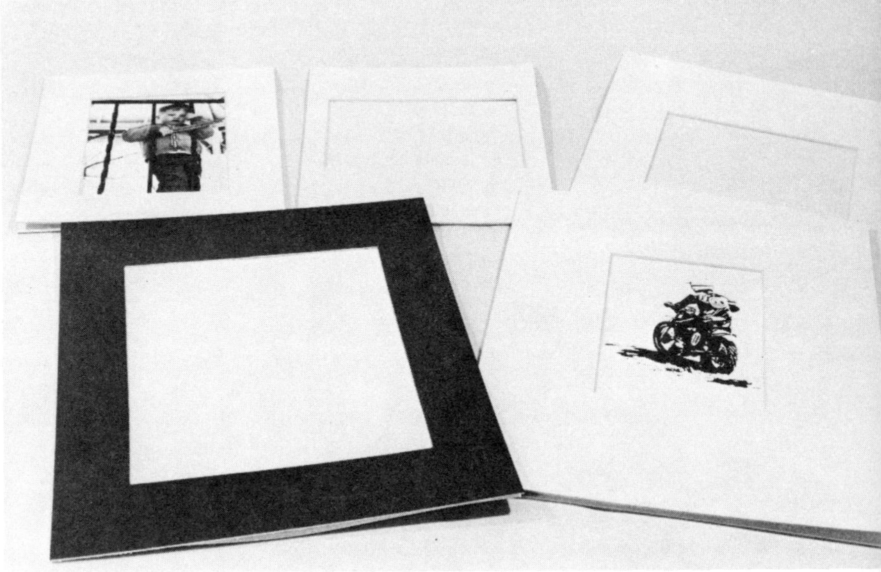

Standardized mats with mounts come in 8×10-, 11×14-, and 16×20-inch sizes.

MATS AND MATTING

Matting your photographic work for display is an important and rewarding endeavor. A mounted print is set off by the mat's border and color. If a matted print is to be framed with glass, the mat will prevent the work from coming in direct contact with the glass, which otherwise might damage the print.

Hundreds of commercial mats are available. They come in an array of cutout-window sizes and shapes. However, the mat's colors are somewhat limited. The most common mat colors are white, cream, off-white, gray, and black. Other colors are available, but it requires trained eyes to match the proper color to blend or enhance the colors of a printed photograph. Matting material can be smooth or have a slightly pebblelike texture.

Commercial photo mats, like mounts, are somewhat standardized for print display. Generally the mat's border is at least one and a half inches wide and no wider than five inches. While prints are made in square, horizontal, and vertical format, consideration should be given to the mat's dimensions so the matted print will be pleasing to look at.

Listed below are basic guides for matting prints. There are many choices, depending on what appeals to the individual's taste.

Horizontal Print, Horizontal Mat: Usually the top and side borders are the same size. The bottom border is noticeably larger, by 25 percent to 35 percent. An alternative is to make all the mat's borders equal in size.

Vertical Print, Horizontal Mat: The two side borders are equal but very wide compared to the top and bottom borders, which are equal to each other.

Horizontal Print, Vertical Mat: The two side borders are equal. The top border is larger than the sides, and the bottom border should be about equal to the mounted print's width.

Vertical Print, Vertical Mat: The top and side borders should be equal. The bottom border should be from 25 percent to 35 percent larger than the other three borders. As with a horizontal print and a horizontal mat, an alternative is to have the four borders equal in dimensions. An asymmetrical arrangement can also be attractive.

Square Print, Horizontal Mat: The top and bottom borders should be narrow and equal, the side margins wider but equal to each other.

Square Print, Vertical Mat: Equal side borders, a wide bottom margin, and a slightly-larger-than-sides top border.

Square Print, Square Mat: All four borders can be equal.

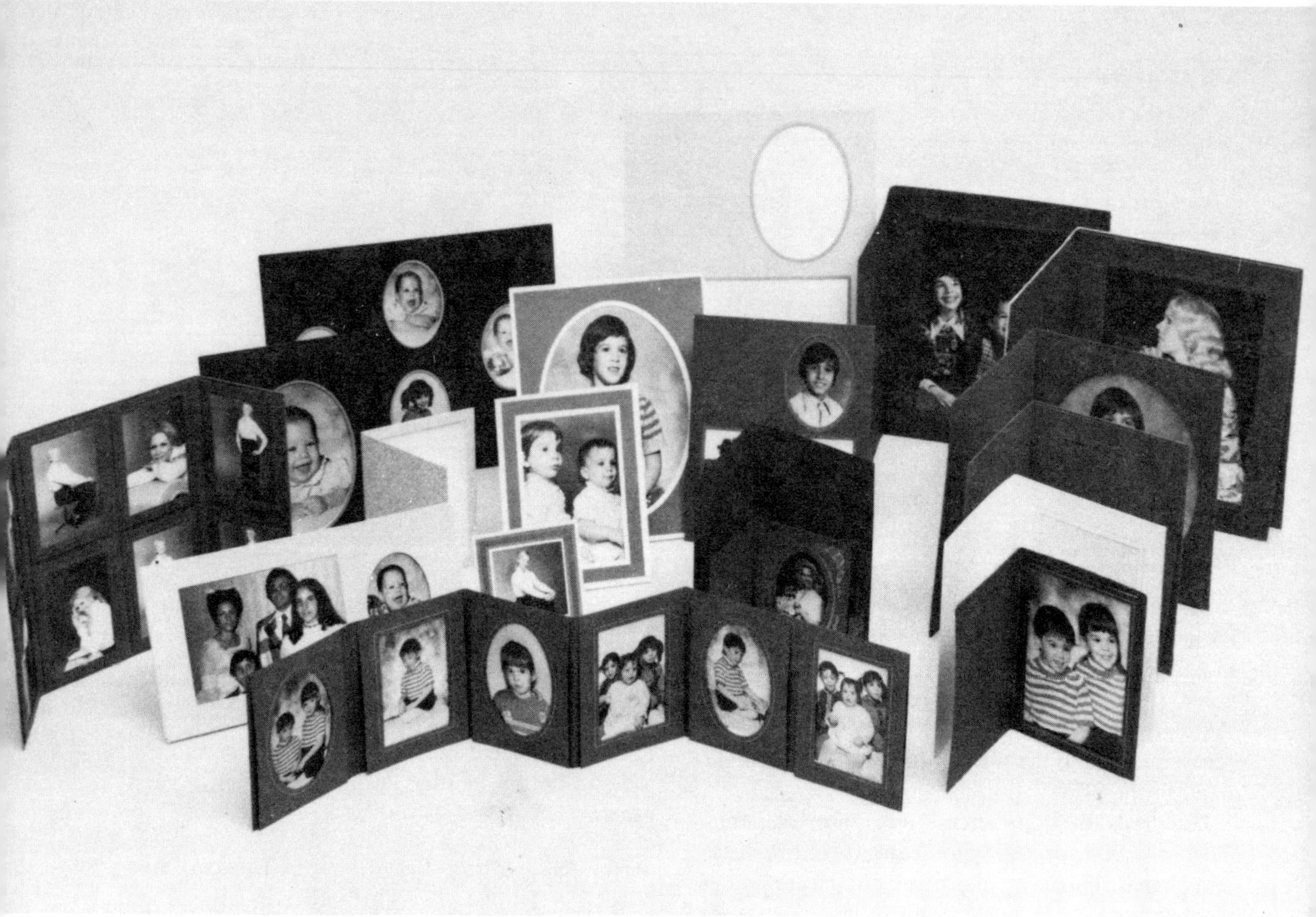

A small sample of folders and mounts available for displaying one print or several. Photo courtesy Callen Photo Mount Corporation.

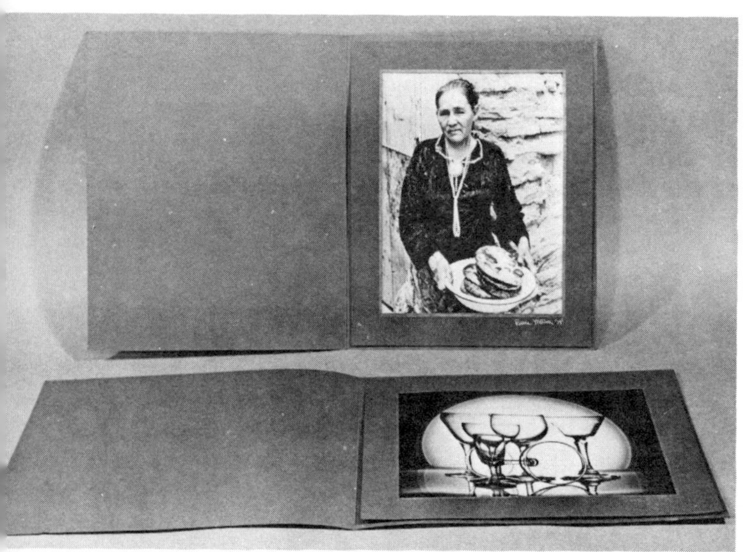

These 8×10-inch photo holders are made for either vertical or horizontal format.

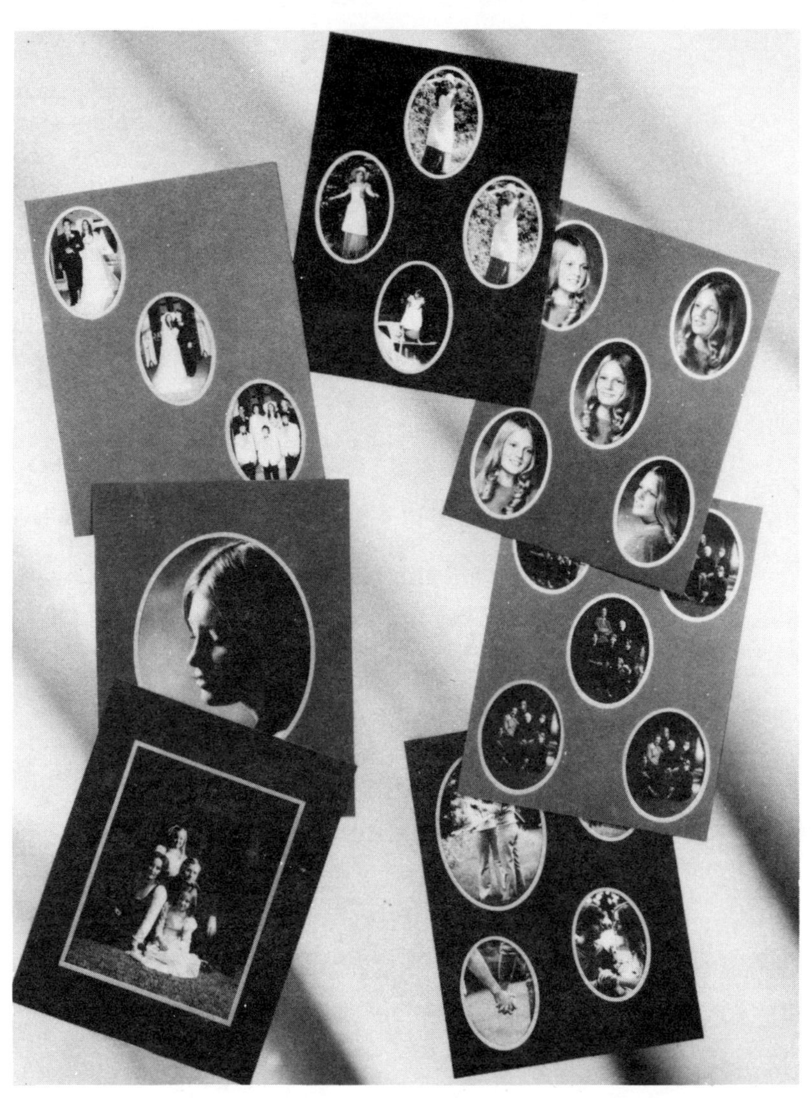

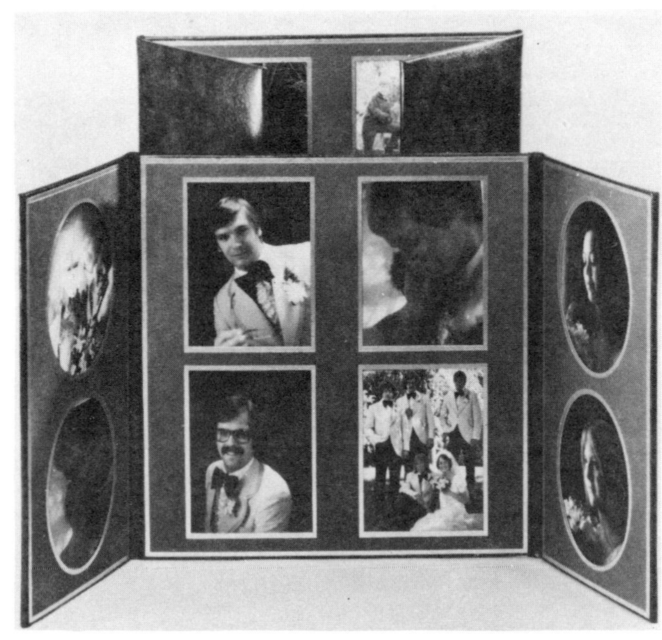

Commercial photographers enhance their products by offering oval and rectangular windowed holders. Photos courtesy the Taprell Loomis Company.

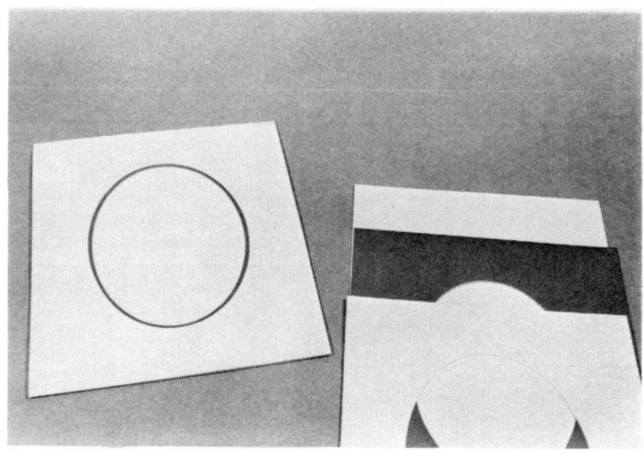

A mat on top of a mat.

Oval window mats are also popular, especially for portraits. The size of the oval window should be carefully considered, so the print to be matted is covered, without the print's edges showing.

MAT OVER MAT

A decorative technique for matting prints is the placement of a mat on top of a mat. The bottom mat is cut so a small portion of it shows when another mat is placed over it. This provides a fine line around the matted print.

An opposite approach can be used to make a thin or wide line around the outside border of the top mat. In this instance, the top mat will be slightly smaller than the mat underneath.

Another line can be added by placing a third mat over the other two. This triple type of matting can detract from the mounted print, but occasionally it may be effective.

RULED BORDERS

Similar in appearance to the mat on mat is the ruled border. A fine line can run close to the print or it can be placed near the outer edge of the mat. A black line is drawn directly on the mat with a ball-point or a felt-tipped pen. Care must be taken to make sure the marking substance does not bleed or run into the mat.

Another approach is to use a felt-tipped pen to darken just the beveled portion of the mat's window.

Fine tape is also available for ruled borders. The tape can be attached to the mat and removed

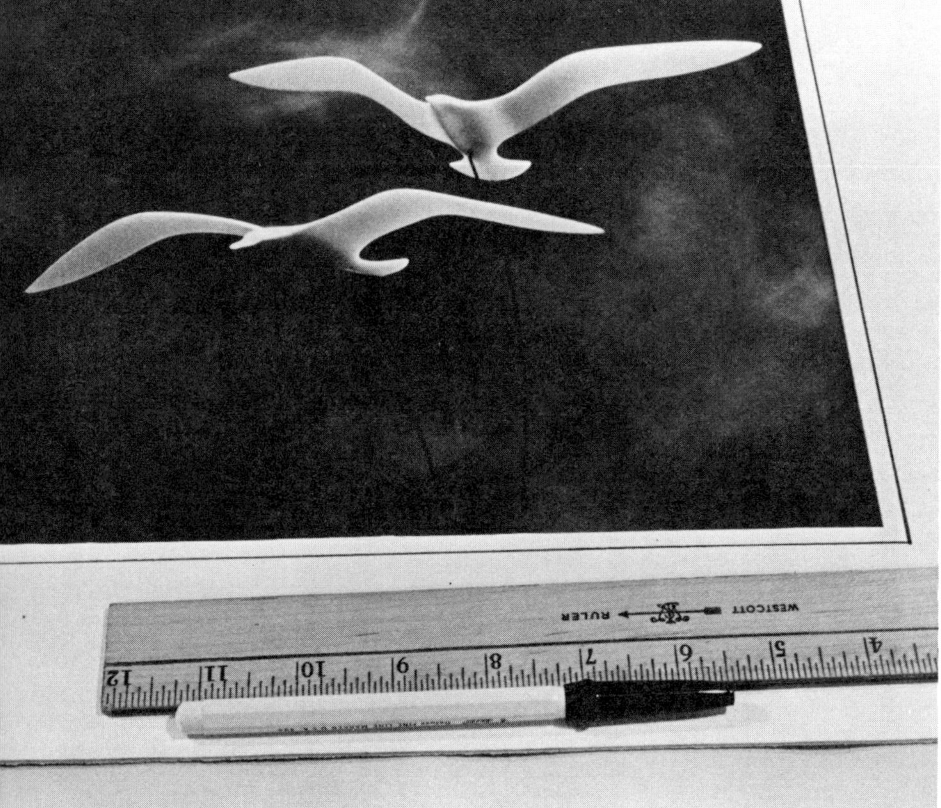

A black line drawn around the print using a marking pen and ruler.

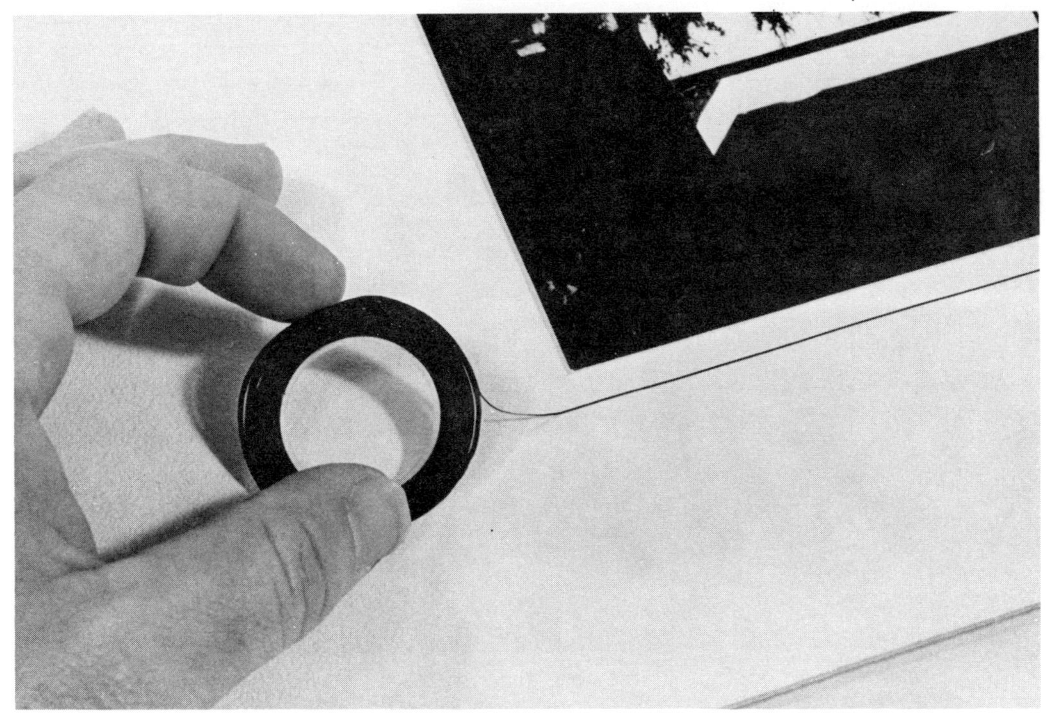

Fine, line tape can be used to add a ruled border that isn't permanent.

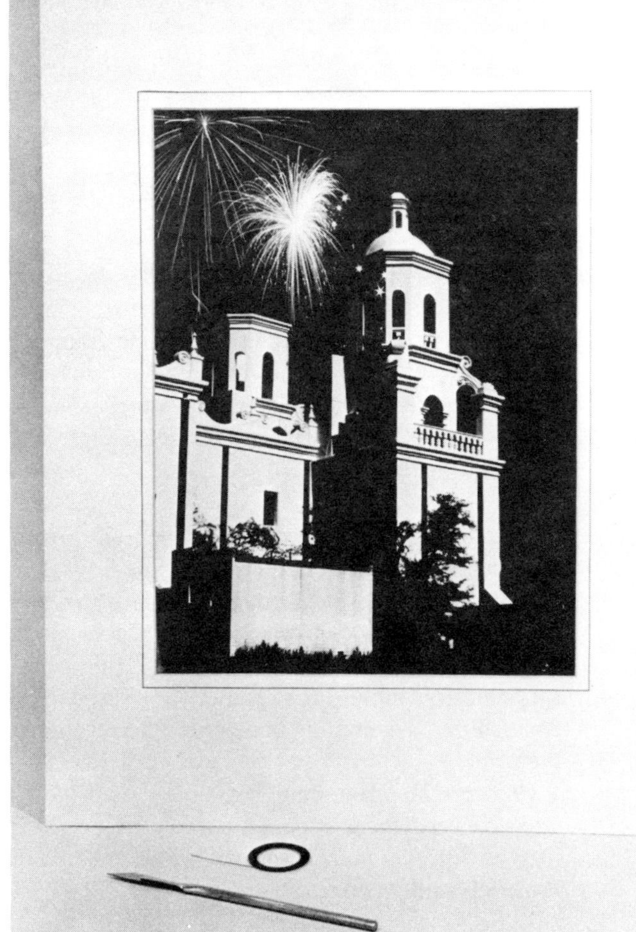

if mistakes in placement are made. When using the tape, one should avoid stretching it unnecessarily, as stretched tape will eventually loosen.

COVERED MATS

Some photographs look better when a texturized or a covered mat is added. Covered mats consist of a cardboard mat covered with fabric such as burlap or linen. Besides fabrics, gift wrapping and contact paper can be used.

The material to cover the mat is cut large so it can be folded over the back of the mat at both the window and the border. The folded covering is held in place using a print-mounting adhesive.

Ademcolor, distributed by Ehrenreich Photo-Optical Industries, allows for the addition of color to mounts and mats by providing a one-sided, adhesive-coated, colored paper. The adhesive-coated paper is for use with a dry-mounting press and is available in a roll of twenty-seven assorted colors.

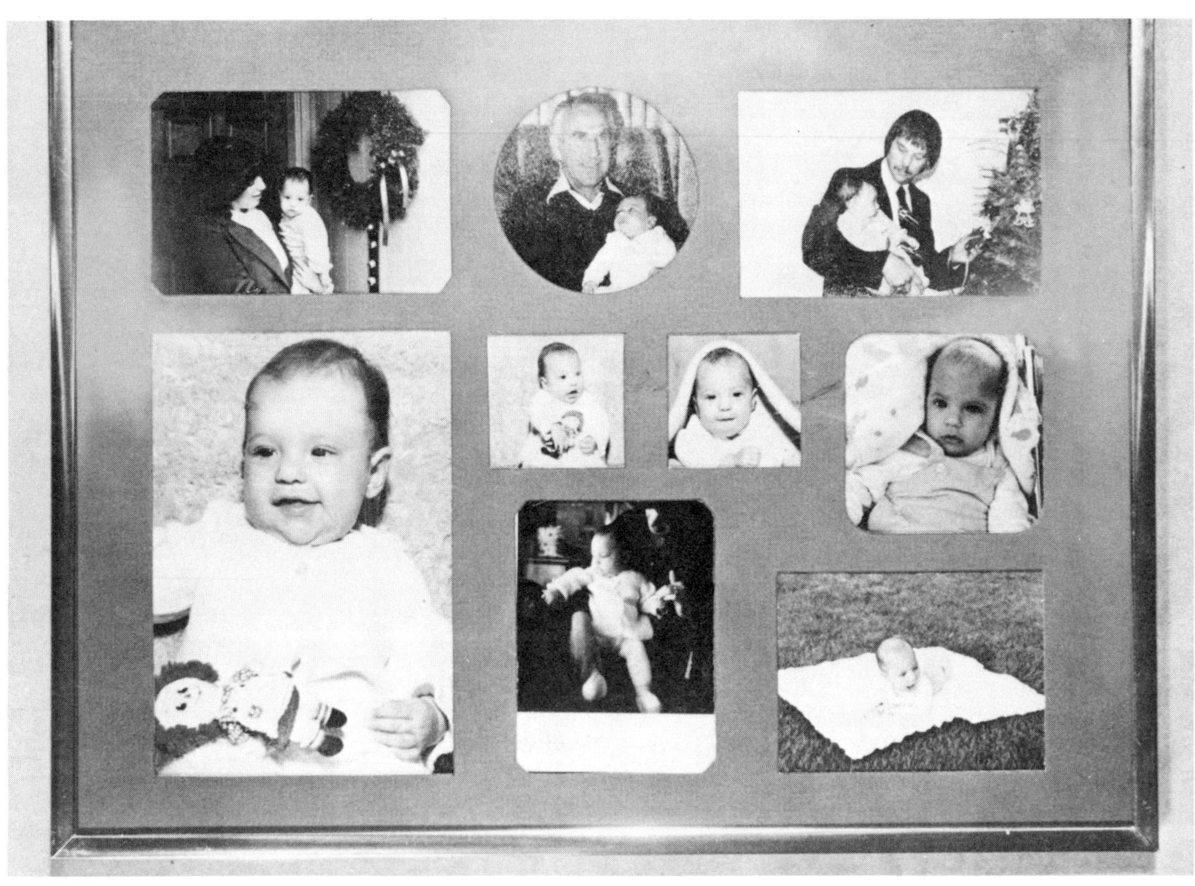

A multiprint mat.

MULTIPRINT MATS

Growing in popularity are the multiprint mats. They can be used as a unifying tool for holding together several photographs within one frame or border. Multiprint mats are useful when grouping family members or single-subject photographs.

A MAT AS A CROPPING TOOL

Since mats are placed over mounted prints, they can be considered a cropping method. The size of the cutout window of a mat can be varied. It can be reduced, allowing only a specific portion of a print to show. Distracting or unnecessary elements around the edge of the print can be covered by the matting material, thus cropping the print.

Commercial mats may not offer the window size you need for cropping a specific photo. You may have to cut your own mat, which requires a few tools and practice.

CUTTING YOUR OWN WINDOWED PICTURE MATS

When you decide on a matting material you would like to use, but find the window size is not appropriate for your needs, you'll have to cut your own.

There are expensive, commercial mat-cutting devices available. For the few mats most people cut, an X-acto or utility knife will do the job. The knives work well for thin-material cutting and non-beveled edges.

For a small investment, the Dexter or the Alto's hand mat cutter will allow for cutting beveled-edge windows.

Besides the cutting tool and blades, a thick, no-skid straightedge or ruler, a pencil, and a level working surface are needed. If you plan on cutting quite a few mats, you may want to invest in a mat-marking scribe and burnishing bone. Both are nice extras, but they are not mandatory for quality mat cutting.

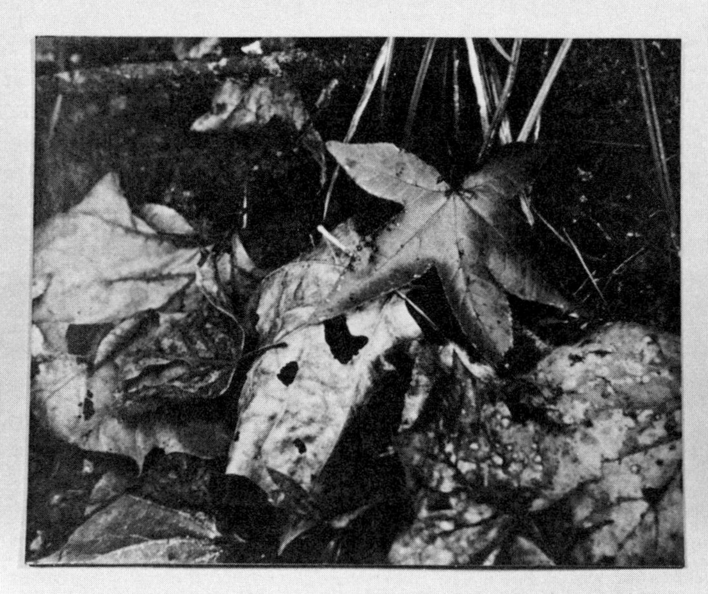

Mat windows come in a variety of sizes and can be used to crop the outer edges of your prints.

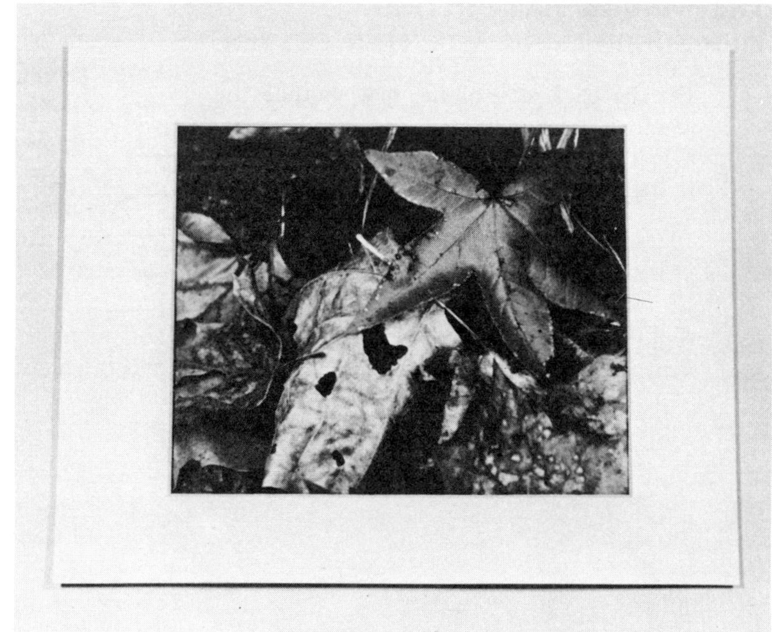

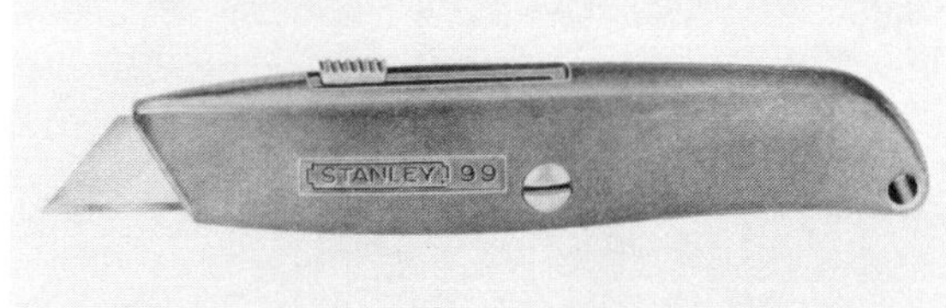

A simple utility knife will help you to cut windowed mats, providing you don't want a beveled edge. Photo courtesy The Stanley Works.

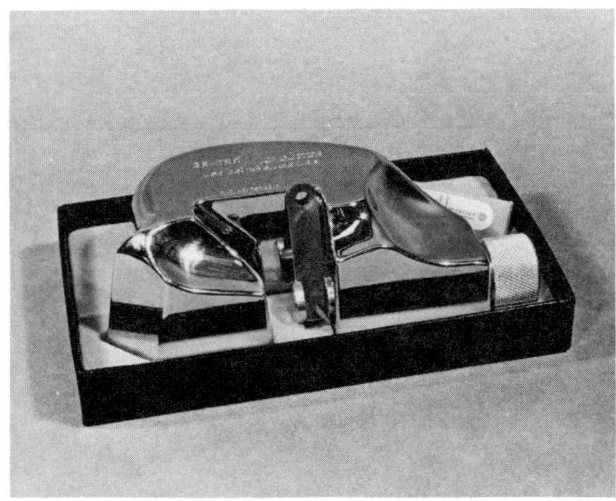

An inexpensive Dexter mat cutter has interchangeable blades and allows for cutting beveled-edged mats.

THE WINDOW MAT-CUTTING PROCEDURE USING A DEXTER CUTTER

1. On the back side of the mat, outline the window, using a pencil and straightedge. When completed, check the widths of the borders for accuracy.
2. Place the mat to be cut on top of a scrap piece of mat or corrugated cardboard. Adjust the cutter's blade so that it will cut slightly through the mat and into the scrap beneath.
3. Align the straightedge with the pencil mark so the cutting blade of the mat cutter will be directly on the pencil mark. The guiding straightedge should be on the border portion of the mat to assure proper direction of the bevel. If possible, clamp the straightedge into place.
4. Make the cut. Using a sharp blade, gently force the sharp edge through the thickness of the mat. Apply a downward pressure on the cutter and push it away from your body, being sure to hold the straightedge in place. CAUTION: AVOID MAKING AN OVERCUT AT THE RIGHT ANGLES (CORNERS) OF THE WINDOW. It's better to finish the cut with a safety-razor blade in order to avoid unsightly overcuts.
5. Continue cutting the mat by rotating it, realigning the straightedge, and cutting.
6. If necessary, trim the corners with a safety-razor blade until the window is removed.
7. To remove any roughness, an emery board or fine sandpaper can be used on the beveled edge.

Overcuts can be avoided with the Dexter mat cutter by placing a piece of light-colored tape on the edge of the mat cutter. After a trial-and-error process, make a small mark on the tape where alignment is made with the edge of the window and the blade touches the corner.

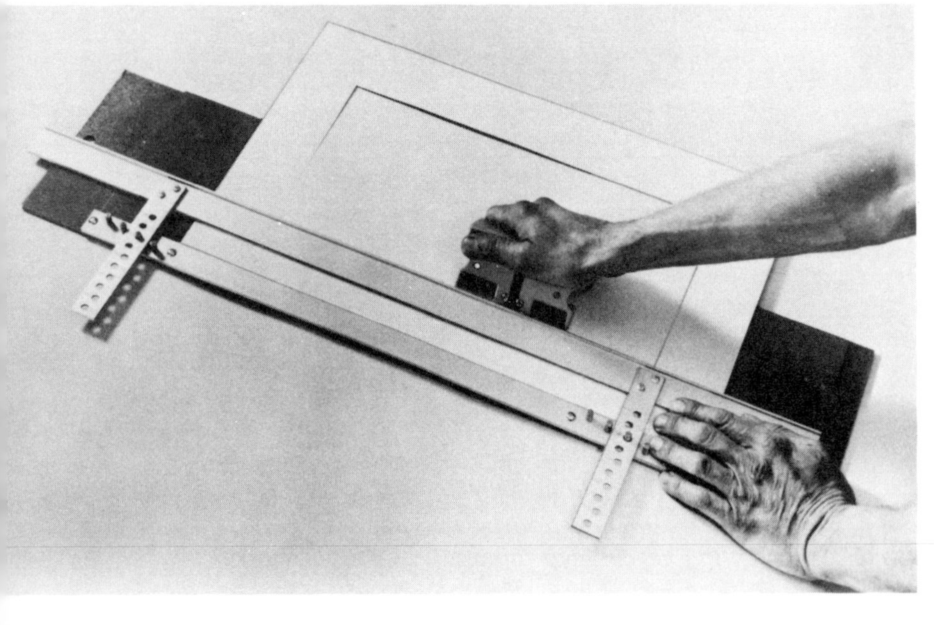

This mat-cutting system offers a straightedge and mat cutter. Photo courtesy the Brookstone Company.

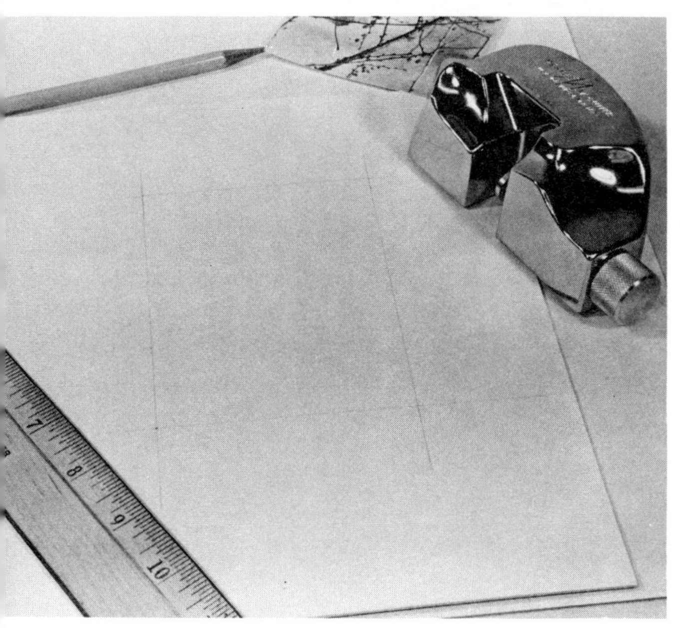

On the back side of the mat, outline the window to be cut out.

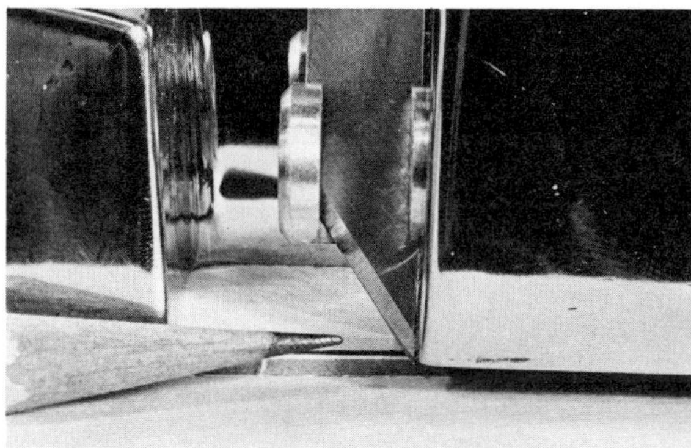

Adjust the cutter's blade so it will cut through the mat and into the scrap beneath.

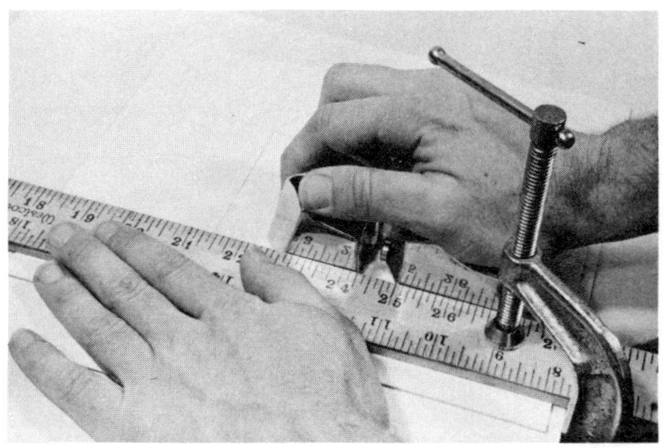

Make sure the straightedge is resting on the outside border of the mat and is held securely in place.

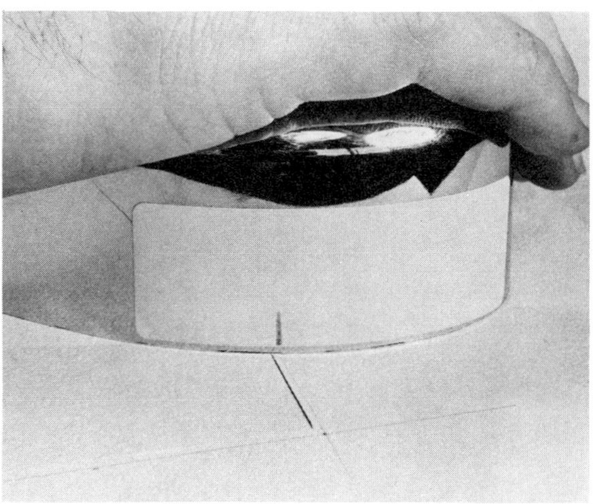

Preventing overcuts with a guiding mark on the outside of the cutter.

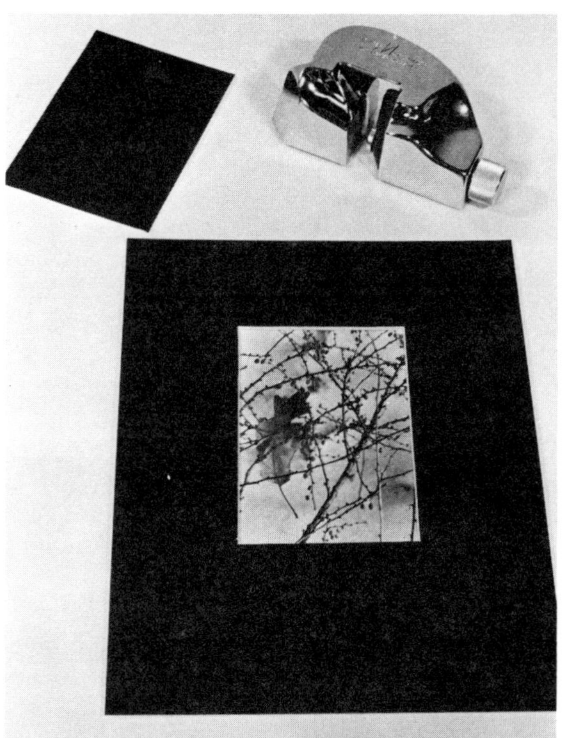

The finished mat will be good, but skills improve with practice.

The first mat you cut will be good but far from perfect. The more mats you cut the greater your chances for a perfect bevel-edged mat.

Square and rectangular mats can be cut fairly easily. Oval and circular mats should be purchased for best results, although a circular mat cutter is available through the Beseler Photo

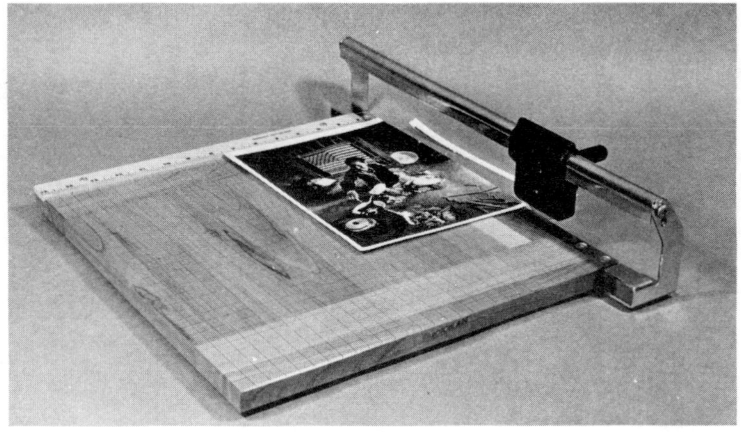

Paper cutters are useful for trimming photographs to desired size.

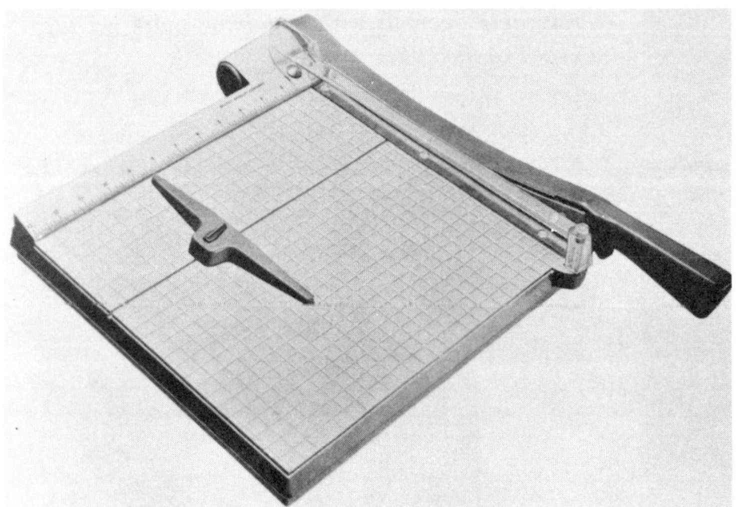

Photograph courtesy the Milton Bradley Company.

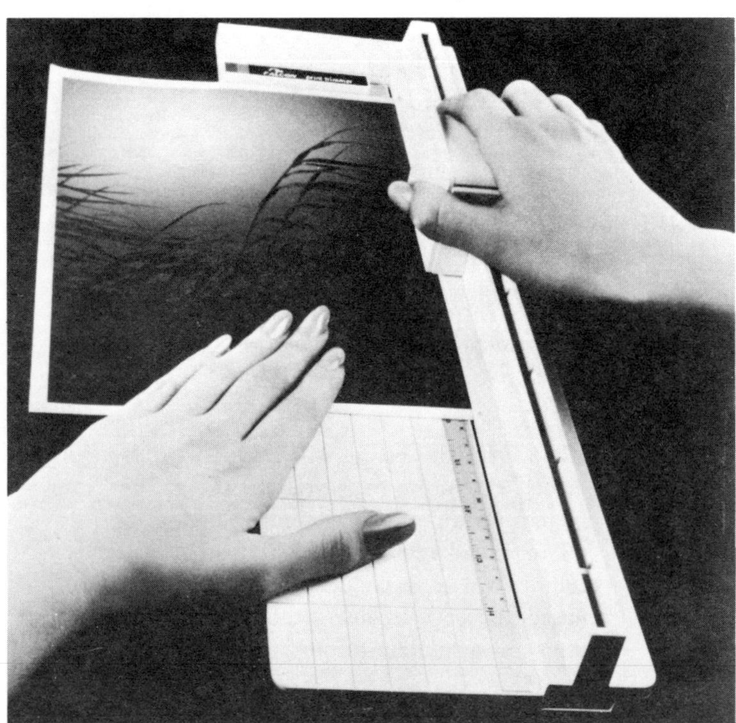

Photography courtesy Falcon Safety Products.

Marketing Company. The Beseler Rotamatte is expensive and impractical for most amateur use.

Mats and mounting boards are both very useful in the art of photographic display. But before they can be used successfully, the print needs to be attached in some manner to the mounting board.

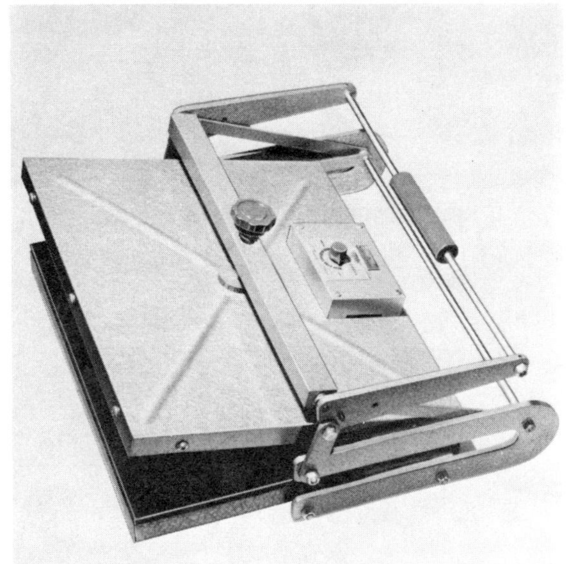

A dry-mounting press. Photo courtesy the Bogen Photo Corporation.

PHOTO-MOUNTING ADHESIVES

Dry-mounting tissue has been a popular device for attaching photographic prints to various mounts. The initial investment for a dry-mounting press is expensive, but you may find one you can borrow from a school or library. If not, a framer will mount your prints for a slight fee.

A thin, dry tissue that becomes an adhesive when heated is attached to the back of a photographic print, using a household iron or a tacking iron specifically designed for adhering the tissue. When necessary, the print and attached tissue are trimmed with a paper cutter.

The print and tissue are then placed on an appropriate mounting board. The print is covered with a protective piece of paper, and the iron is placed on the paper to melt the tissue beneath the print. The print is now in place on the mounting board. The temperature setting should coincide with the instructions supplied by the dry-mounting-tissue manufacturer. High heat can melt resin-coated prints.

Finally, the print and mounting board, covered by a protective piece of paper, are placed in a dry-mounting press. The press is closed, and the tissue heats and melts, making a permanent bond. The mounted print is removed and set on a flat surface with heavy objects on top to prevent warpage of the mount while it cools.

A household iron can be used in place of a dry-mounting press, providing prints no larger than 5×7 inches are being mounted. It becomes cumbersome and sometimes impossible to get a picture mounted flat if a large print is attempted with an iron.

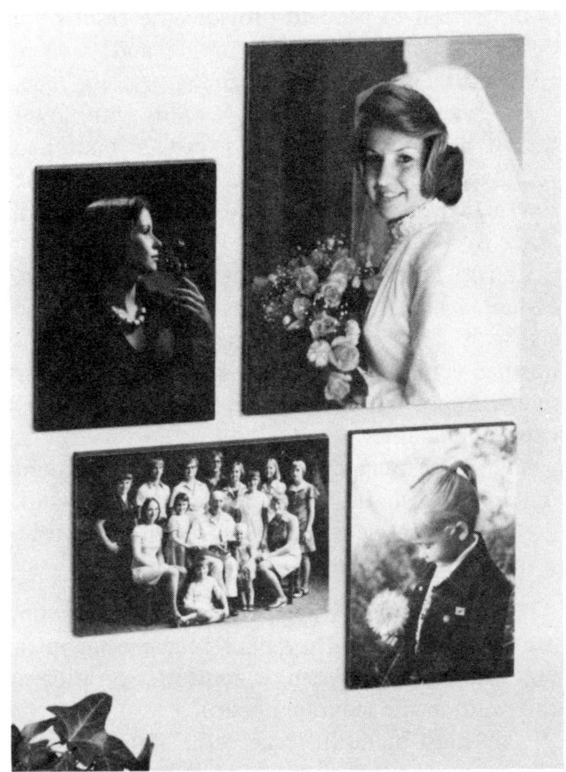

These photo blocks come complete with self-sticking adhesive. Photo courtesy the Taprell Loomis Company.

Cold-mount adhesive for attaching prints is an alternative if the individual doesn't own or have access to a dry-mounting press. There are a variety of cold mounts available at your local photo supply retailers. It's best to experiment with a variety of cold-mount materials to see which one

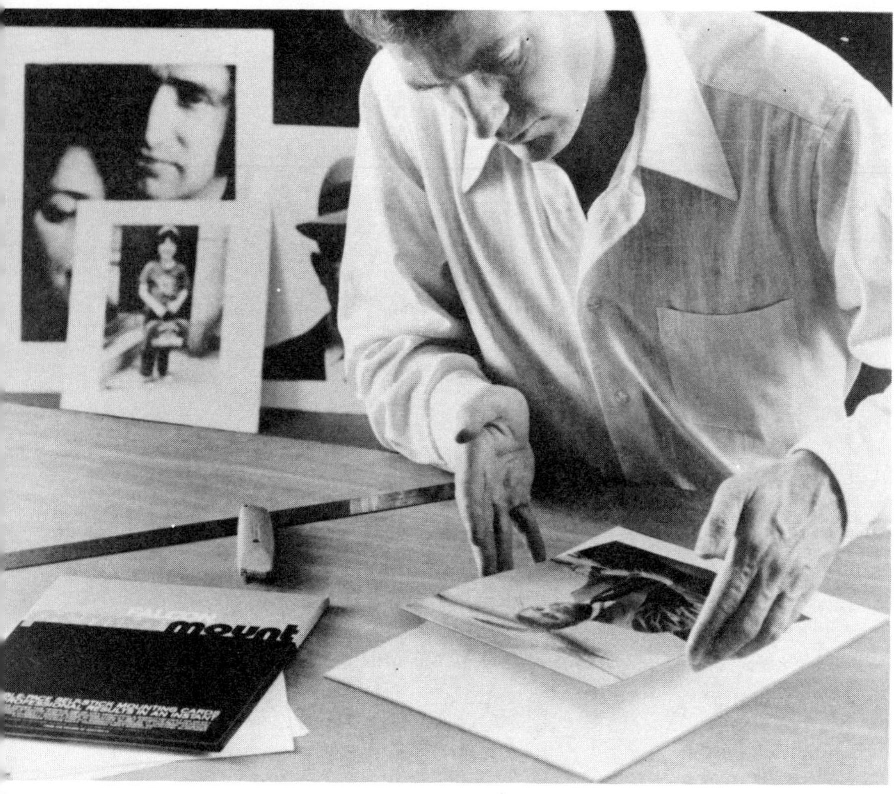

Falcon Safety Products manufactures two-sided self-stick adhesive cards and positioning T square for mounting prints. Photos courtesy Falcon Safety Products.

is the easiest to use and provides the results you desire. All are considered durable and have no effect on the print, such as staining or color fade.

One method uses mounting boards with an adhesive already attached. It's just a matter of removing the protective covering from the adhesive and then placing the print and securing it in place by using a rubber roller.

Falcon Safety Products manufactures Perma/Mount, which is a double-faced, self-stick adhesive card. The adhesive is permanent, and if a mistake is made while aligning the print, it is virtually impossible to remove the print without causing damage.

The 3M Company offers positionable mounting adhesive sheets. They offer accurate positioning of the print before it is secured in place using a roller, or squeegee.

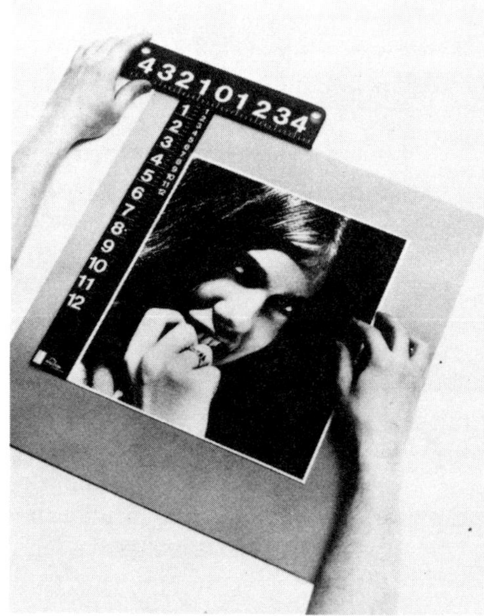

Spray adhesives designed for print mounting are also available. They offer secure attachment but can be tricky when it comes to positioning the print on the mounting board.

Care must be taken to keep the spray adhesive away from the face of the print. When the print is positioned on the mount, it should be covered with a clean piece of paper before applying pressure with a roller. The paper will catch any adhesive that is pushed out the print's sides, and help to keep the roller clean. You won't have to worry about damaging other prints when you go to press them on the mount with the roller.

If accidental adhesive spotting occurs, it can usually be removed with nail-polish remover or whatever substance the spray-adhesive manufacturer designates.

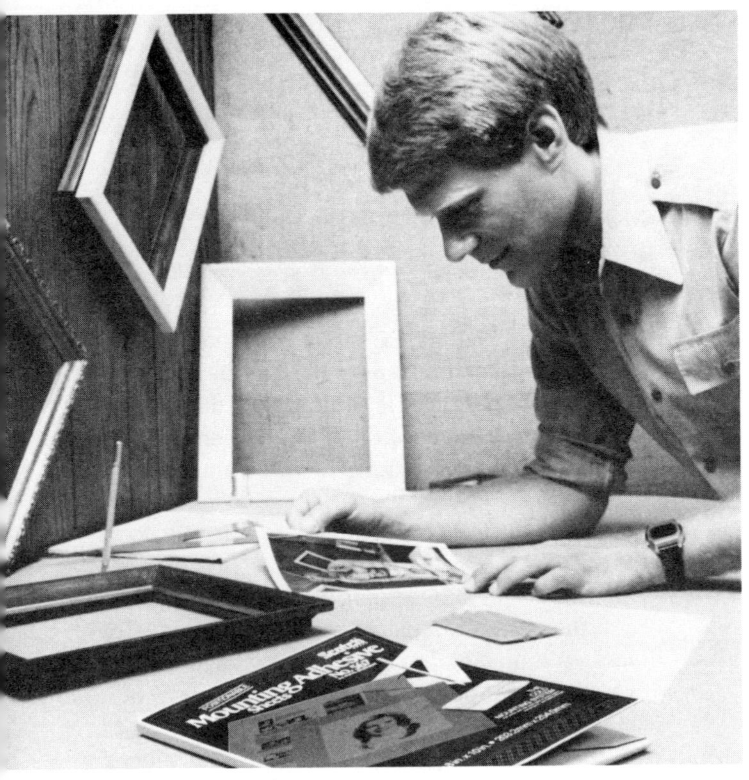

Using positional mounting adhesive sheets. Photo courtesy the 3M Company.

A heavy roller for mounting prints.

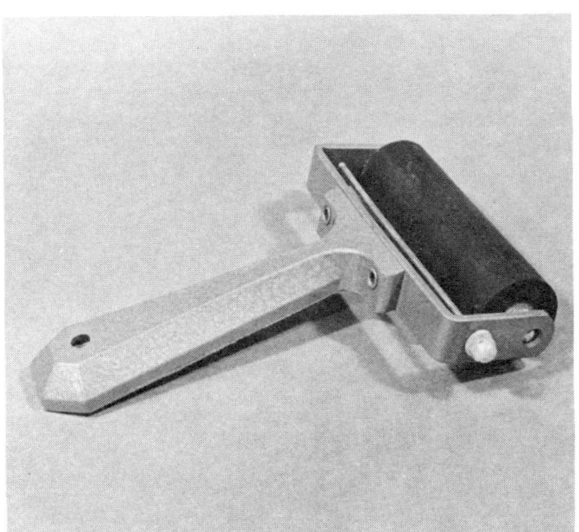

Two coats of spray adhesive allowed to become tacky before print attachment is considered a stronger bond than one coat of adhesive.

Glues and rubber cement will work for print attachment, but they have a tendency to dry out, releasing the bond. These adhesives may also discolor the print they are adhering to the mount. So, unless you are in a hurry or only need a temporarily mounted print, use a spray, dry-mounting, or cold-mount adhesive.

Linen tape can be used for nonpermanent mounting of photos. Linen or other tape can be placed around the edges of the print, securing it in place. The mounted print will have to be covered with a mat to hide the tape.

MAT ATTACHMENT

When a mat is to be placed over a mounted print, it might need to be attached to the mount

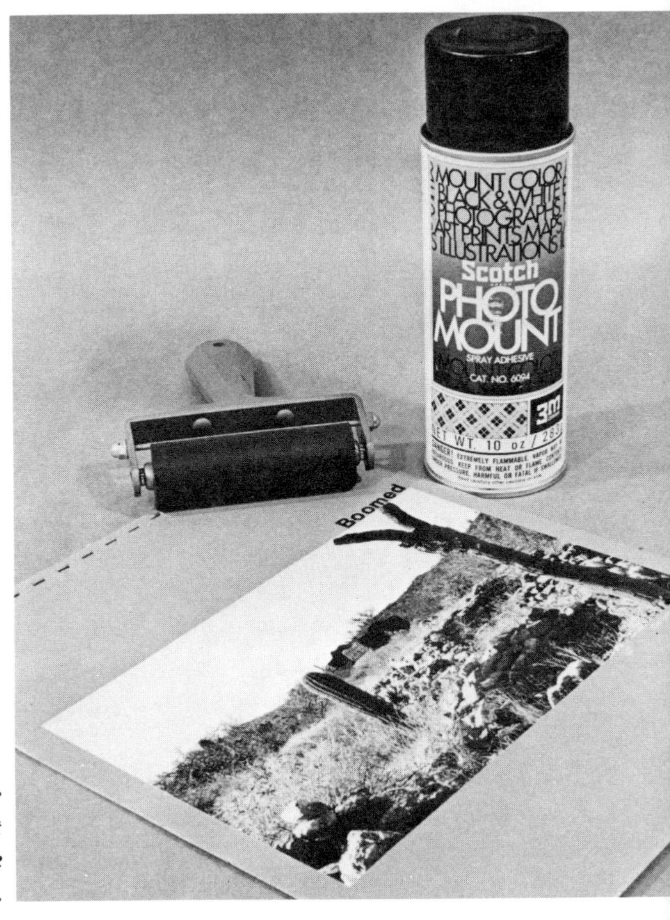

Spray adhesives offer secure print attachment but often require first-time alignment.

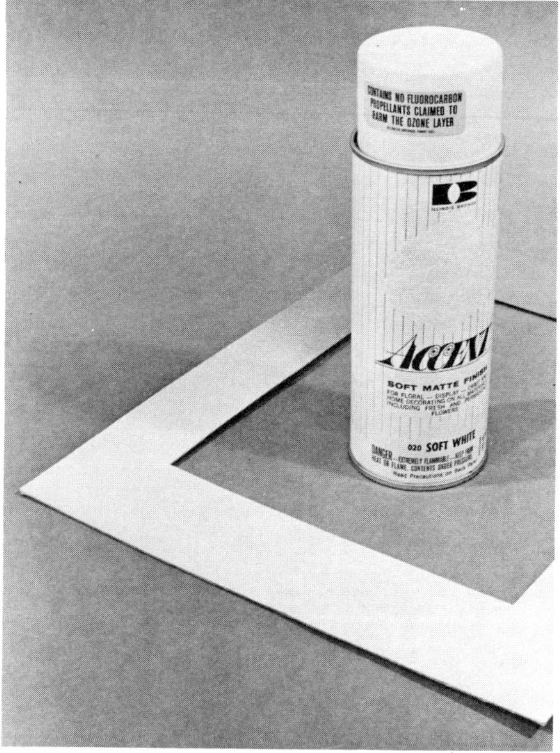

Spray paint for mats.

beneath. Any of the previously mentioned adhesives for print mounting can be used for mat attachment.

If the matted photo is to be used in a frame, it may not be necessary to attach the mat to the mount. The frame should hold the mat and the mount in alignment.

Linen or other tapes can be used as hinges so the mount will stay in relative alignment with the mat. The arrangement may not work as well as permanent mat attachment, because the mat may not lie as close to the mount as possible.

MOUNTED OR MATTED PRINT CARE

As with all photographic images, care must be taken when handling the mounted prints. Mounting is a permanent arrangement and usually cannot be undone if there is some sort of damage.

Clean hands should be used when handling the mounted or matted prints, to avoid unnecessary marking from dirt or grease. On occasion, a mat may become soiled or yellowed and detract from the appearance of the print.

If the mat is not permanently attached, it can be removed and replaced by another mat. At times, it's possible to place a new mat directly over the old. Sometimes you can remove a permanently mounted mat by using a sharp knife to cut the adhesive bond between mat and mount. Then a new mat can be used.

Another approach to repairing a soiled mat is with the use of special mat spray paints. Extreme care must be taken to completely cover the mounted print before spraying with paint. Masking tape and heavy paper can be used.

Mounting and matting prints is not difficult. Anyone can get professional, long-lasting results with a little practice. If your photographic display is limited to just a few large prints, you can pay a framer for the service, or some custom processing labs will do the work if you include the instruction in your order.

4

FRAMES: MAKING, HANGING, AND DISPLAYING

Frames have always been the most feasible and acceptable method of photographic print display. There are certainly thousands of different frames to choose from, with all shapes, sizes, and colors to fit any home or office environment. A frame helps set off the photograph by isolating it. This enables the picture's shapes, tones, and content to be easily seen and studied. A frame is nothing more than an outline for the picture—an outline that helps draw the viewer's eyes to the photograph, almost as if it were saying, "Look at me."

There's no secret to selecting the proper frame for a photograph. It's simply a matter of choosing one that is plain or basic in design. Fancy frames are fine for paintings, but for photographs an ornate surrounding will detract from the photos themselves.

Photographic frame selection can be simplified by using the customary photo frames. If there is a gallery within your city that specializes in selling or displaying photographic prints, pay them a visit. You'll find the framed and matted prints enclosed in a narrow, usually silver-colored, aluminum border. It's nothing more than readily available sectional framing.

There are several manufacturers that sell these metal frames. They are sold in packages containing two sections of equal length. Many lengths are available, and one needs to buy two packages to complete a frame. The joining hardware is also included. If you plan to cover the matted print with glass, you'll have to purchase it separately.

Frame selection can be just that simple if you are willing to standardize your print display technique. But why standardize when there are so many attractive alternatives in frame selection? Even the sectionalized metal frames are available in gold, black, and an array of other colors. Besides metal, frames can be made of plastics, ceramics, and the traditional wood.

To obtain a precise photo/frame match, take your photo and mat to the nearest framing store and actually test frames to see which one adds to the photo's visual appeal. The trained personnel will help you in the proper frame selection and, if need be, mount, mat, and frame your picture for you. Of course, you'll need your checkbook to compensate the framer for the service.

Large photo supply stores will have an assortment of framing apparatus. The popularity of picture taking has encouraged the development of specialized framing and display products and kits

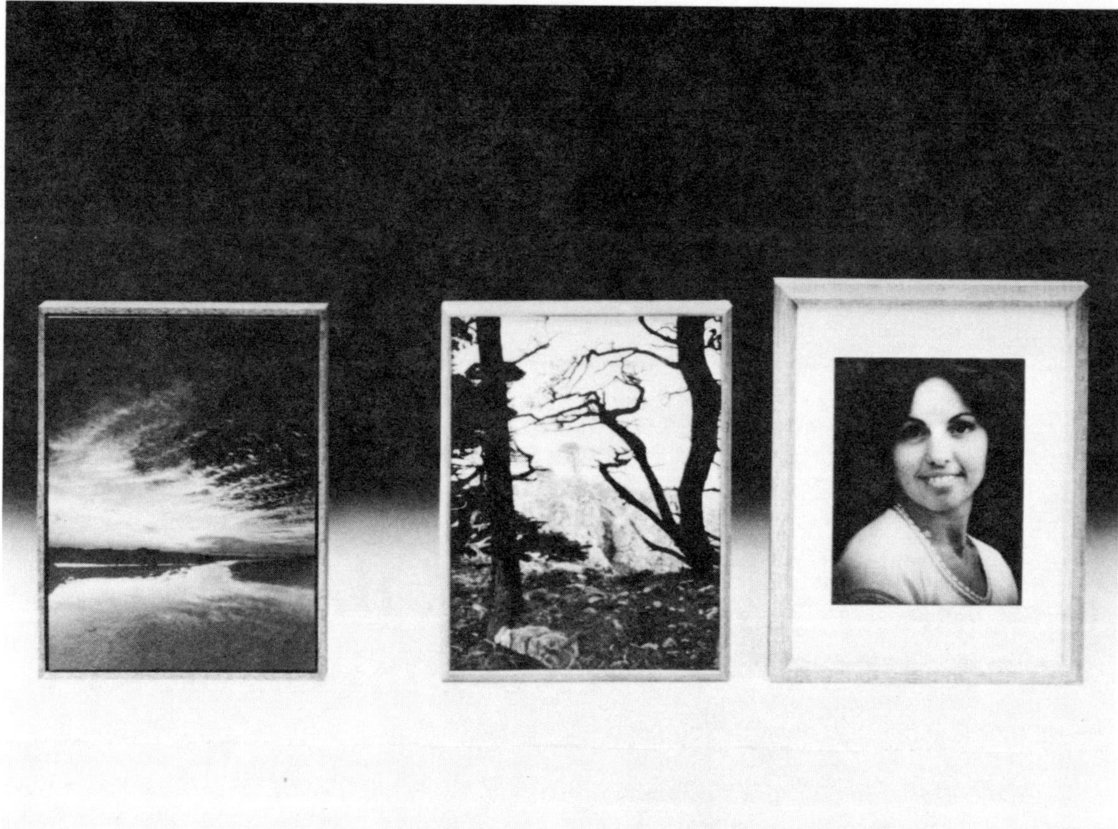

Frames that are simple in design enhance photographic images. Photo courtesy Photo Art Frames, Inc.

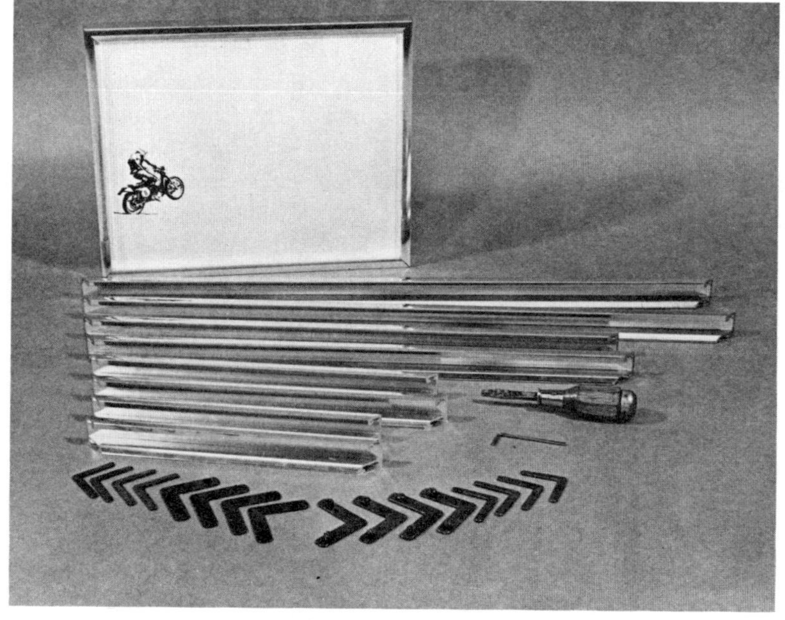

Sectional metal frames come in a variety of sizes and colors for quick, standardized photo display.

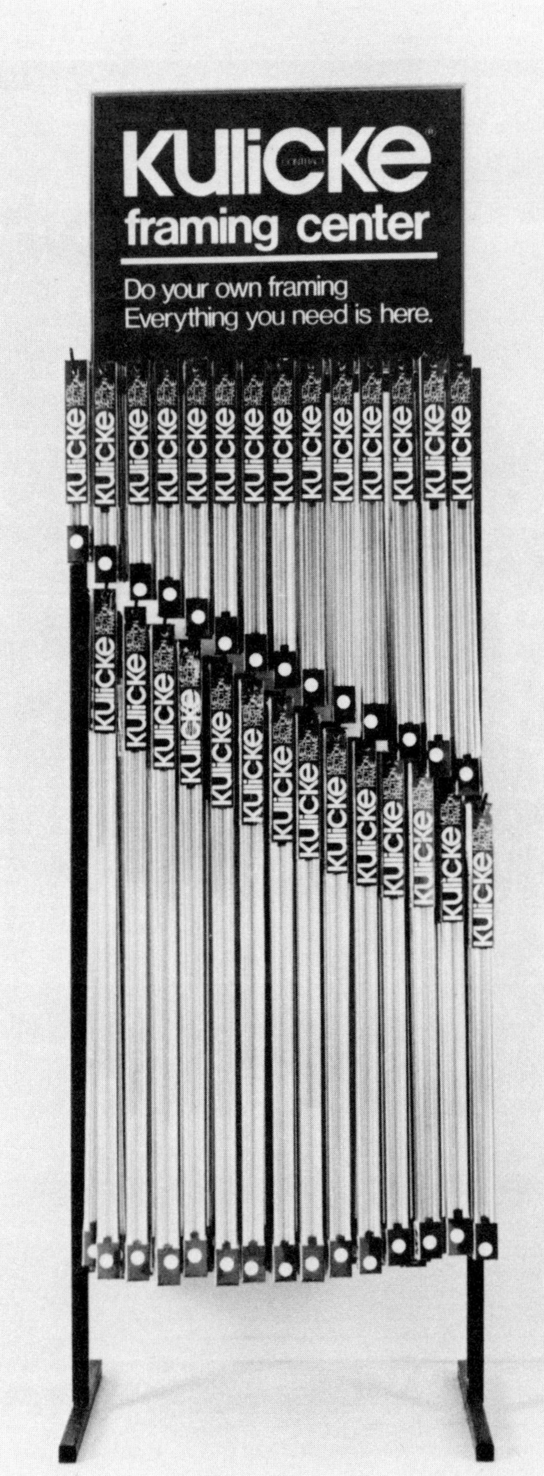

A display of sectional metal frames generally sold in a package containing two framing strips. Two packages are needed to frame a picture. Photo courtesy Kulicke Frames Inc.

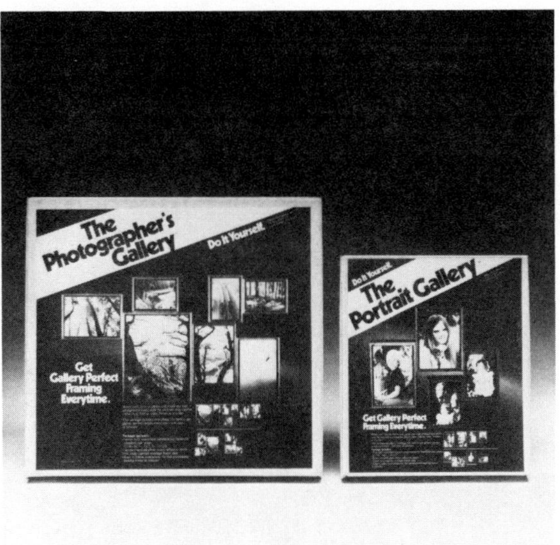

Framing kits such as these provide everything you need but the prints. Photo courtesy Photo Art Frames, Inc.

just for photographic prints. Many of the kits offer a natural wood frame, an oversize sheet of photo mounting adhesive, a nonwarping Masonite mounting board, plus the necessary but often neglected instructions—everything you'll need to properly frame a particular-size photograph.

The Gallery Series, by Photo Art Frames, includes kits with various-size wood frames, mounting adhesive, instructions, and special montage frame clips for quick joining of the frames. You'll be able to manipulate a whole group of framed photos for display on a wall. Simple—and relatively inexpensive for what you get.

Other photo product manufacturers, such as Falcon Safety Products and Coda Inc., sell three-dimensional boxes with mounting adhesive for print display. The various-size boxes are easy to hang, due to their light weight. One small push-pin inserted into a wall is capable of holding the box in place.

Simple plastic boxes by Dax and Kulicke are easy to use. A removable cardboard box is inside a larger plastic box. A print is inserted between the plastic and cardboard box and you're ready to hang the three-dimensional creations, or stand them on a table.

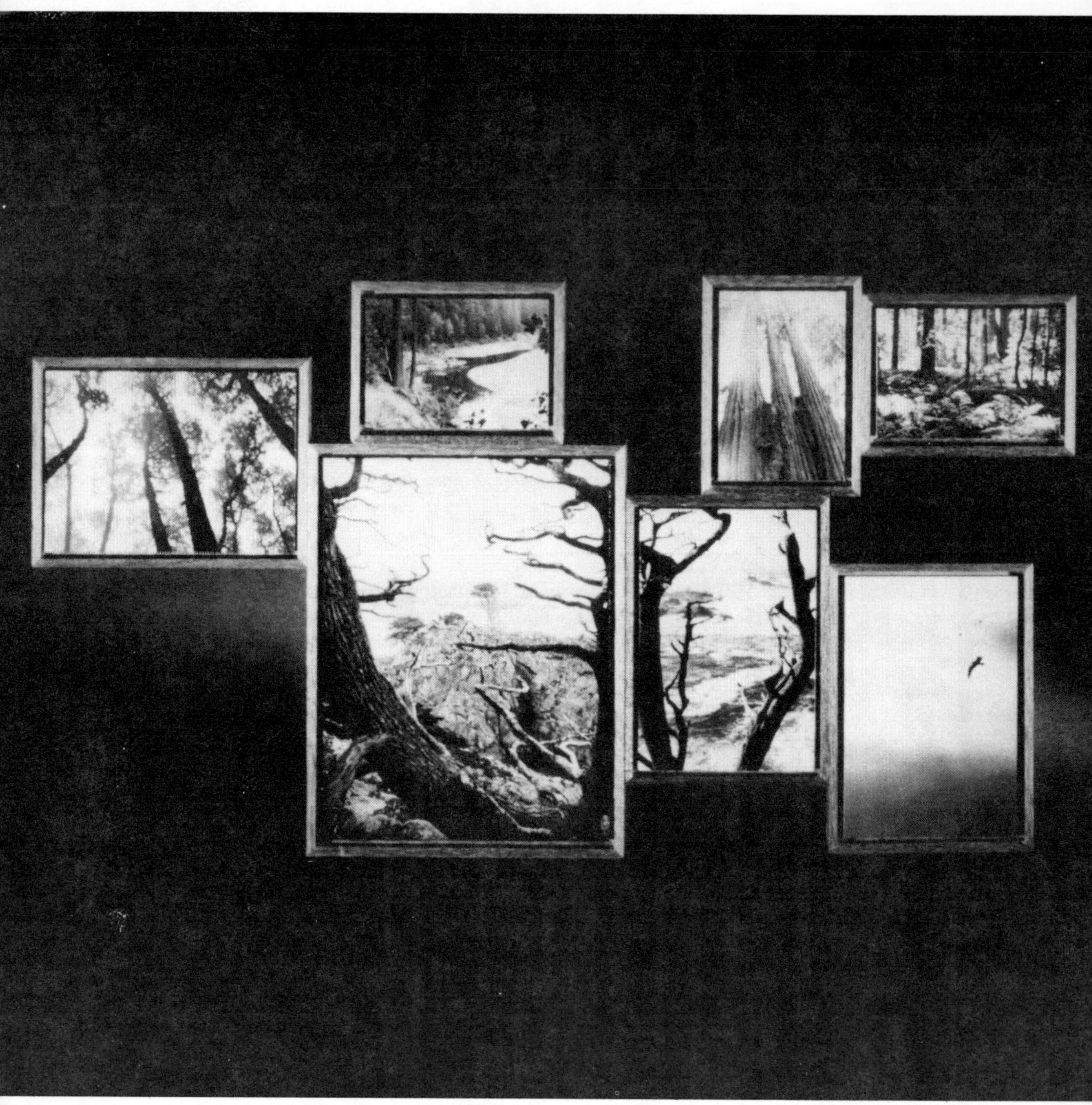

The Gallery Series includes several frames for displaying grouped pictures. Photo courtesy Photo Art Frames, Inc.

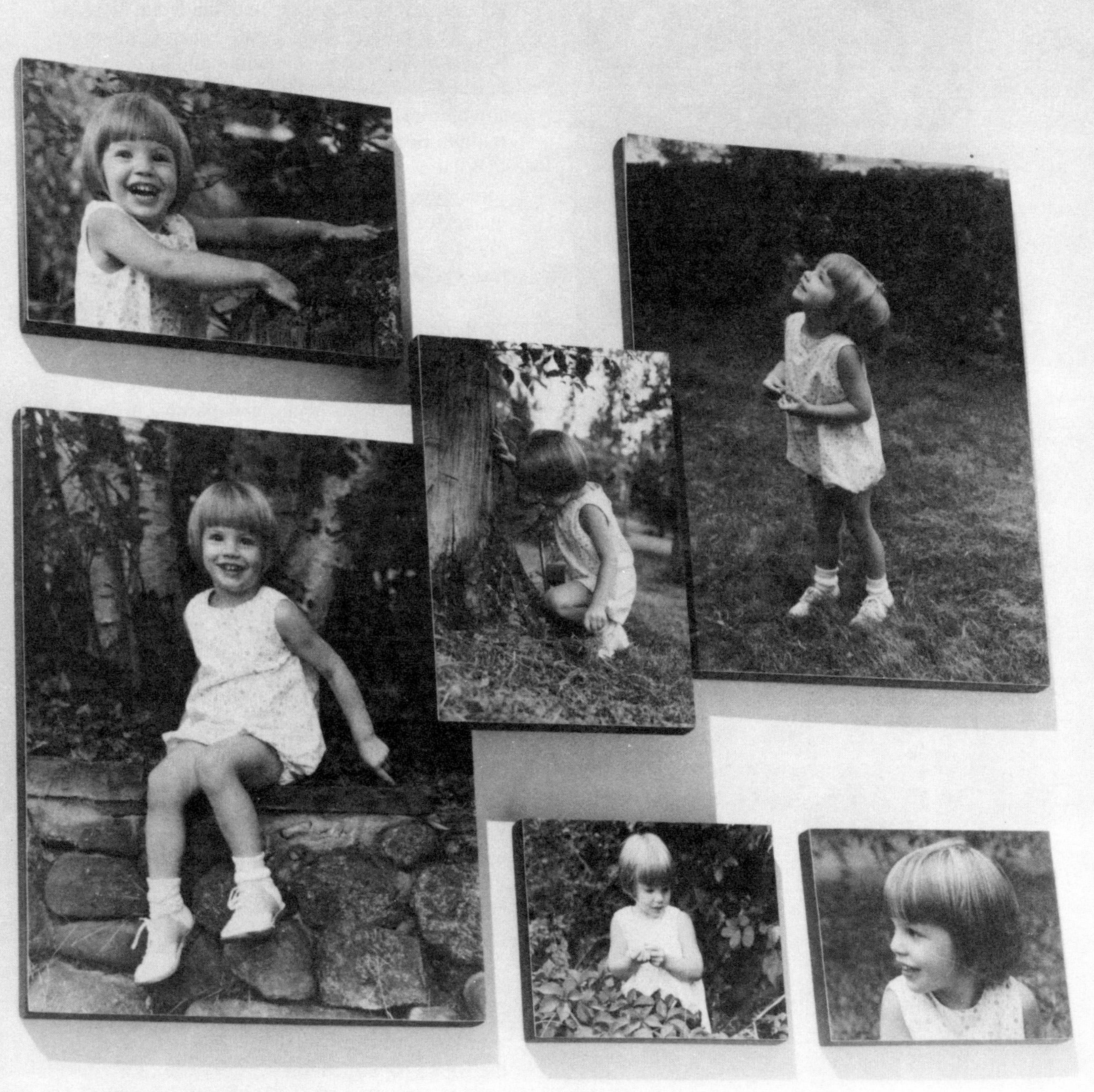

Coda's Galerie® is three-dimensional with adhesive already attached. Photo courtesy Coda Inc.

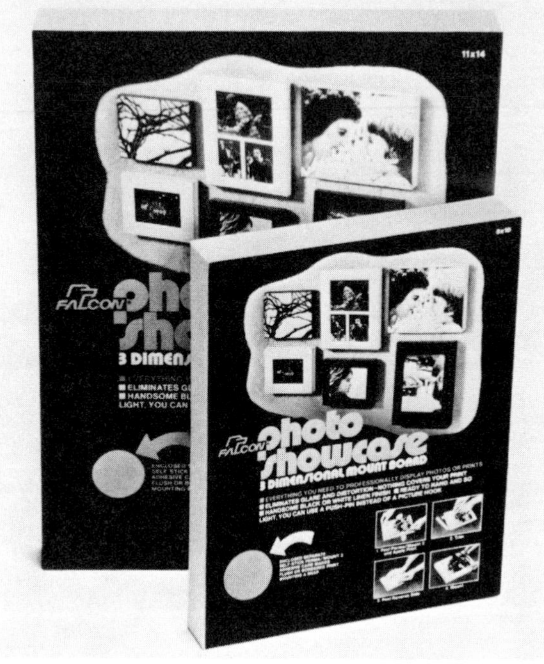

Falcon's Photo Showcase is a box with cold-mounting material included. Photo courtesy Falcon Safety Products.

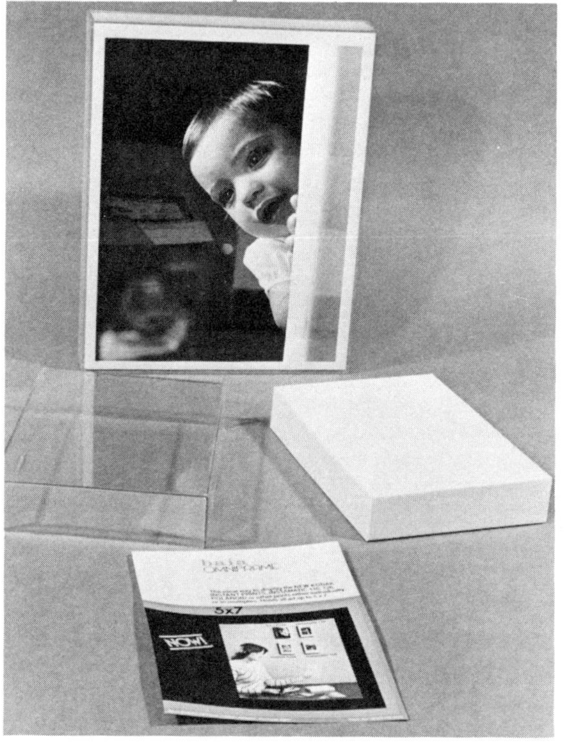

Plastic boxes make photo display as simple as possible.

Besides the acrylic boxes, there are a number of tabletop plastic frames on the market. They are usually self-standing and made to fit standard-size photos. Their rigid construction makes it possible to slip in an unmounted photo for a finished display. Removal of the print may be troublesome if it sticks to the acrylic due to a buildup of heat and moisture.

Whatever the photo's content or size, there is some type of frame available for enhancing the image for display. The selection of the framing material is strictly personal, relating to one's own tastes and surroundings. Frame selection is like selecting a photograph for display. The composition, construction material, and quality of the frame should be considered. Most important is whether or not the frame serves its purpose. Is it supposed to hold the framed photo on the wall without really being noticed, or is it there to help draw a viewer's eyes to the image it surrounds?

If the frame does what it is supposed to do without detracting from the appearance of the photograph, it is a good frame. If by chance you can't purchase a frame to fill your needs, you can invest in a few tools and make your own, unique wood frames.

MAKING YOUR OWN, UNIQUE WOOD FRAMES

You've taken the photograph, possibly made your own print, mounted the photo, and selected a mat. Now you may want to make your own wooden frame for that very special image. There are hundreds of wooden frames to choose from in the nearest frame shop. But the cost might be prohibitive, and there is always the chance you just can't find what you want.

Simple, photo-enhancing frames are easy to make if you have a few necessary tools and a place to work. Below is a list of tools you might need and descriptions of the tools' functions during frame construction.

THE MITER BOX

Most frames fit tightly together to form a rectangle. The joints are 45-degree angles. The 45-degree angle is the most difficult and important aspect of quality wood frame making. The angle must be accurate and tight-fitting to give a handcrafted frame the look of quality.

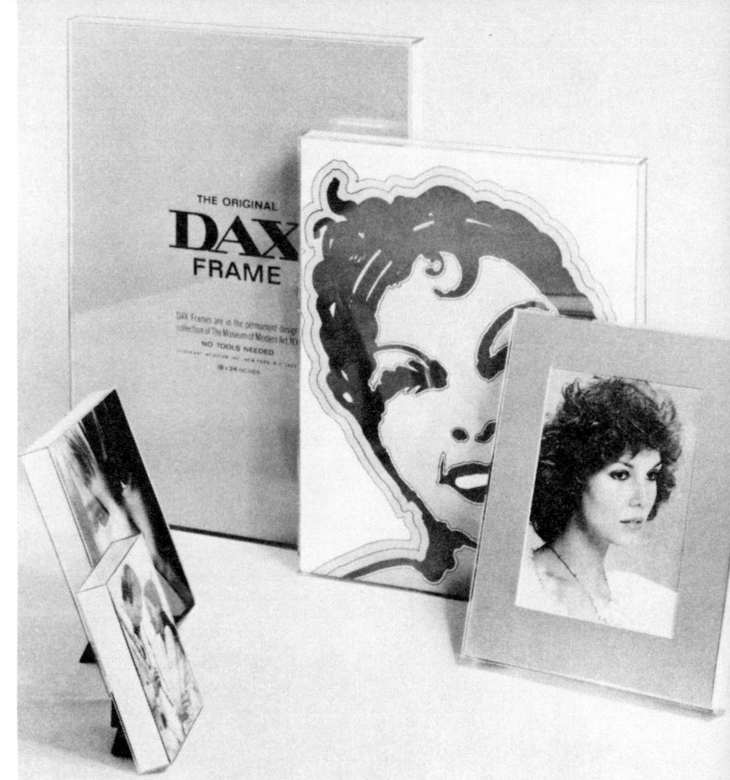

The original plastic box frame by Dax. Photo courtesy Dax Manufacturers, Inc.

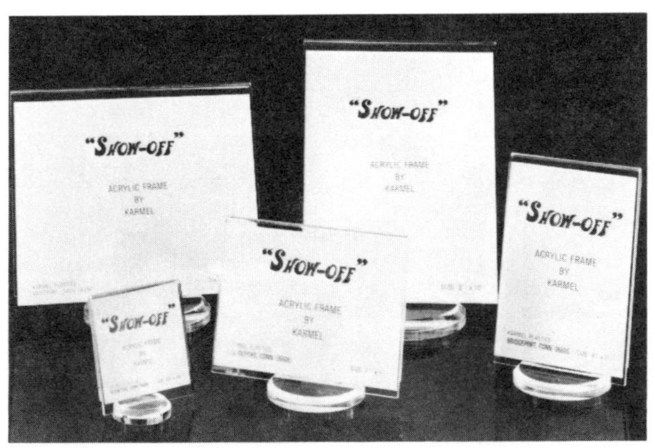

ABOVE AND RIGHT: *Acrylic frames.* Photos courtesy Karmel Plastics.

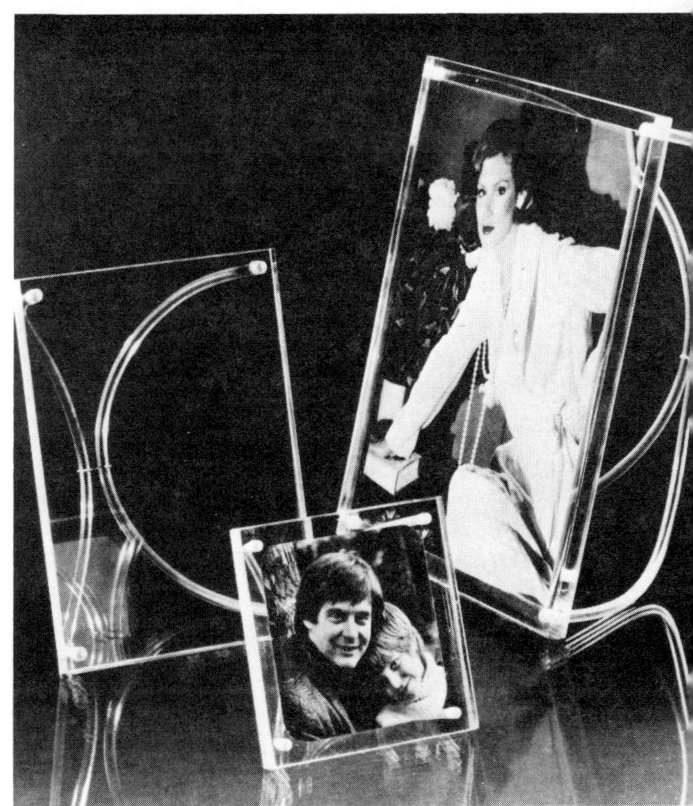

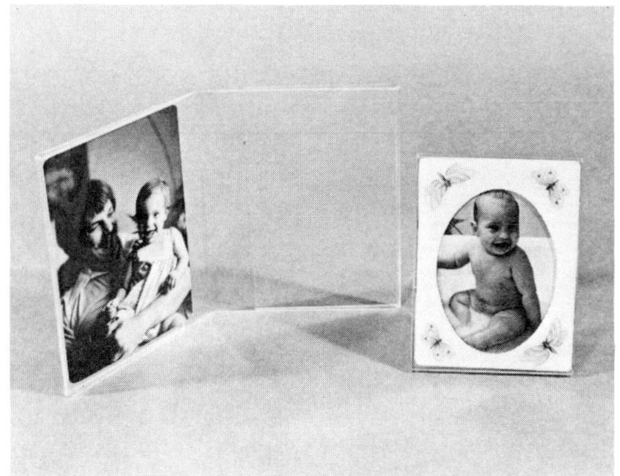

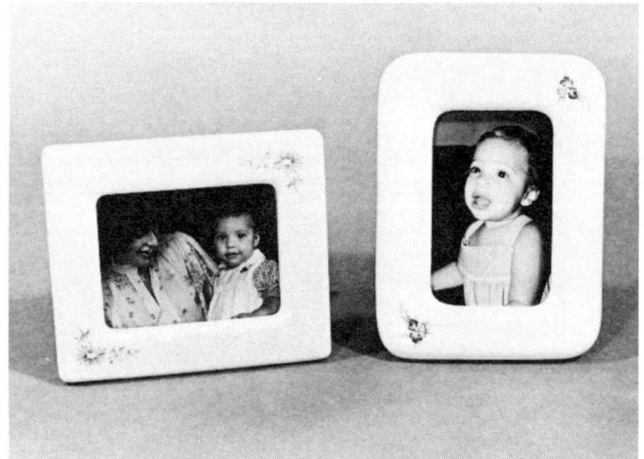

Samples of other commercial frames.

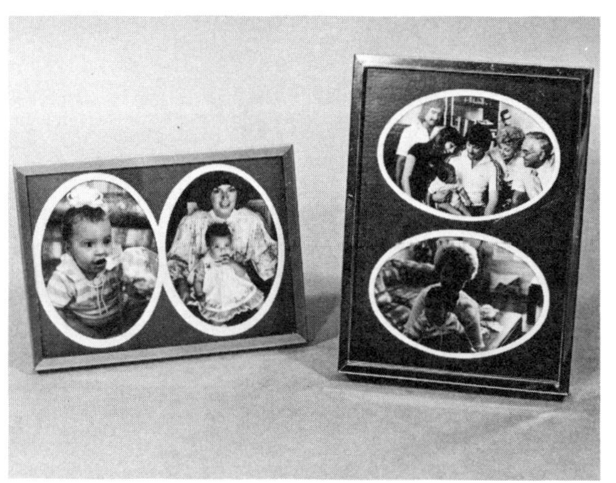

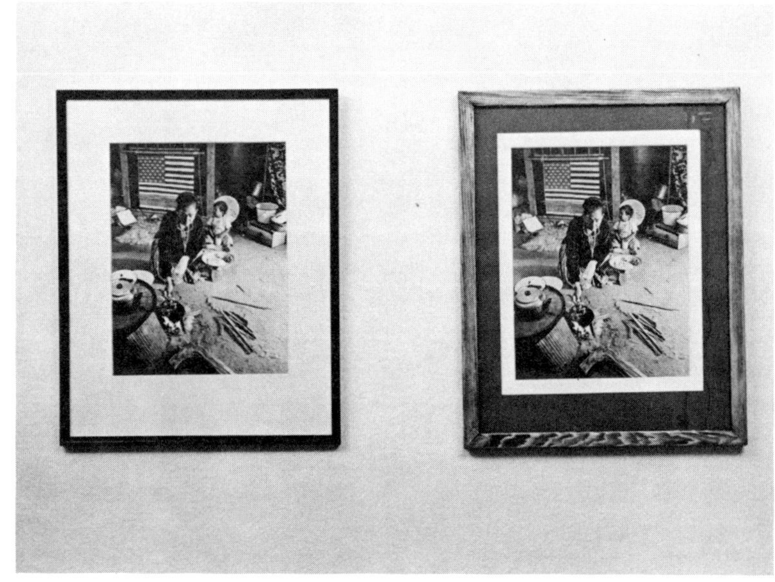

A purchased frame on the left, a handmade frame on the right.

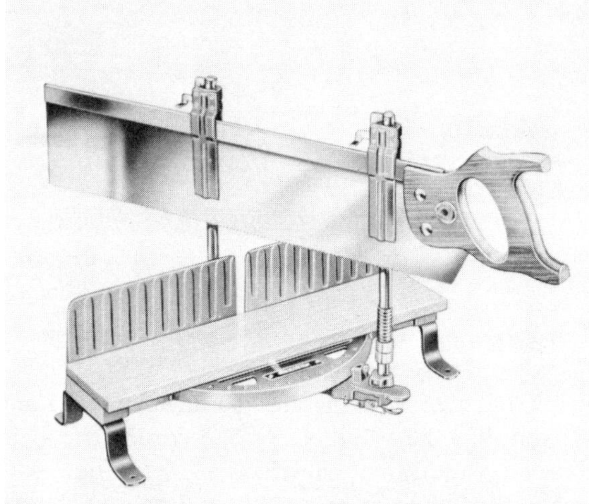

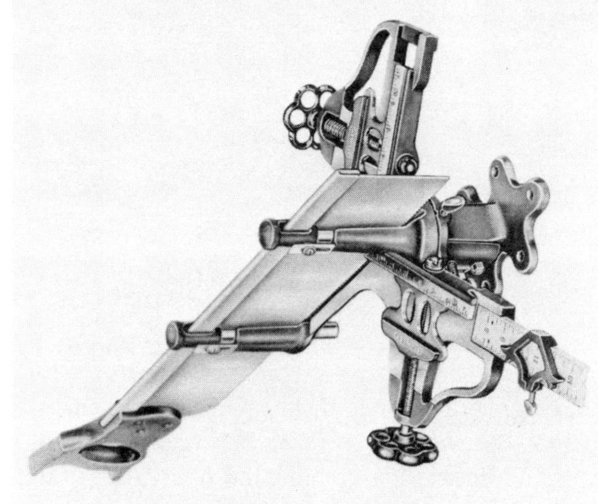

Samples of miter boxes. Photos courtesy The Stanley Works.

The miter box is designed for cutting 45-degree angles accurately. The selection of miter boxes on the market is vast. What you buy is based on what you can afford and how much use the tool will get. There are inexpensive wooden and plastic miter boxes, and there are heavy, durable metal miters. As with most items, you get what you pay for.

The purpose of the miter box is to guide the saw you are using. The cut will be straight and accurate if you use a miter box. When you butt two 45-degree angles together, the joint will be nearly invisible.

THE BACKSAW

Backsaws are designed for making mitered cuts. They can be used freehand but function best when used in conjunction with the miter box.

When you cut with the backsaw, use smooth, long strokes with as little pressure as possible. Let the saw's weight and teeth do the cutting. That's what it is designed for. To prevent excessive splintering of the wood when you near the end of the cut, cut slowly and be sure the material you are cutting is held firmly in place.

C-CLAMPS

These clamps are useful in many frame-making operations. They can hold the wood you are cutting in a miter box to free your hands and help place your concentration on the cut you are making.

C-clamps can also be used to hold glued pieces of wood together while it is drying. (Caution: The clamps are made of metal and can mar the wood, so protective pieces of scrap wood should be used between the clamp and the wood being held in place.)

HAMMERS

Everyone knows what a hammer is, but they do come in various sizes. A heavy claw hammer is useful for driving and removing nails quickly. The tack hammer, which is considerably lighter and has a smaller driving head, is useful when accuracy is important and you are limited in the area in which to hammer.

NAIL SET

This small, pointed tool is used to drive finishing nails below the surface of the wood you are

This chopper trims mitered molding for accurate frame construction. Photo courtesy the Brookstone Company.

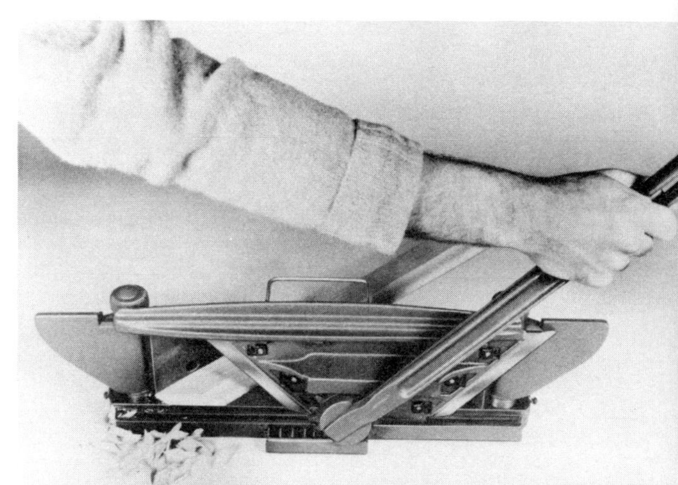

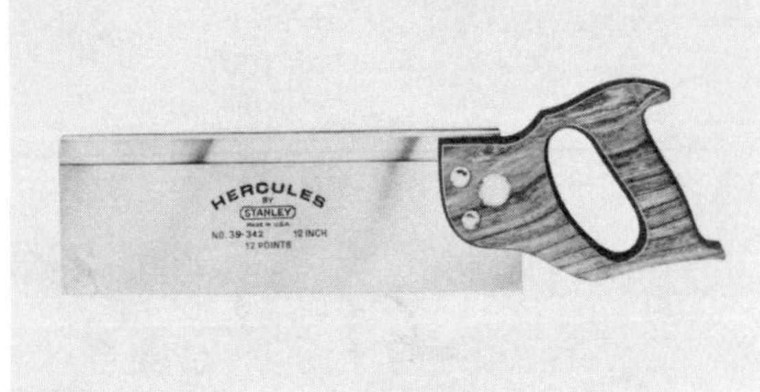

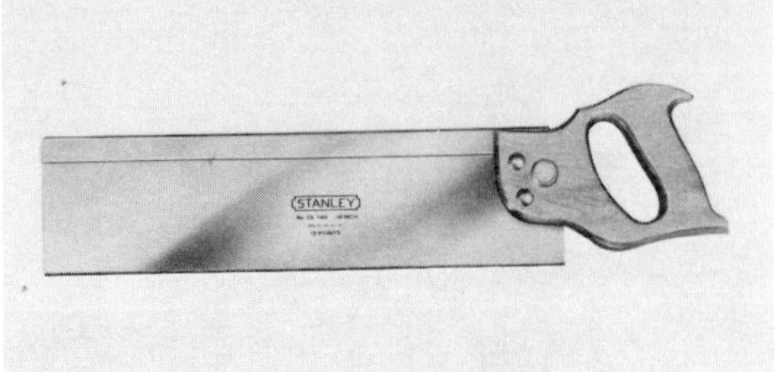

Backsaws. Photos courtesy The Stanley Works.

making your frames from. Once the nails are below the wood's surface, the remaining holes can be filled with a commercial filler. After sanding and finishing, the holes will be unnoticeable.

CORNER CLAMP

The specially designed corner clamp is for holding the mitered ends of the frame together while the glue is drying and the finishing nails are driven into the wood. Only one corner clamp is needed for frame construction, but four will make the job go more quickly and help in checking squareness of the frame.

Small C-clamps hold glued material together while the adhesive dries.

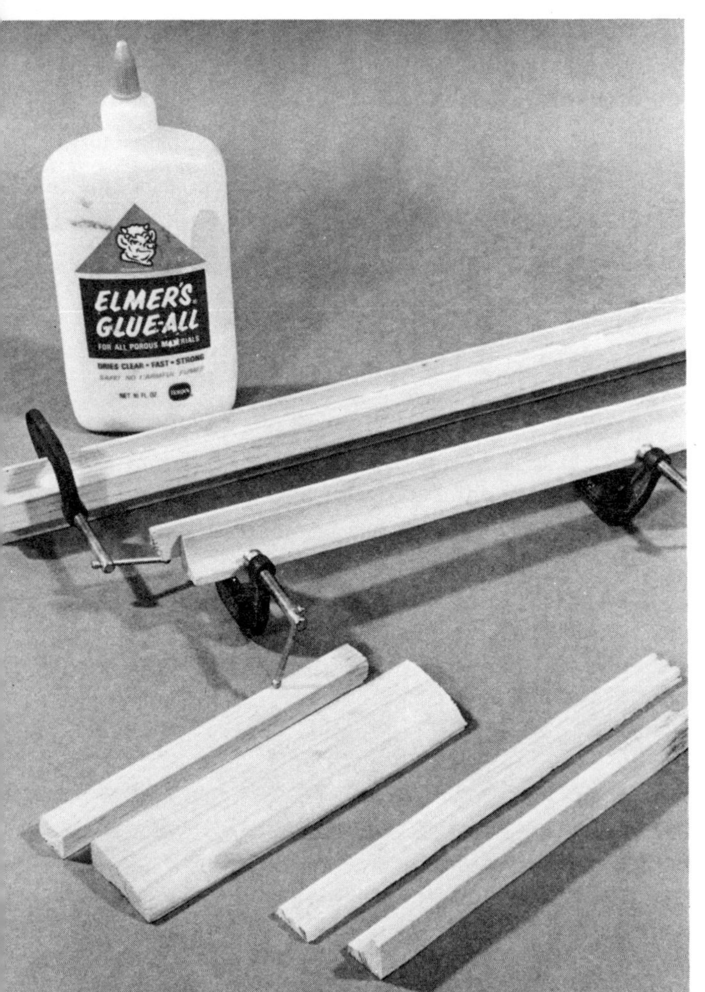

OTHER EQUIPMENT

A measuring device of some type is needed to figure out the dimensions of the frame so guiding marks can be made and accurate cuts can follow. A flex tape, yardstick, or wooden ruler will work.

Other materials you'll need to complete the handcrafted frames are *a pencil, finishing nails, wood glue, filler,* and *sandpaper.* The frames that you construct will have to be sanded smooth before they can be painted or stained. A small *sanding block* will make the job easier. *Paint* or *stain* can be applied with either spray aerosol or by using a brush.

If you plan to protect the framed print with glass, you may need a *glass cutter.*

A final touch to any framing job is the application of a protective backing using *kraft paper.* This is the heavy brown paper used for wrapping packages for mailing. The kraft paper is attached to the back side of the finished frame to help keep out dust and dirt.

You'll also need some sort of *picture hangers,* which can be wire and screw eyes or one of the many other picture-hanging devices available.

The most important part of frame construction is the selection of wood molding. You have a choice of either purchasing picture-frame molding from a frame shop or visiting your nearest lumber supply dealer to survey the carpenter's molding. The lumber yard's molding is the least expensive. At first glance, carpenter's molding may seem inappropriate for frame construction. However, using a little imagination and the com-

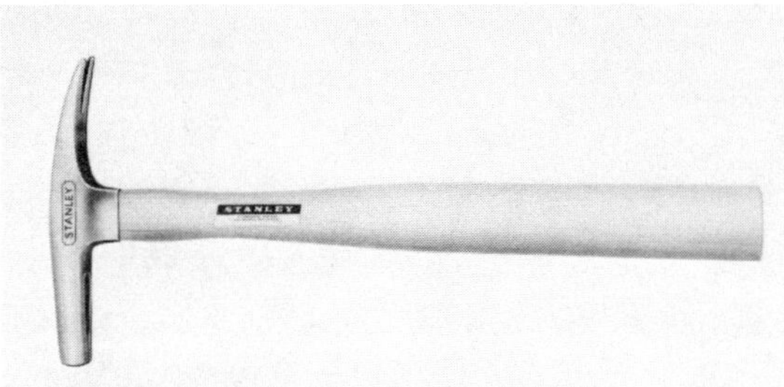

Small tack hammer is useful in driving finishing nails into wood molding. Photo courtesy The Stanley Works.

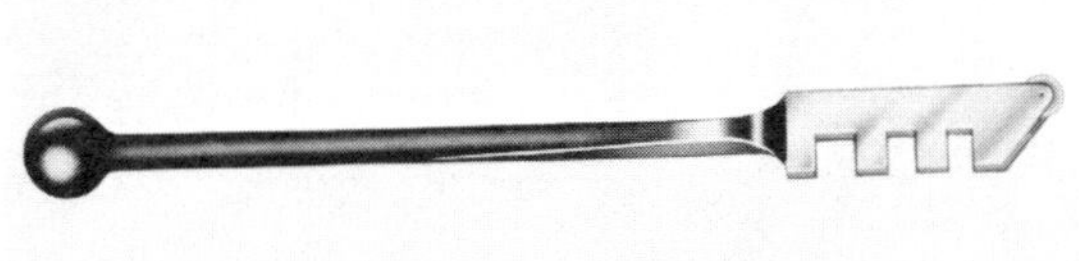

An easy-to-use glass cutter. Photo courtesy The Stanley Works.

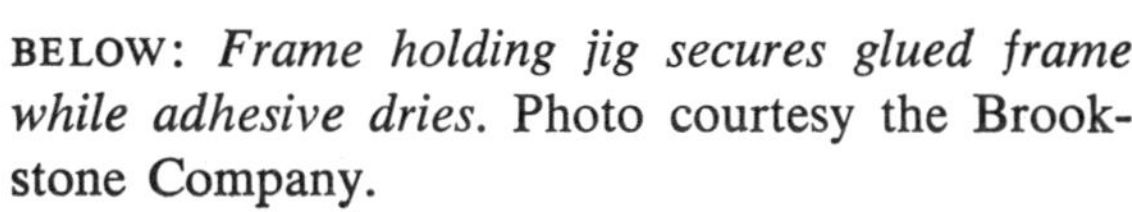

BELOW: *Frame holding jig secures glued frame while adhesive dries.* Photo courtesy the Brookstone Company.

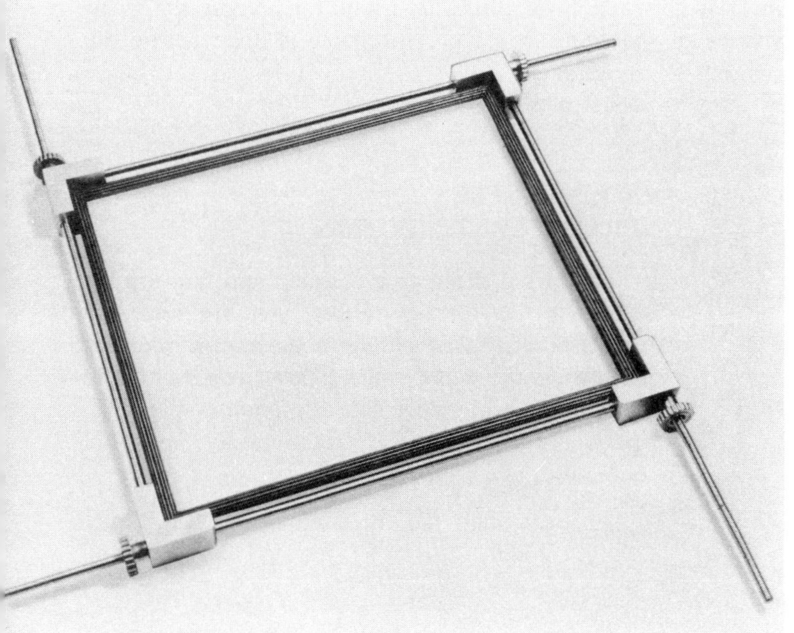

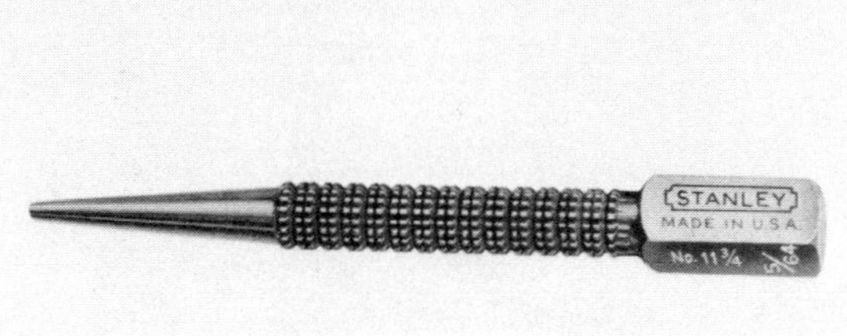

A nail set. Photo courtesy The Stanley Works.

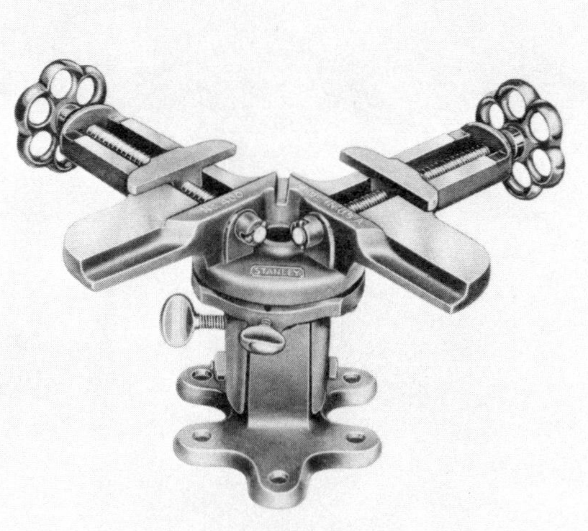

ABOVE AND BELOW: *Samples of corner clamps.* Photos courtesy The Stanley Works.

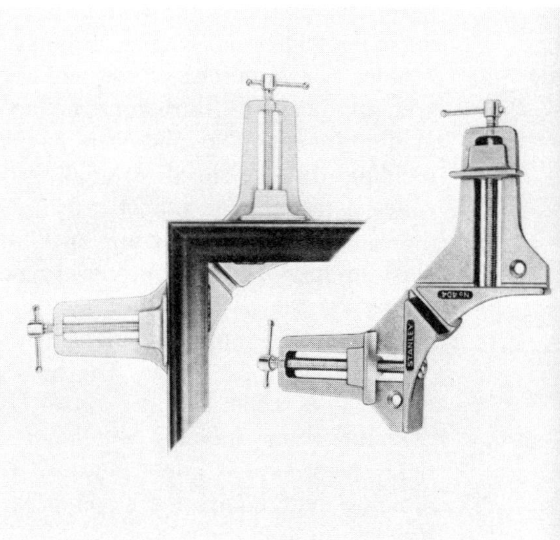

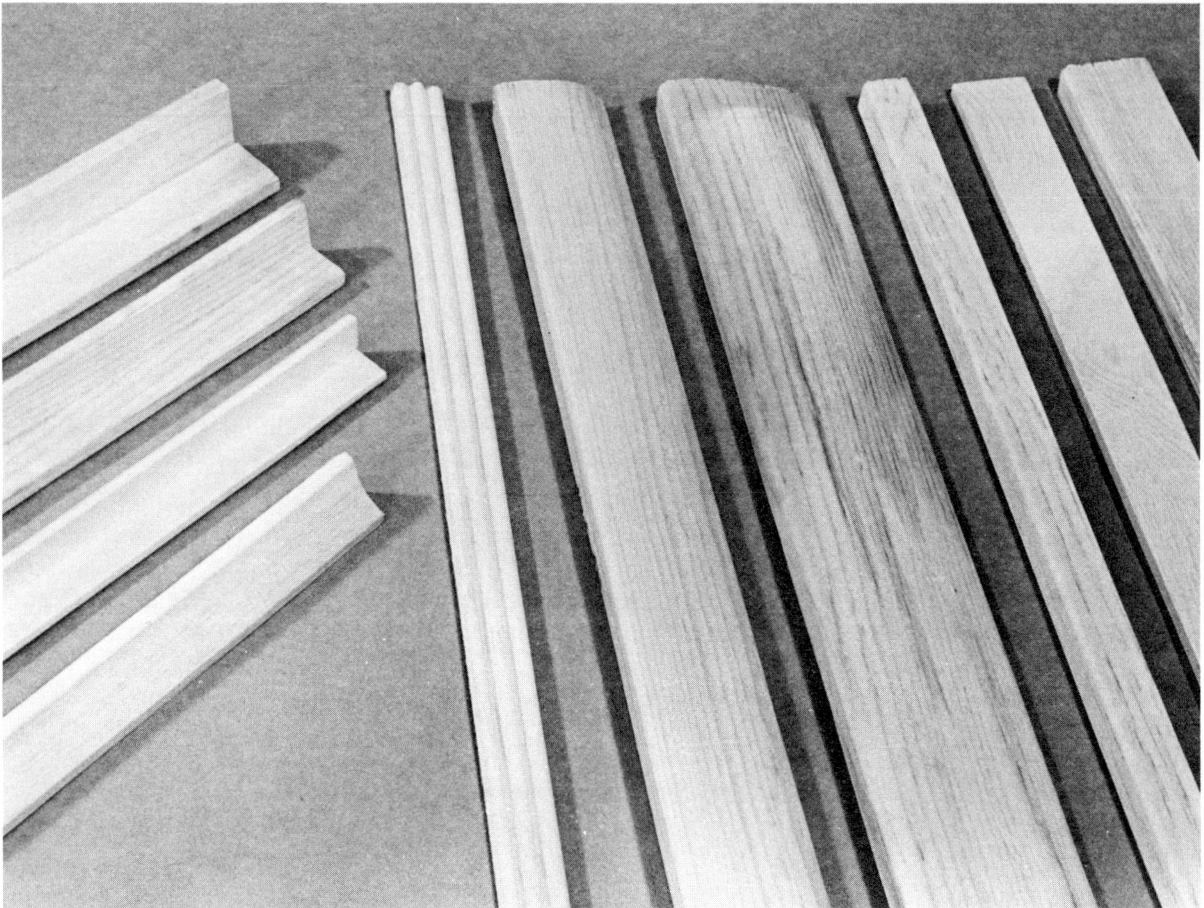

A few random samples of molding found at lumber supply dealers.

bination of one or more moldings, you can create any type of frame you desire. (There are many picture-frame books available at your local library that illustrate the various frames you can make combining molding from the lumber yard.)

Once you've purchased the molding you want, you are ready to start constructing your own, unique frames. The first step is preparing the molding. Frames need a small groove or lip called a rabbet. The rabbet provides a place for the mounting board, picture, mat, and optional glass to rest. The majority of frames have the rabbet on the back side of the frame. Others, which can be almost borderless, have the rabbet on the front of the frame. The mounted print is glued to the rabbet, and glass is not used.

Picture-frame molding will have a rabbet already incorporated into the wood. Lumber-yard molding may require the attachment of strips of molding to form the rabbet.

Small strips of wood are glued and nailed, if necessary, to larger pieces of molding forming the rabbet. C-clamps are useful for holding the glued molding in place. The gluing is done before the molding is cut to the proper length for frame construction.

STEP-BY-STEP FRAME CONSTRUCTION

Once your molding is selected and built up for design or to form a rabbet, you are ready to begin cutting the molding to the proper size. By following the steps listed below, you can build and finish a simple frame for photographic display.

1. Decide what size the frame has to be to surround the mounted or matted photo. When measuring, always allow enough

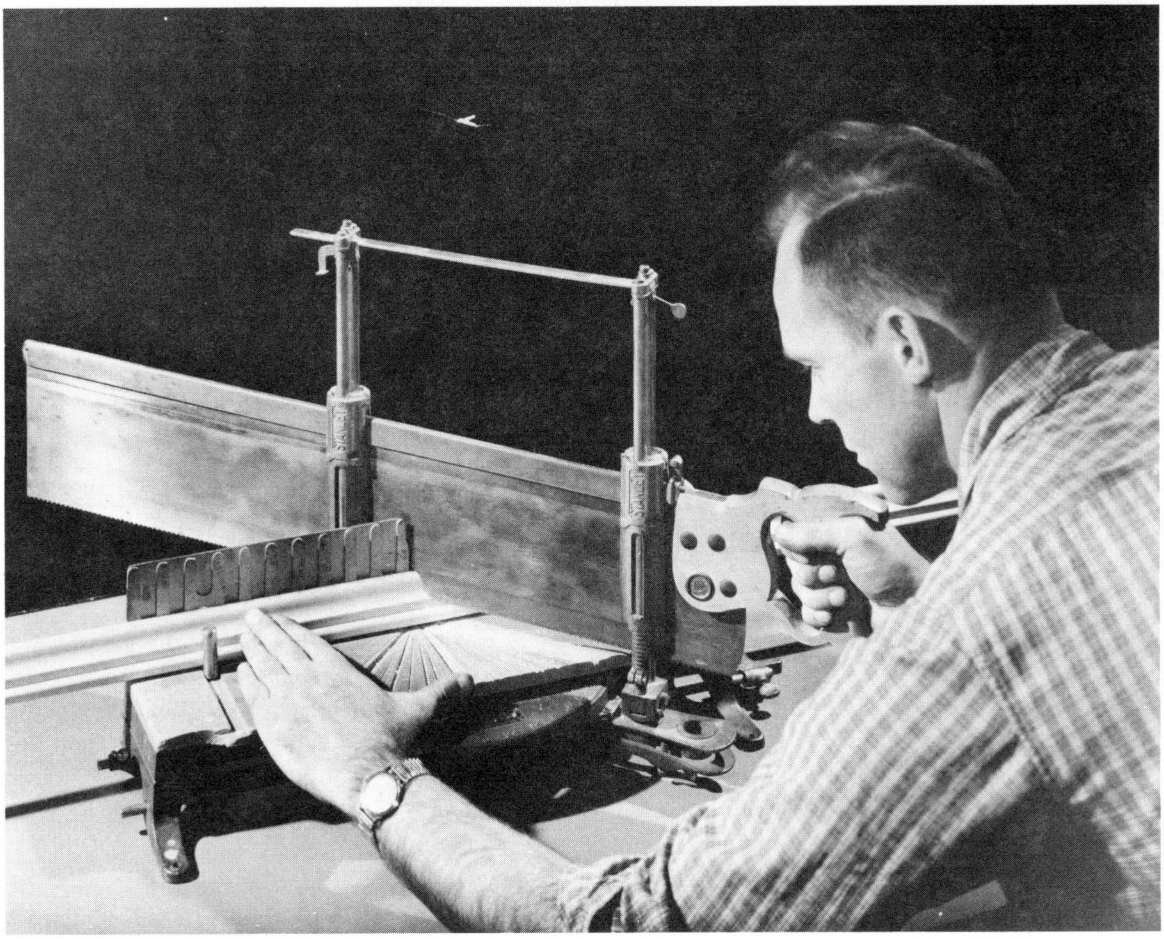

The measured molding is placed in a miter box and the 45-degree angle is cut using a backsaw. Photo courtesy Western Wood Moulding & Millwork Producers.

room for error by adding an extra ⅛ to ¼ inch. Cut the longer sides of the picture frame first. That way, if you do make a mistake, the length can be used for the shorter sides of the frame. This helps prevent wasting molding material.

2. Place the measured length of molding in a miter box and cut it with the backsaw. Make sure the molding is held in place, using clamps or by exerting pressure with your free hand. Once the 45-degree angle is cut, move the molding so you can make another 45-degree angle. The two angles should slope toward one another for proper frame construction.

3. Once both 45-degree angles are cut, use the finished piece of molding as the guide for the next section of frame you will need. Make the cuts with the backsaw and miter box.

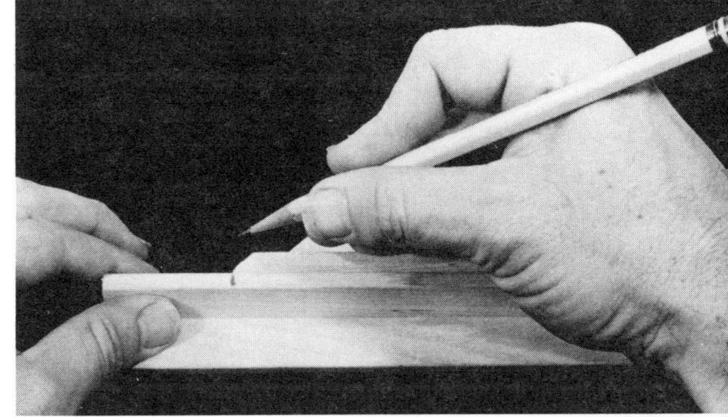

Use a finished piece of molding to measure the second section.

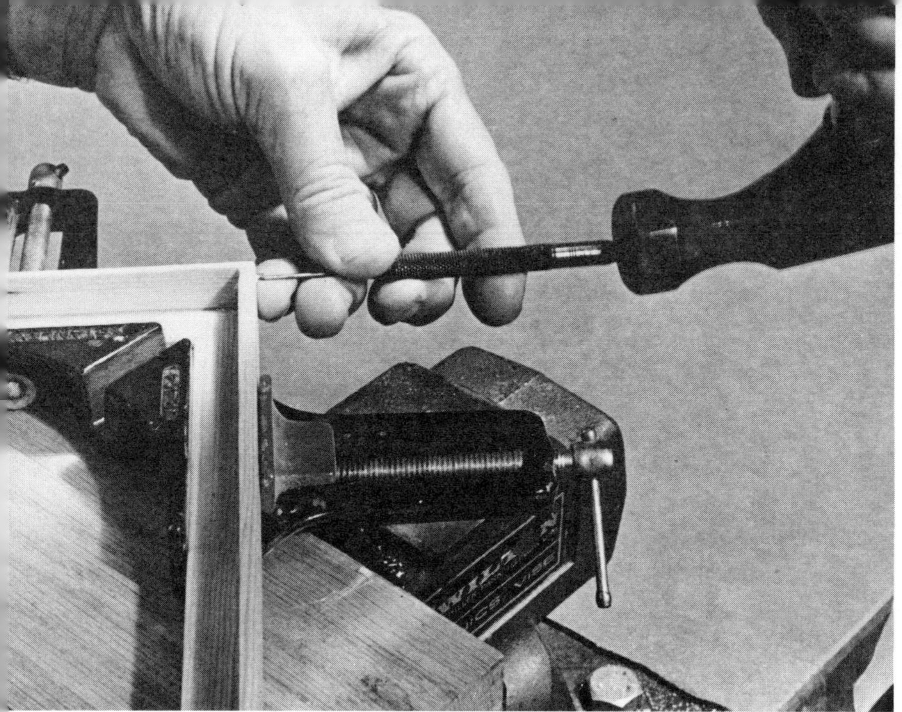

Once a corner of the frame is glued, drive a finishing nail beneath the wood's surface with a nail set.

4. Repeat Steps 1 through 3 for the shorter sides of the picture frame. Again, be sure to use the finished piece of molding for a guide to cut the second short length of molding.
5. When all four sides of the frame are cut to size, you are ready to put the frame together. Using a corner clamp, place a long and a short length of molding so the 45-degree angles come together. Check to make sure there is a tight fit between the two butted angles.
6. If the two pieces of molding come together tightly, you are ready to add glue and secure the pieces of molding in place by tightening the two clamps.
7. Small finishing nails are hammered into the molding to add strength to the corner. One nail is driven through one side of the corner and another is driven around the corner on the other piece of molding. A nail set is then used to drive the finishing nails beneath the surface of the wood.
8. Each of the three remaining corners is treated in the same manner if you are using one corner clamp. If you are using four corner clamps, the frame can be glued and secured in place. Then the nails can be driven with a hammer and a nail set.
9. Allow plenty of time for the glue to dry. Make sure the corners of the frame form exact 90-degree angles when completed. A sloppy-looking frame will show up quickly when hung on a wall.
10. Wood filler needs to be forced into the holes made by the nails and the nail set. You can use your finger or a knife blade. When the filler is dry, sand it smooth along with any other areas of the frame that look rough.
11. The frame is completed except for the finish. Remember: Frames used for enhancing photographs are fairly simple in appearance. A stain or black paint might be better than a loud color like red or yellow.

When the finish is dry, the frame is completed, except for inserting the mounted photograph. Adding picture glass or plexiglass is your option. For odd-size frames you make, you'll either have to pay someone to cut the glass to size or cut your own.

THE VALUE OF PICTURE GLASS

Covering a matted and framed picture with glass provides added security to your favorite prints. Glass is a protector. It can help to keep

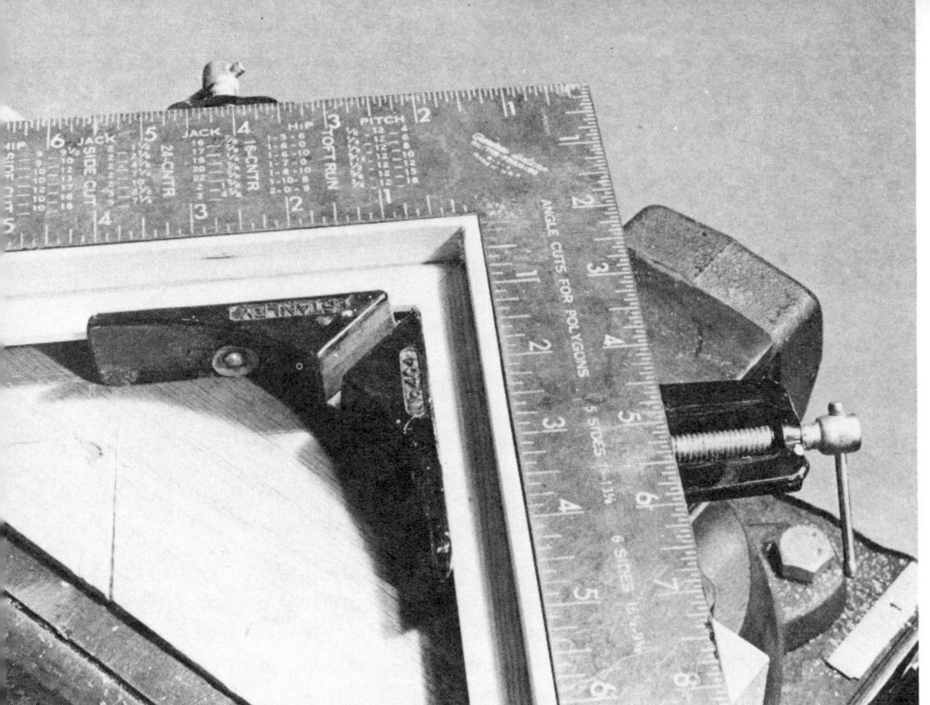

Double-check your measurements for accuracy and frame squareness.

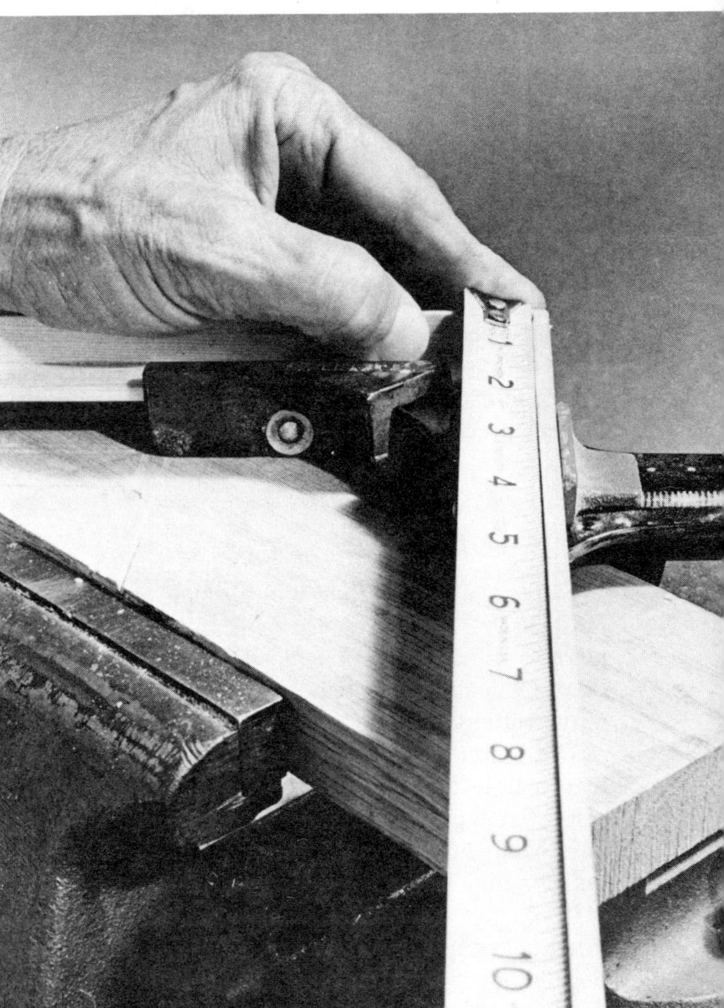

Applying the wood filler.

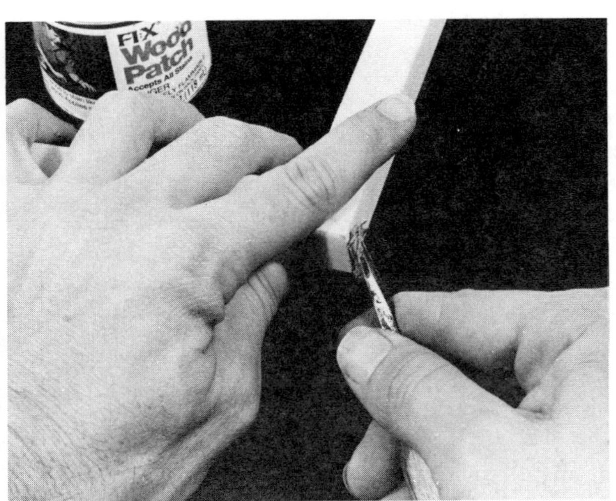

dust, dirt, and moisture off the print. It's simpler to clean the glass with a lint-free cloth and cleaning substance than it is to replace a mat or print.

Two types of picture-framing glass are available. First, there is picture glass. It is thinner than conventional window glass, therefore offers greater optical clarity.

Another type of display glass is the non-glare variety. It reduces obtrusive reflections that can distract attention from the photographic image. The non-glare glass reduces reflections, but its special design also decreases image clarity. The newest protective glass for prints is Denglas, introduced by Edmund Scientific Company. An antireflection coating is added to the glass to cut down glare and screen out ultraviolet rays, which cause prints to fade.

Adversely, glass never offers the clarity an uncovered print will. Before you commit yourself to using a protective piece of glass, you'll have to decide whether the print is going to remain behind the glass forever or whether it is going to be replaced by another print after a few weeks. Are you sure the print is worth the protection?

If you own an expensive or especially valuable photographic print, by all means use any method of preservation at your disposal.

Many of the frames you might purchase for print display include a protective piece of glass. Others, especially the metal sectional frames, do not. Glass is not expensive, especially if you are willing to cut your own. With the right tools and diligent practice, you can cut your own glass to any size you need.

GLASS CUTTING

The actual glass-cutting tool is small and very inexpensive. A straightedge or T square and a place to work are the prerequisites for the procedure. Optional glass pliers are available to help in the cutting.

The secret to successful glass cutting, other than a little training, is not to be afraid of the glass. Far too often, people worry about cutting their hands instead of concentrating on the process of cutting the glass.

If you are willing to follow the simple rules listed below, you should have little problem cutting the glass you require for any photographic display methods you can devise.

1. Always use a flat, clean surface to work on when cutting picture glass.
2. Make sure the glass you are cutting is clean. Rubbing alcohol is a good cleaning substance because it doesn't streak and dries quickly.
3. Make sure the glass cutter you are using is sharp and rolls smoothly. A drop of oil at the axle of the wheel may help it to roll smoothly.
4. Dip the glass cutter in kerosene or turpentine before you make your cut.
5. When making the cut, pull the tool toward you with a fair amount of pressure on the glass you are cutting. Use a smooth pulling action and DO NOT stop until the glass is completely scored with the cutter.
6. Make the cut correctly the first time. DO NOT go over the same cut twice.
7. You may want to wear a pair of heavy protective gloves as a safety precaution when you go to break the glass.
8. Place the scored glass with the excess piece hanging over the edge of a table. The cut, or scored, side should be facing up.
9. Raise the glass a little off the table as you grip the excess piece. Bring it down sharply onto the table and the glass will break.

Sometimes you may find small chips of glass still remaining along the break. Glass pliers with a flat-nosed jaw are used to nibble off the bits of glass after a bad break.

The glass must be kept clean when you are using it for framing and display. Try to handle only the edges, to prevent unnecessary fingerprints. Make sure the glass is free of lint, dust, dirt, and smudges before a matted photograph is placed behind it.

There is nothing more disappointing than finishing a framing job to find there are needless pieces of lint and dirt inside the frame.

You should always use a protective covering mat between the print and the glass. Condensation and heat can cause the print to stick to the glass and cause damage when it is removed from the frame.

Using a straightedge, pull the glass cutter toward you with ample pressure applied to the cutter.

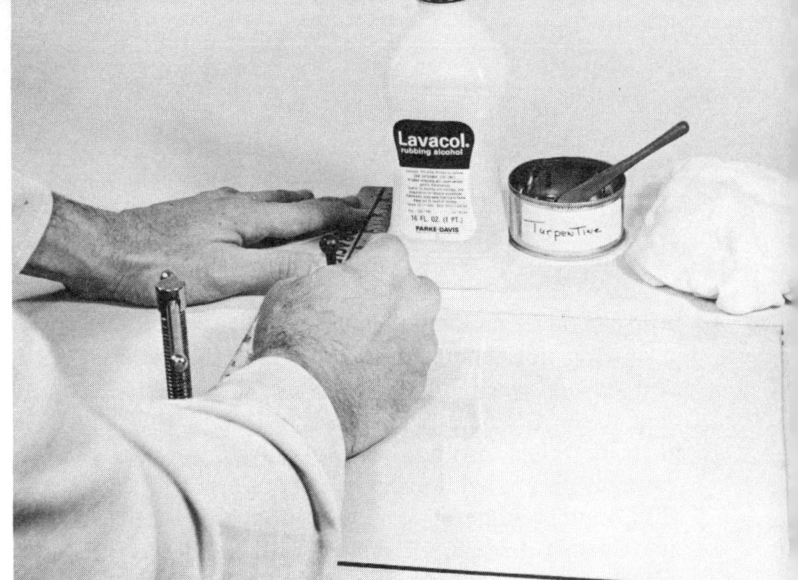

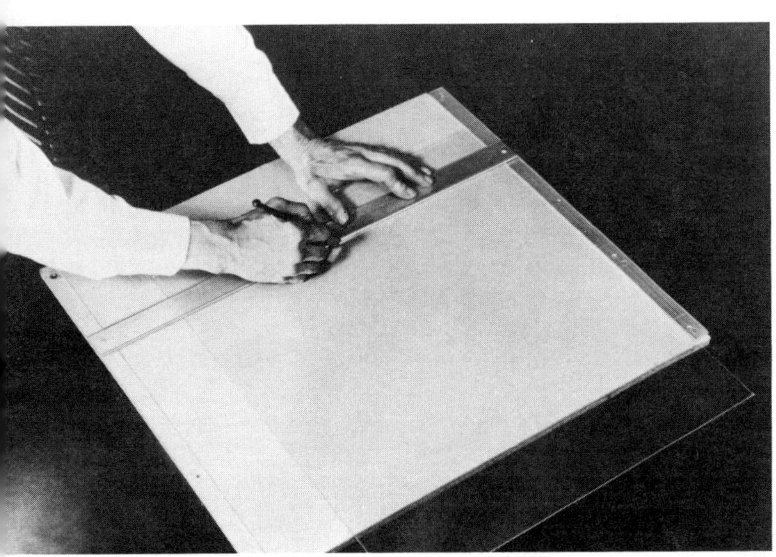

A glass-cutting guide will help assure a straight score. Photo courtesy the Brookstone Company.

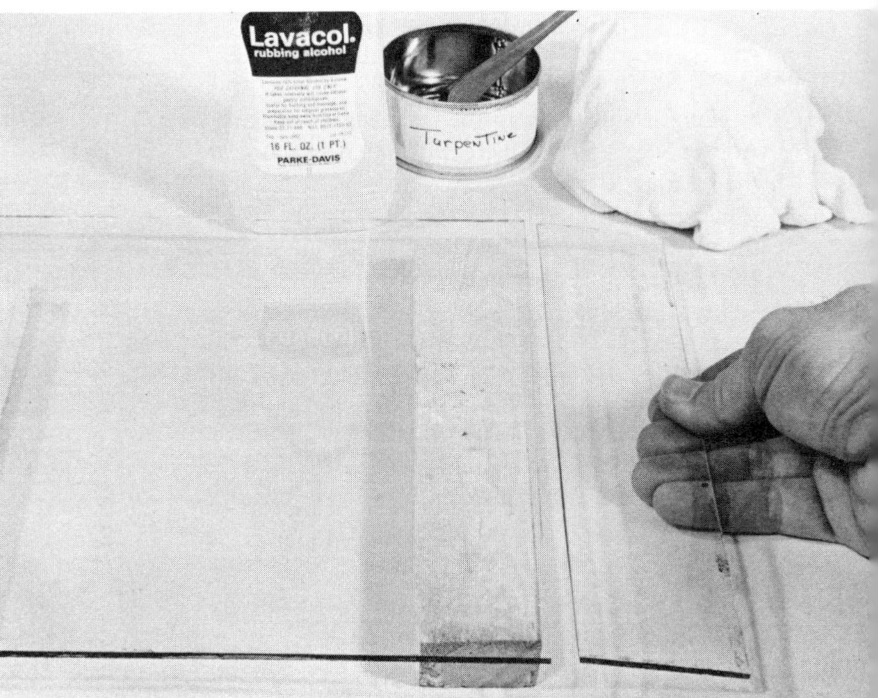

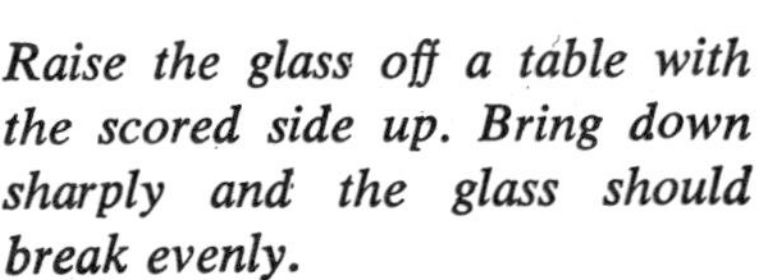

Raise the glass off a table with the scored side up. Bring down sharply and the glass should break evenly.

PLEXIGLASS: THE ALTERNATIVE TO GLASS

Besides glass, ready-cut plexiglass sheets are available for covering prints used in a frame. As with glass, plexiglass is available with non-glare characteristics. Another variety of plexiglass is a specially designed ultraviolet filter. The advantage to the UV filtration is the added life it gives to color prints that are being displayed. All the plexiglasses are lightweight and shatterproof. The disadvantage is the possibility of scratching when it's cleaned. Special formulated substances such as Brillianize, offered by Light Impressions, should be used for cleaning plexiglass.

When the glass has been cut or the plexiglass selected, you are ready to insert it into the frame.

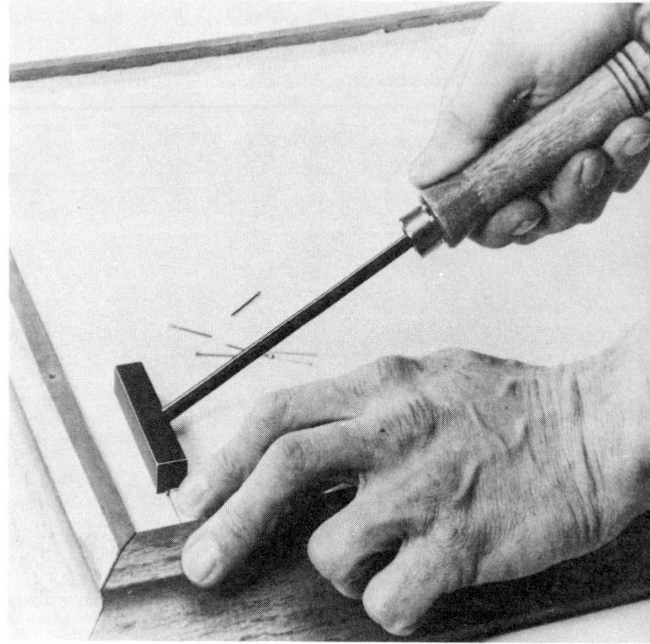

A flat hammer or a special framing tool for driving nails will secure the mounted print in the frame. Photos courtesy the Brookstone Company.

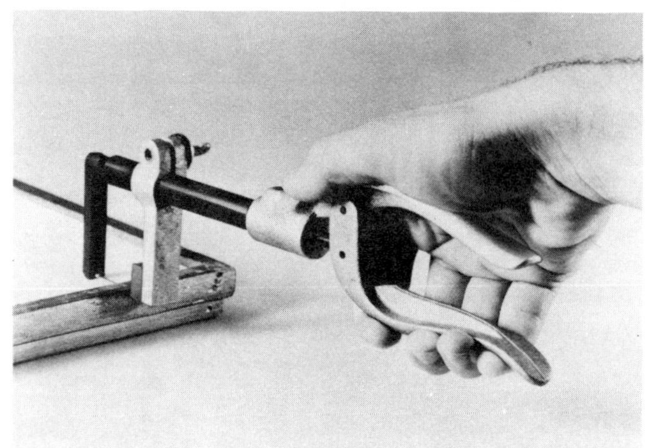

PICTURE FRAMING

The glass or plexiglass is slipped into place in the frame. Care must be used in handling the material so there will be no fingerprints or unsightly dust marks.

The matted photo is placed behind the glass. Remember: To prevent sticking and eventual print damage, photographs should not touch glass, so a cutout mat is needed to keep the glass from touching the mounted print.

A heavy piece of cardboard can be cut to fit snugly behind the mounted print. This will help in keeping the mount flat.

Once everything is inserted into the frame, it can be secured in place using small nails or staples. Nails can be driven into the edge of the molding right next to the cardboard backing. Add enough nails so there will be no chance for the backing to bend or warp. The same will apply to using a staple gun. Don't let the staples go all the way into the wood, or there will be nothing to hold the cardboard backing in place.

As a finishing touch to frame construction, a protective piece of kraft paper can be glued to the back of the frame. An oversize piece of kraft paper is glued to the rim of the molding and then trimmed with a razor blade.

The actual framing is now completed, but to hang the framed photo from a wall, some sort of hanging device is needed. The standard method is by inserting two small screw eyes into the edge of the molding and then attaching light, flexible picture wire.

Another method for attaching a frame to a wall is by using a saw-toothed hanger. The small metal bracket attaches to the edge of a wooden frame. Small nails hold the hanger in place. The saw-toothed edge is slipped over the head of a nail that has been driven into the wall. The several grooves in the hanger allow for movement of the framed picture so that it hangs perpendicular to the floor.

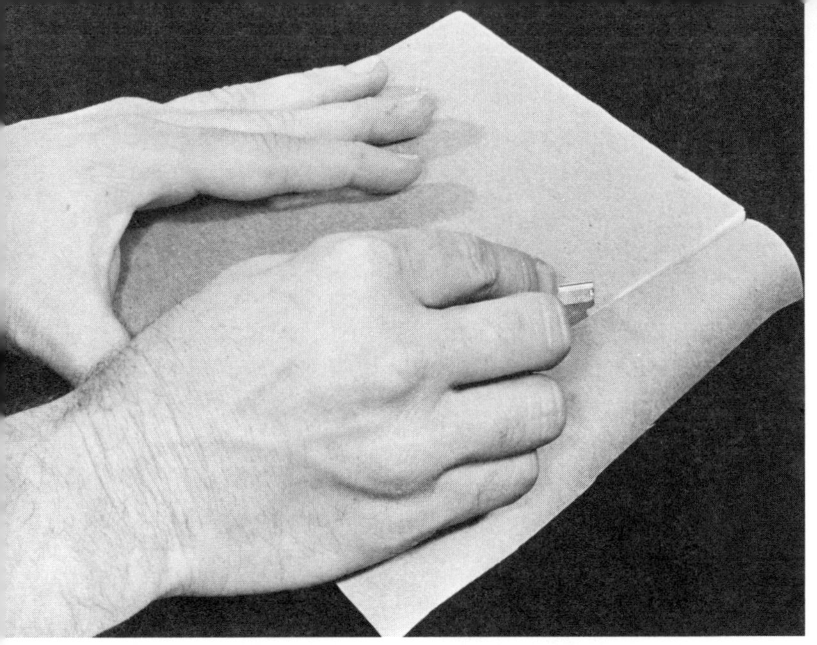

Kraft paper glued and then trimmed on the back side of the frame will help keep out dust, plus give a professional, finished look.

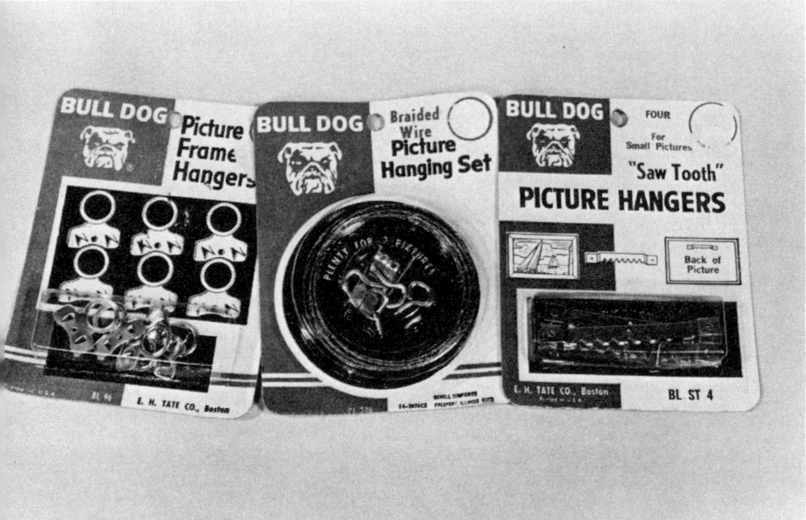

A few picture-hanging devices available from frame and hardware stores.

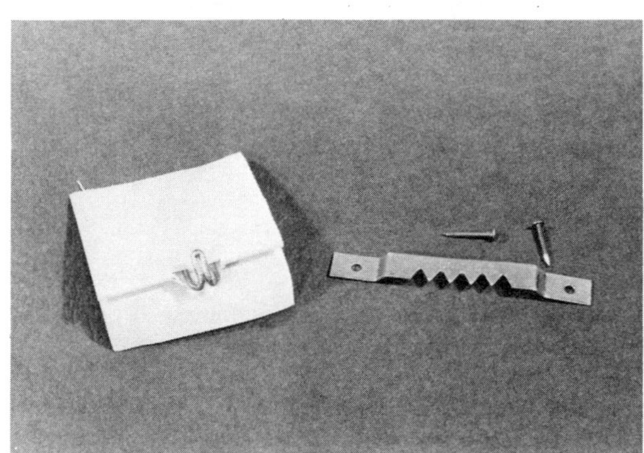

The adhesive tab is used for lightweight prints, while the saw-tooth hanger works on heavier, framed prints.

For lightweight picture frames and mounted photos, you can use glue-on tabs. The small piece of fabric has a small hook protruding from it. You can attach the tab to the back of a framed picture.

HANGING THE FRAMED PHOTOGRAPH

Once the photo is attractively framed, you are going to have to hang it on a wall. There are several ways to do it.

THE NAIL

This is one of the simplest and most common methods of hanging framed photographs. Simply drive a small nail into the wall so that it is slanted upward. Then you can either set the frame's edge over the nail or, if the picture has been wired, slip the wire over the nail and position the frame.

WALL HANGER

This is nothing more than a hook and nail. The nail is easily removed, so the wall hanger can be reused. The picture's frame wire or a saw-toothed hanger is slipped over the hook.

HEAVY-DUTY HANGER

Very similar to the wall hanger, this one has more than one nail holding it in place. This is used for exceptionally heavy framed or mounted photos.

Diversity—creativity—is the secret to hanging your framed photographs. Don't let your enthusiasm for getting the picture on the wall influence your common sense. There are all types of adhesive materials available, but that doesn't mean they can all be used to hang photographs. All adhesives come with instructions for their proper use and warnings against their misuse. Read the labels, and use the adhesives correctly.

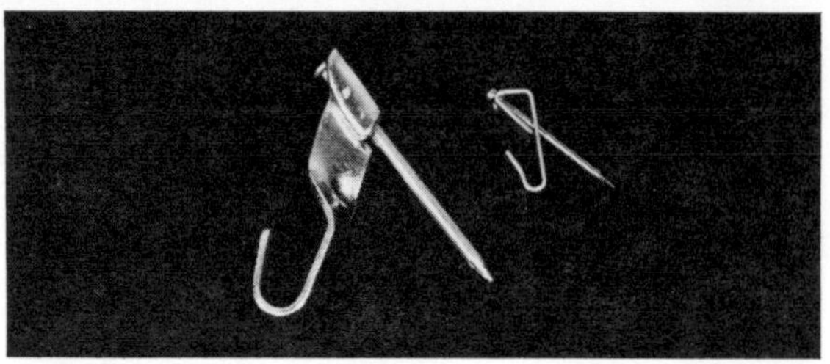

Wall hangers vary in size to accommodate the weight of the framed print.

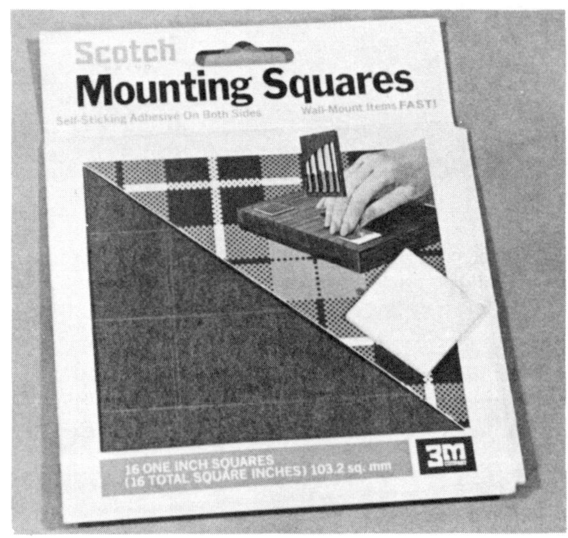

Adhesive mounting squares to prevent frames from slipping.

PREVENTING FRAME SLIPPAGE

Many framed photos you hang may have a tendency to slip when an airplane flies over or a door is slammed. It can become quite troublesome if you have to straighten your framed photographs every day.

There are two very simple ways to eliminate frame slippage. The first is to purchase self-adhesive pads that can be attached to the bottom corners of the frame. They will help prevent the framed photo from slipping and also prevent the wall from becoming marred.

Another method is using reusable adhesive similar to a piece of sticky clay. Roll it into a small ball and stick it to the bottom corners of the frame. Then push the frame back against the wall, and it will stay in place. When you wish to remove the frame from the wall, the remaining adhesive can be removed by using another piece of the same adhesive to pick it up. If there is an oily residue, it can be cleaned off with lighter fluid. Permabond International manufactures the

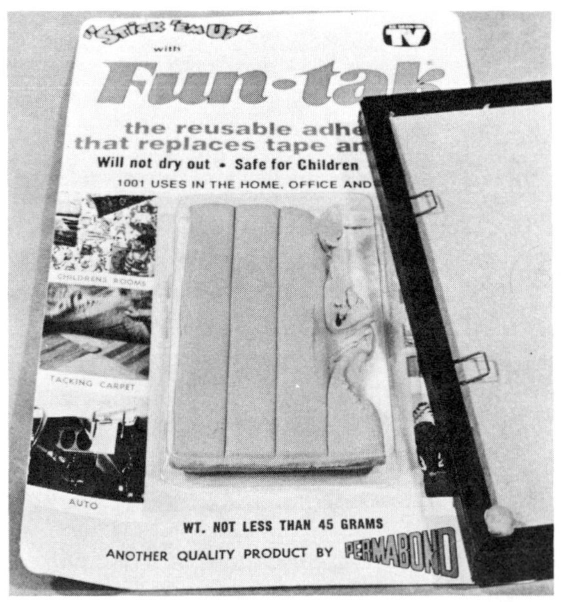

Fun-tak or similar adhesive will help to keep frames in place.

adhesive under the name Fun-tak, and Eberhard Faber, Inc., offers a similar material under the name of Holdit.

Before you start driving nails into your walls for hanging framed photos, you should give considerable thought to the actual placement of the images.

FRAMED PICTURE PLACEMENT

Where you hang your framed pictures is up to you. Certainly you won't hang them in a closet where they can't be seen. You should also realize there are walls in the home or office that are not conducive to good photographic print display.

CONSIDER THE LIGHTING

Before you hang a photograph, be sure to consider the lighting. Good lighting is important if the picture's content is to be appreciated.

Natural light from windows is great during the day. However, you must not forget that sunlight fades color photographs. Therefore, you don't want direct light falling on the photograph. Instead, window light that is indirect or at least filtered through curtains is more appropriate for print display.

Artificial light sources such as table lamps and ceiling fixtures should also be properly placed for good lighting. Obtrusive shadows caused by lampshades and other objects can detract from a hanging photograph. Even light is the key to displaying photographs so they can be enjoyed.

The ultimate in artificial lighting for photo display is track lighting. Small floodlights can be moved along a stationary track that is positioned on the ceiling above the wall where photographs are to be hung. The installation of track lighting can be a little costly, so for displaying just a few framed photographs it might be impractical.

Some frames for artwork have their own little light attached to the top of the frame. This type of lighting looks awkward on the simple lines of a frame used for photographic prints. Plus, you have an obtrusive electrical cord that runs down the back of the frame and then into the nearest electrical outlet.

Lighting is extremely important for good photographic display. Make sure there is sufficient light for easy viewing in both day and night before you hang your photographs.

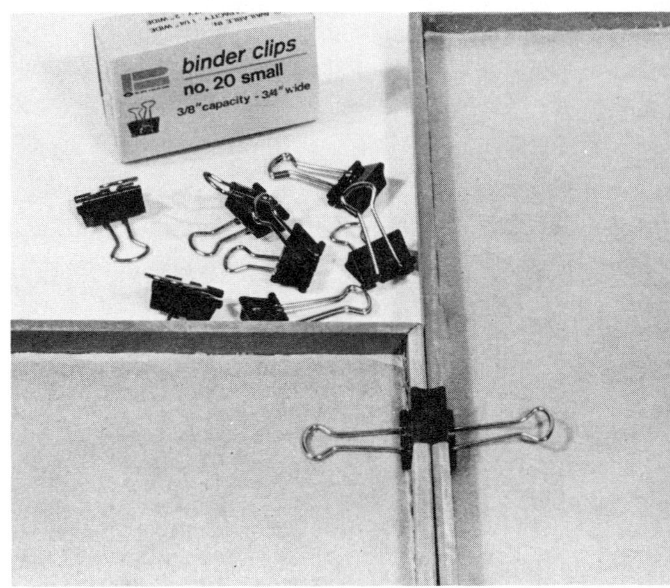

Binder clips can be used to join some frames for a grouped look.

FRAMED PICTURE ARRANGEMENT

Once your selection of prints is framed and ready to be hung on a wall, you must give careful consideration to their arrangement.

Large photographic images can stand on their own. The large size makes them noticeable whether they are visually pleasing or not. Images such as 5×7s or 8×10s may need to be grouped to produce an effective display.

Some frames can be attached together using small metal clips purchased at a business supply firm. The grouped frames can then be hung on a wall as a single unit, creating the impression of one large photo.

The possibilities for arrangement of framed photographs on a wall are unlimited. What's important is that the photos be visible and blend with the decor they are to share.

Try to hang the photographs as close to eye level as possible. The viewer should not have to stoop or stretch his neck to see or study a photographic image placed on a wall. However, eye level is just a starting point. Not all framed pho-

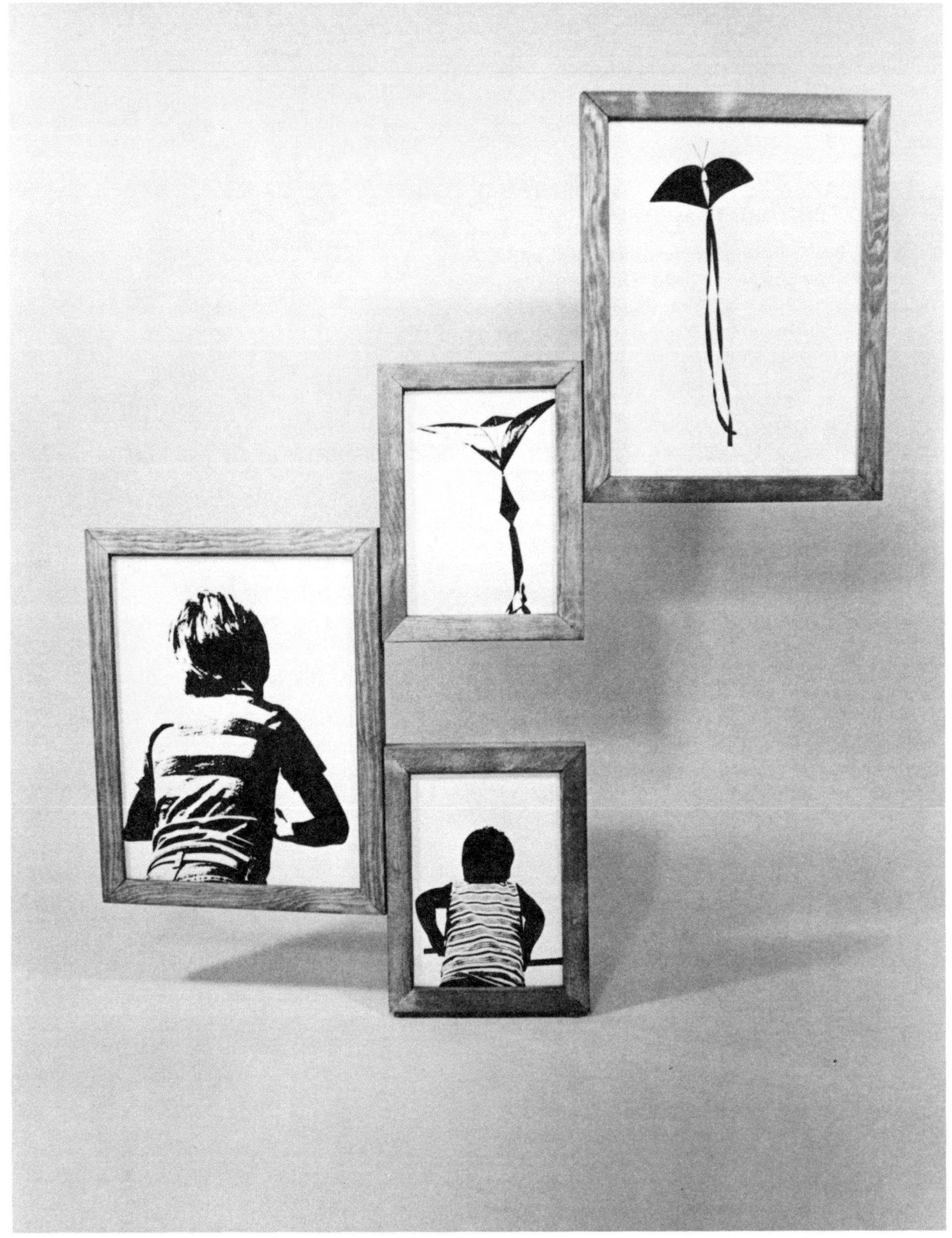

These photos are held together using binder clips.

Paper, cut to the size of the frame, can be attached to the wall, using tape to give you help in deciding a desirable photo arrangement.

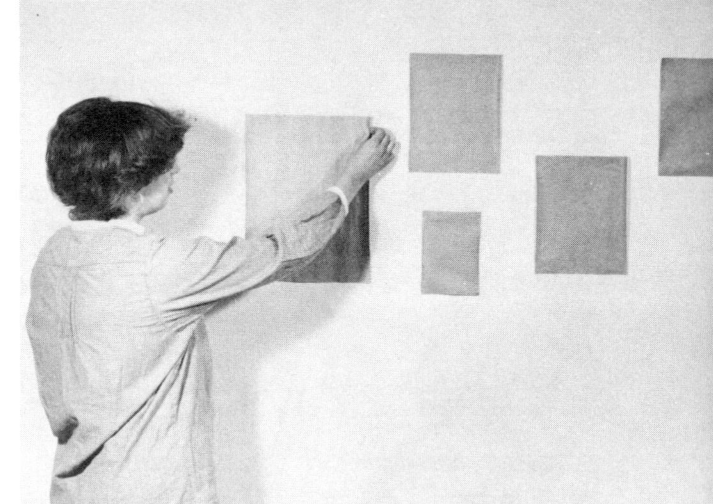

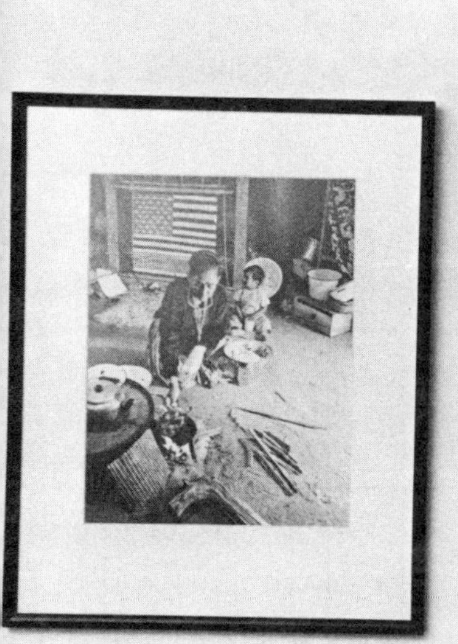

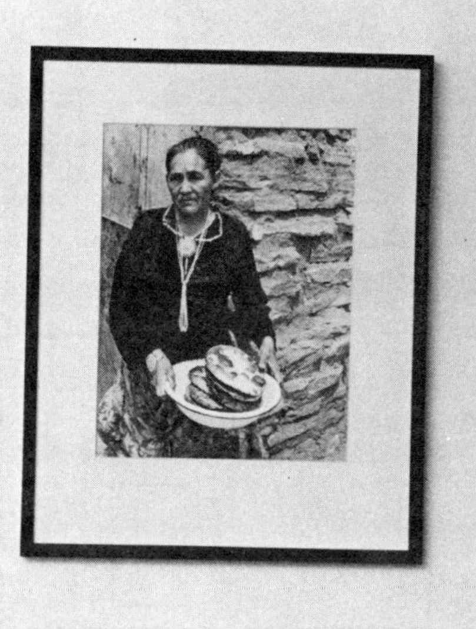

Photos do not have to be even but can be staggered to add to their visual appeal.

tographs need to be displayed at eye level. Oftentimes, placement depends on the furnishings and decor of the office or home where they are to be displayed.

For example, photos hung on a wall above a sofa may be a little lower than eye level when standing. This allows for easy viewing from a sitting position and helps eliminate any wide vacant area between the sofa and the hanging photo.

Always start with the premise that the photos should be hung at eye level or close to it. When necessary to blend with furnishings or make for better viewing, alter the premise to fit your specific photographic display needs.

CREATIVE EXPERIMENTATION

Design your framed photo display before you attach a wall hook or drive a nail. It will take a little time to plan in advance but help eliminate unnecessary holes in your wall and unsatisfactory results.

Take your framed photos and arrange them on the floor until you develop a design you like. If you're sure it's the arrangement you want, you can then begin to hang them on the wall, using an imaginary line at eye level as a guide.

If you still can't be sure you'll like the arrangement as it looks on the floor, go to the trouble

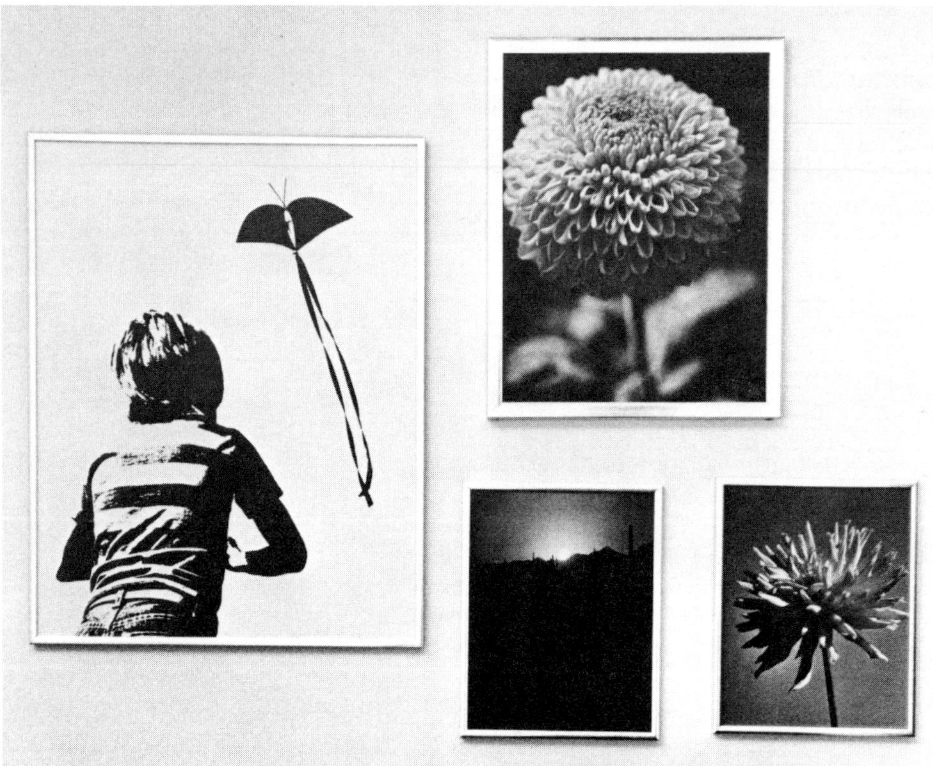

Grouping four photographs isn't too difficult. Hanging more than four can be troublesome due to the great number of arrangement possibilities.

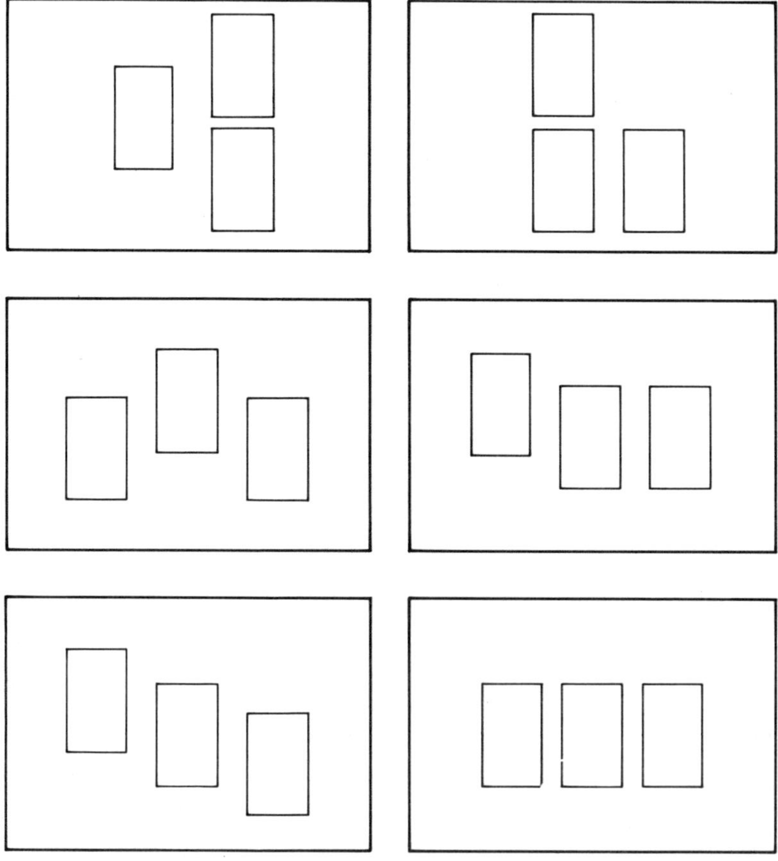

Photo Arrangements

of cutting pieces of paper the same shapes and sizes as the frames you are going to hang. Once you have the paper cutouts, attach them to the wall by using tape. Then stand back and look at your work. It will give you the best idea of how the photos will look once they are attached to the surface of the wall.

If you are still unsatisfied, just rearrange the paper cutouts until you get exactly what you want.

The rule for hanging framed photographs is simple: Arrange the photos so they are visually pleasing. Grouping two to four framed pictures is not difficult. Grouping more than four pictures can be bothersome due to the great number of possibilities. Pencil and paper will help you come up with a design. Just draw the various arrangements on paper as I did with three equal-size photos.

Remember: Pictures are to be seen. If you don't want them seen, then stick them back in drawers, closets, and cookie jars. If the photographs are pleasing, let the viewer have a chance to see the photograph and study its content.

5

CREATIVE DISPLAY

Creative display is for anyone with a little imagination and the willingness to follow through with any idea he may originate. Framing techniques and photo albums are without a doubt the most common methods for print display, but that doesn't mean they are the only methods that will work effectively.

This chapter will give you a variety of other options for displaying many of your favorite pictures. Some of the ideas may appeal to you; others will not. However, they should help give you incentive to try your own personal forms of creative display.

WHERE TO GET IDEAS

Ideas for photographic display are not always easy to come by. It takes some sort of catalyst to get one's thought waves heading in the right direction. The more you see, participate, and live, the more opportunity to find the ideas you may be able to use.

Ideas can come from anywhere: your neighbors, your work, or from books and magazines. Looking through magazines is an excellent source for ideas. Many of the pictures found in magazines may have content that you can adapt to your own photographic display needs.

When you pursue an idea through to the finished product, don't become discouraged if the display technique doesn't turn out as well as it could. Make the necessary changes and try again. Sometimes you'll find your creative display methods to be unsatisfactory. They just don't work. However, you should not be discouraged; creative display is often a series of trials and errors until the right combination presents the photograph(s) in a pleasing manner.

On the following pages are numerous ideas that have been tried, thought about, observed, and even some that were tried and discarded. This chapter is an attempt to compile a comprehensive list of the common and the not-so-common means for photographic display.

PERSONALIZED GREETING CARDS

Every Christmas, the seasonal greeting cards arrive in the mail. Many people like to send cards that have a photograph of the family and the printed words "Merry Christmas" or "Season's

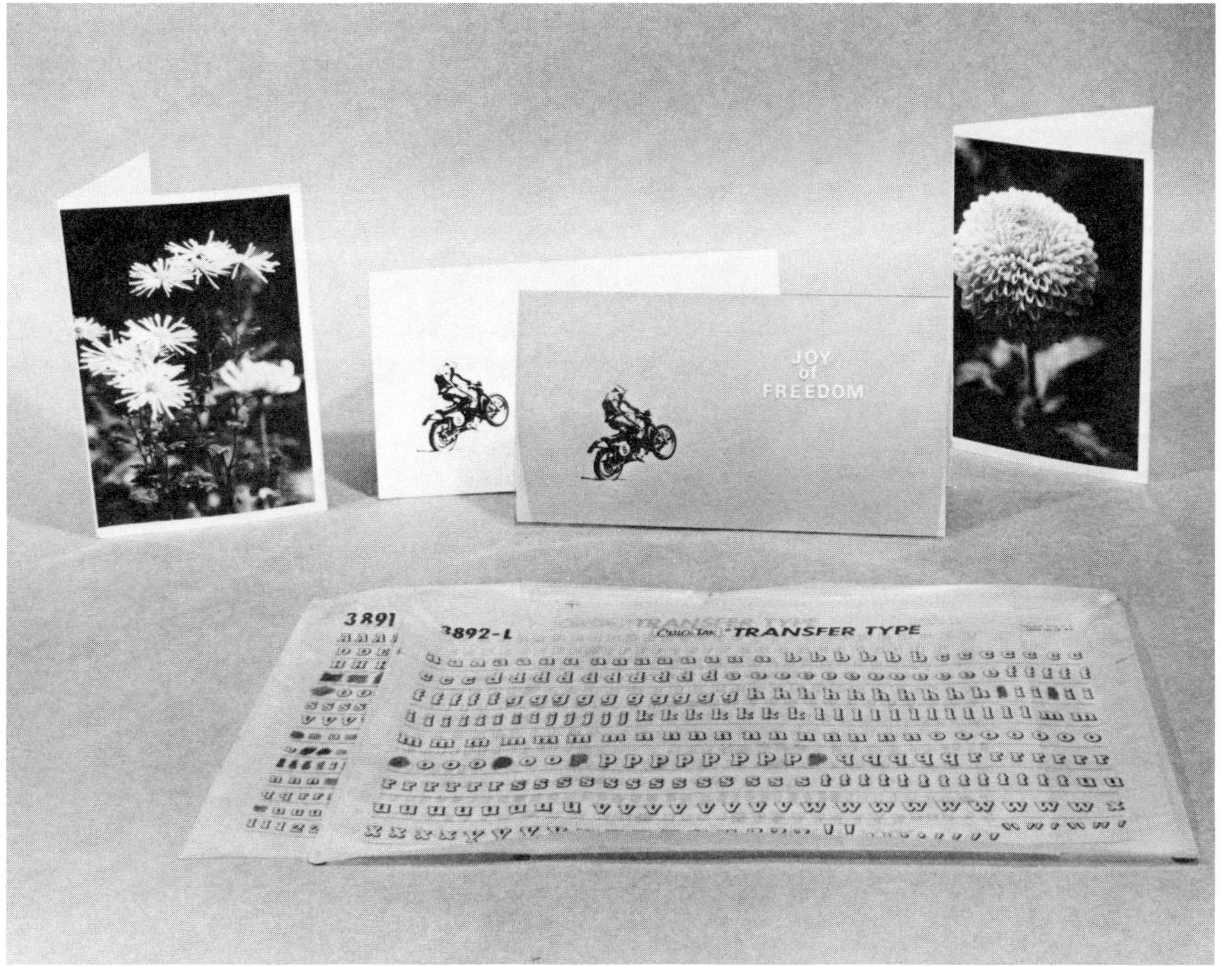

Transfer type, heavy paper, and your favorite prints make interesting, personalized greeting cards for any occasion.

Greetings." Various photo-processing labs offer the service. This type of card has become somewhat of a tradition in many families.

With a touch of creativity and advance planning, you can make your own, personalized greeting cards, not just for Christmas but for any holiday or occasion.

The quickest way to produce a personalized card is to take an appropriate photo and attach it to a fairly heavy grade of construction paper. You can add a few choice words and a happy note with a pen or marker, and it's ready to be stuffed in an envelope and mailed.

If you have just a few cards to prepare, you might want to add transfer type, which is purchased from an art store.

For a larger number of cards, as with Christmas greetings, you can become your own layout artist and design your greeting cards with printed wording. Decide on the size of the card you need, allowing for later attachment of a snapshot-size photograph. Add the words you want and then take it to a printer. Have the wording set in type and have it printed on plain or colored paper. When you get the printed material back, you can attach any photo you want by using a mounting adhesive. (You might decide to use photo-album adhesive corners for attaching the photos. That way, the recipient can remove the photo and keep it in an album or have it framed.)

For more ideas to help you produce imaginative greeting cards, pay a visit to any store that sells commercially produced cards. You will get hundreds of ideas you can put to good use.

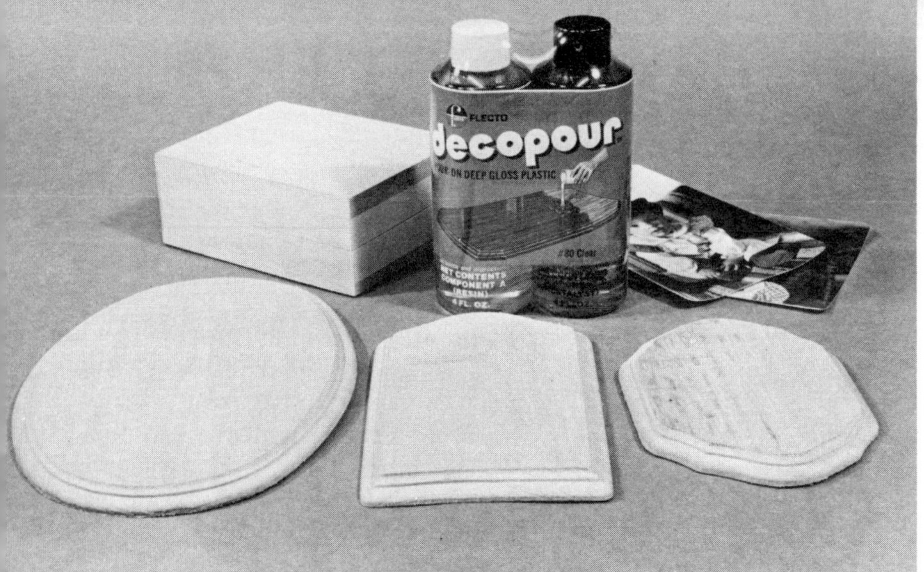

Wood plaques, boxes, and tabletops can be covered with photos and sealed using Decopour liquid plastic.

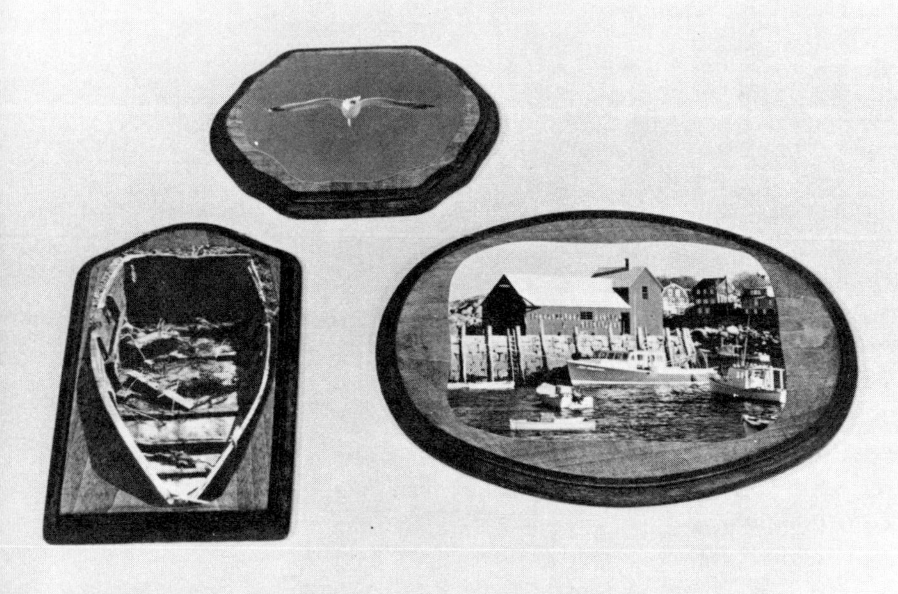

These stained plaques and mounted photographs are ready to be covered with Decopour.

DECOPOUR

Wooden boxes, wooden plaques, and many other items can be decorated with photographs and then covered with a pour-on plastic called Decopour. Photographs are trimmed to the desired size and then mounted to the top of a box or wooden plaque. Cold mounts or spray adhesive can be used to attach the photos.

The photograph must be perfectly flat, and any excess adhesive should be removed from around the photo's edges. The Decopour is mixed and then poured onto the photo to give a protective coating of plastic.

Decopour can be purchased in various amounts to cover from three to seventy-two square feet. An eight-ounce kit will cover three square feet if just poured on and nine square feet if poured and then spread. A sixteen-ounce kit will cover six square feet if poured and eighteen square feet if spread.

Complete instructions are included with the Decopour kits. Read the instructions carefully before starting and be sure to have spare photos and old wood to practice on before a special project is started.

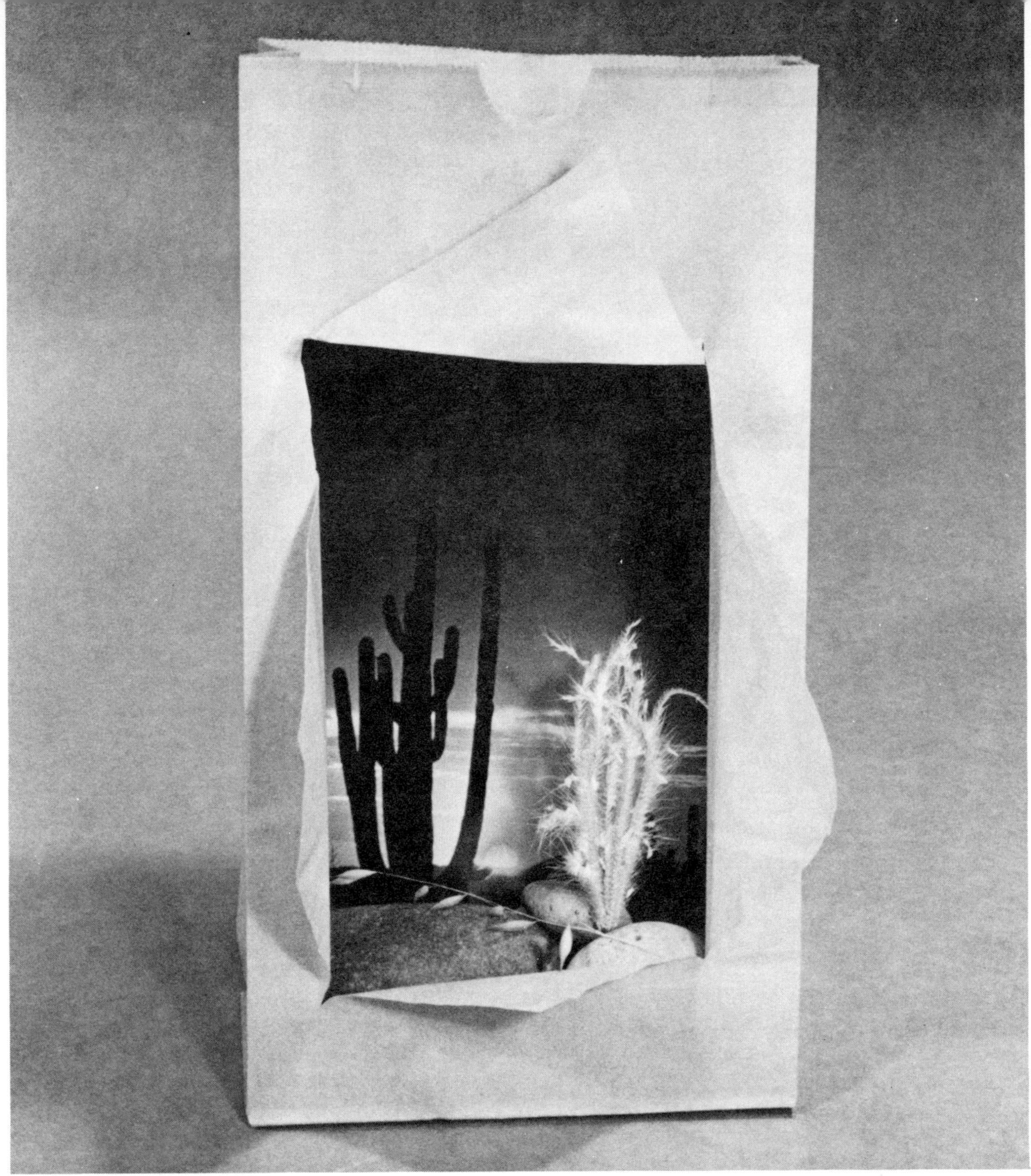

A brown paper bag has been transformed into a tabletop display using a cropped and mounted 8×10-inch print. The rocks add stability to the paper-bag display.

PAPER-BAG DISPLAY

The brown or white paper bag you use to pack a lunch can be used for creative photo display. With your imagination and the right photo, there's no telling what you might create.

A window needs to be cut through one side of the paper bag. You can use scissors or, for a rustic look, you may want to try tearing a window. The flaps need to be folded back against the bag so they don't block the view of the picture that will go inside.

The display bag illustrated here uses an 8×10 photograph attached to a mounting board. The photo was trimmed to fit in the bag. Small strips of adhesive were used to hold the mounted photo to the back side of the bag.

Rocks and a selected weed were added to help

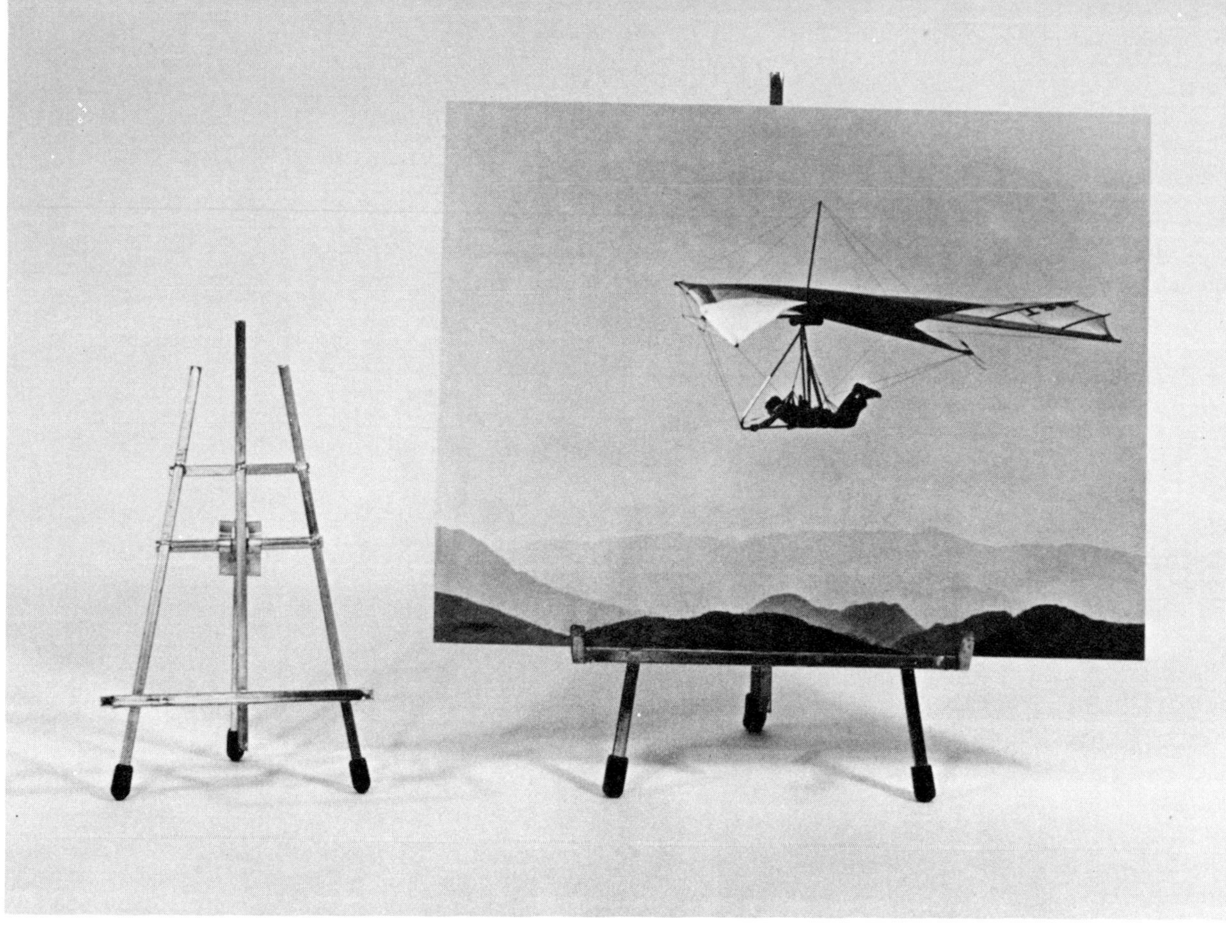

Easels come in a variety of sizes and help your photos to stand out on shelves and tables.

hold the bag in place and give the impression of "the desert in a bag."

The bag was left natural, but you may want to paint the bag to match the color scheme of your home's decor, or you can spray the bag with clear lacquer to give an added gloss.

EASEL DISPLAY

Artists' easels come in all sizes, from small tabletop to large canvas-holding models. Whatever size photograph you have, there's an easel available for creative display.

Good photography is like quality artwork. Your best photos can be given the recognition they deserve by displaying the photo on an easel. The photo can be framed or it can be mounted and matted and then set on the arms of the easel. Art supply stores and many import shops will have easels to choose from that are made of wood or metal.

PERSONALIZED CALENDARS

Few homes seem to be without at least one calendar. Most calendars, especially those that are hung on walls, have either one scenic picture or a different photo for each month.

You can have one of your own favorite photos converted into a calendar. You might check with your photo dealers to see if they know of a lab that offers the calendar-making service. If not, you'll have to watch for advertisements in magazines and mail-order catalogs that offer calendar production from prints, negatives, or slides. The ads usually start appearing about three months before the end of the year. Below is a list of five companies that have offered calendar-production services.

Jay Norris Corporation
31 Hanse Avenue
Dept. 6-208
Freeport, New York 11521

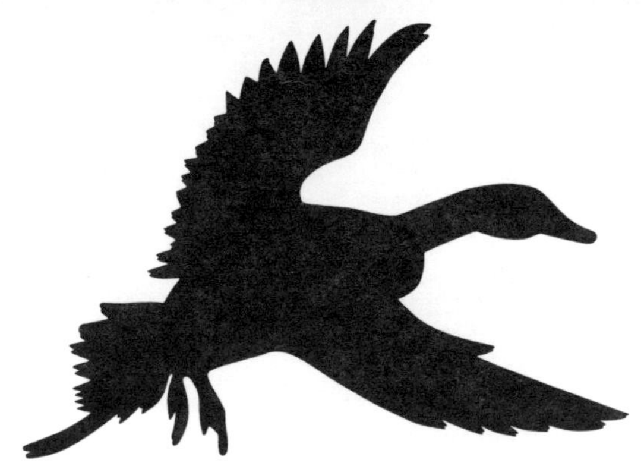

January

S	M	T	W	T	F	S
1	2	3	4	5	6	7
8	9	10	11	12	13	14
15	16	17	18	19	20	21
22	23	24	25	26	27	28
29	30	31				

February

S	M	T	W	T	F	S
			1	2	3	4
5	6	7	8	9	10	11
12	13	14	15	16	17	18
19	20	21	22	23	24	25
26	27	28				

March

S	M	T	W	T	F	S
			1	2	3	4
5	6	7	8	9	10	11
12	13	14	15	16	17	18
19	20	21	22	23	24	25
26	27	28	29	30	31	

April

S	M	T	W	T	F	S
						1
2	3	4	5	6	7	8
9	10	11	12	13	14	15
16	17	18	19	20	21	22
23/30	24	25	26	27	28	29

May

S	M	T	W	T	F	S
	1	2	3	4	5	6
7	8	9	10	11	12	13
14	15	16	17	18	19	20
21	22	23	24	25	26	27
28	29	30	31			

June

S	M	T	W	T	F	S
				1	2	3
4	5	6	7	8	9	10
11	12	13	14	15	16	17
18	19	20	21	22	23	24
25	26	27	28	29	30	

July

S	M	T	W	T	F	S
						1
2	3	4	5	6	7	8
9	10	11	12	13	14	15
16	17	18	19	20	21	22
23/30	24/31	25	26	27	28	29

August

S	M	T	W	T	F	S
		1	2	3	4	5
6	7	8	9	10	11	12
13	14	15	16	17	18	19
20	21	22	23	24	25	26
27	28	29	30	31		

September

S	M	T	W	T	F	S
					1	2
3	4	5	6	7	8	9
10	11	12	13	14	15	16
17	18	19	20	21	22	23
24	25	26	27	28	29	30

October

S	M	T	W	T	F	S
1	2	3	4	5	6	7
8	9	10	11	12	13	14
15	16	17	18	19	20	21
22	23	24	25	26	27	28
29	30	31				

November

S	M	T	W	T	F	S
			1	2	3	4
5	6	7	8	9	10	11
12	13	14	15	16	17	18
19	20	21	22	23	24	25
26	27	28	29	30		

December

S	M	T	W	T	F	S
					1	2
3	4	5	6	7	8	9
10	11	12	13	14	15	16
17	18	19	20	21	22	23
24/31	25	26	27	28	29	30

Some photo labs will transform color or black-and-white negatives into one-of-a-kind calendars.

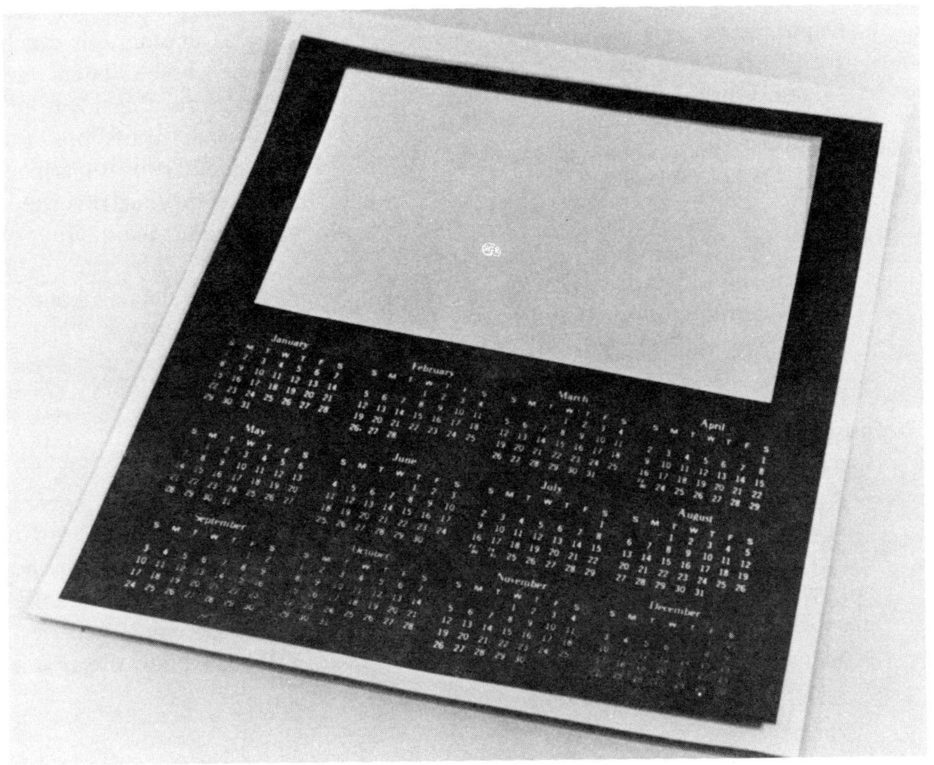

A calendar mask.

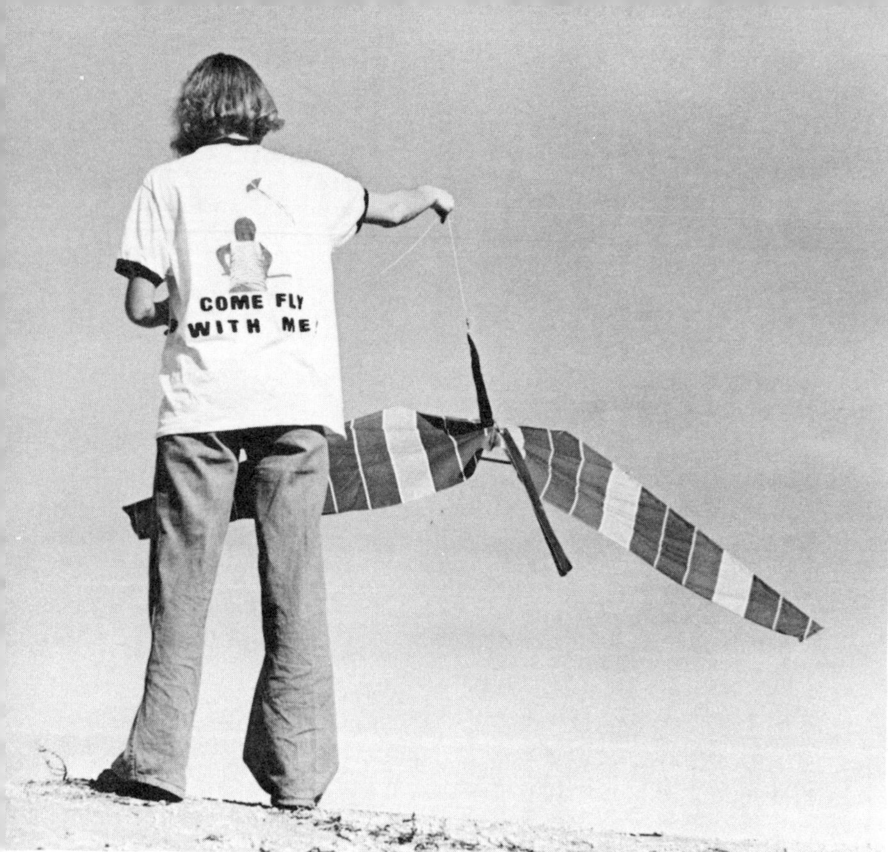

T-shirts become works of art when you have your own photos and message on them.

Romar Sales
Dept. 3688
380 Madison Avenue
New York, New York 10017

Bennett-Graf, Inc.
Dept. 3672
1450 N.E. 123rd Street
Miami, Florida 33161

Spencer Gifts
C-21 Spencer Building
Atlantic City, New Jersey 08411

Deluxe Color Photo Lab
Dept. PP
27 West 27th Street
New York, New York 10001

If you do your own darkroom work, you can produce your own calendar. All you need is the special mask that comes in either 8×10- or 11×14-inch size. Either color or black-and-white images can be produced. Your photo supply dealer may have the calendar mask you need. If not, watch the ads in the back of photographic magazines for companies that sell the calendar-producing masks.

PHOTO T-SHIRTS

T-shirts with words, sketches, and pictures have always been popular with the younger generation. It gives them a chance to promote a cause, product, or even themselves. Your own color photograph can be printed on a T-shirt of your choice. Then you can add a few press-on letters for the slogan or saying you want.

Some printshops can handle the process or locate a store that specializes in printed T-shirts. Take in your favorite photo or slide and they'll tell you if the quality is good enough for a T-shirt transfer. The store will also have a selection of shirts to choose from.

SILK SCREEN

If you plan to produce a great number of T-shirts with a specific photograph or message, it might be less expensive to have a silk screen made. The quality of reproduction will be better than the transfer method.

Many of the T-shirt specialty stores will have silk-screening services available. The Eastman Kodak book *Creative Darkroom Techniques* has

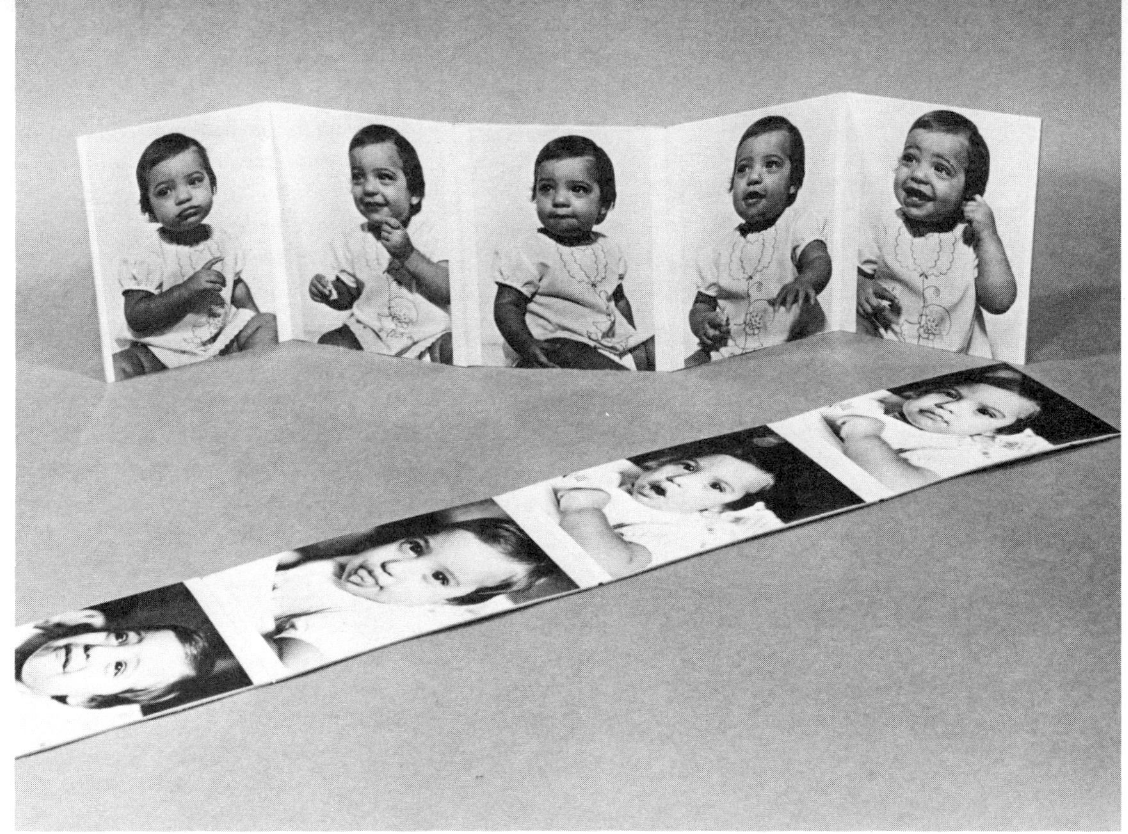

Mounting board, tape, and a selection of photos help create either horizontal or vertical foldouts for free-standing or hanging on a wall.

a chapter on photo silk-screen printing. It will give you an idea of the work involved in producing a silk screen and may help to ease your apprehension about the cost.

PICTURE FOLDOUTS

Special photo mats can be purchased that hold several photographs. The mats allow for the pictures to be folded like an accordion. With a little tape, mounting board, and adhesive, you can create your own.

Several pictures are needed. They should all be vertical, horizontal, or square for proper construction.

The photographs will need to be mounted to identical pieces of mounting board. Once the pictures are mounted, they are joined together, using a plastic or cloth tape. The color of the tape should blend with the color of the photographs. A little space must be left between the photos to allow the mounted pictures to be folded.

When the construction is completed, the foldouts can be attached to a wall, or they will stand on their own on any flat surface. For the best results, the pictures in a foldout should be related.

BASKET FRAMING

For a different approach to framing, small inexpensive baskets can be used. All types of baskets are available from many import merchants.

Some home decors have a grouping of baskets adorning their bare walls. You can do the same thing, but instead of just baskets, you can have a gallery of photographs and basketry.

The photos to be framed in a basket should be cropped and mounted. Depending on the size of the basket, the photo can fill the bottom of the basket or it can fill just a portion, allowing the basket weave to act as a mat.

Two approaches to basket framing can be used. The photo can be placed inside the basket, or it can be placed on the outside so that the basket sides hold the photo a few inches from the wall.

Experimentation with photos and baskets will

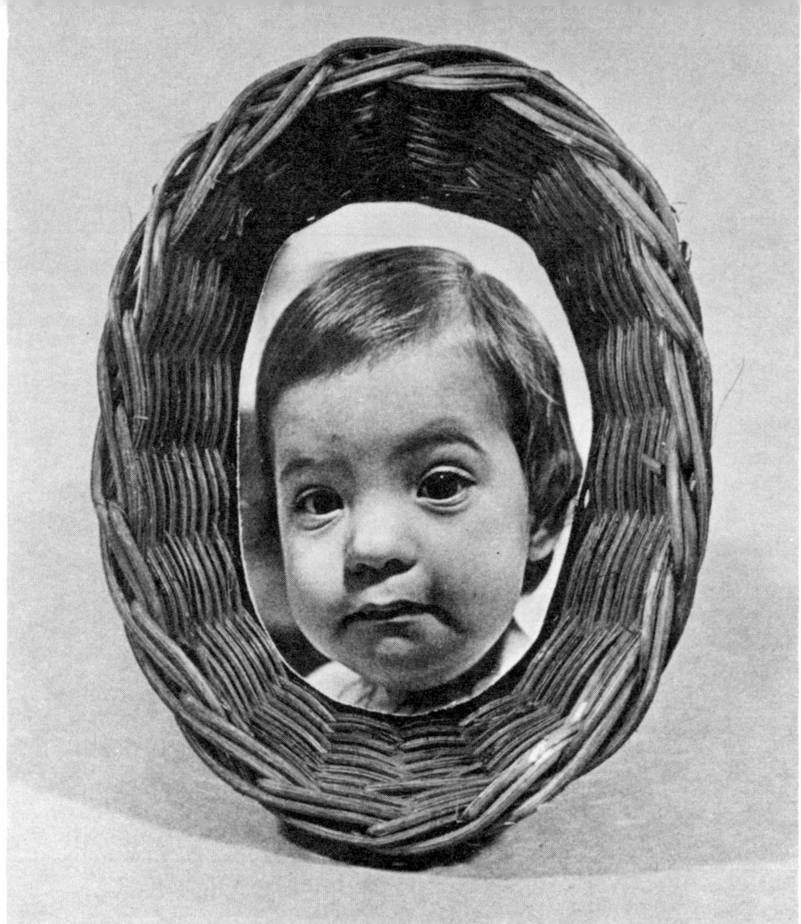

This is just a sample of what you can do with baskets and prints. A whole wall can be decorated using prints and various-size baskets.

help you decide which is the more desirable method for your display.

The mounted photograph can be attached to the basket using removable adhesives. That way, the photos can be changed without damaging the basket. The 3M Company manufactures one-inch mounting squares that are a two-sided adhesive. The one-inch squares can be cut to any size you might need.

THE PHOTO BOX

Plastic photo cubes are popular for photo display on a desk or tabletop. Instead of purchasing the plastic cubes, you can make your own photo box, using mounting board, adhesives, and plastic or cloth tape.

Five or six photographs are needed—five if you plan on leaving the bottom of the cube open. Keep in mind that the photo on the bottom will not be visible at all times. Prints that have borders will work best, because you can cover the border area with tape without covering any of the image.

Equal-size photos will be needed, preferably square. You can cut the photos to equal size with a paper cutter or scissors. Mount the photographs on five equal pieces of mounting board with any of the mounting adhesives discussed in Chapter 3.

Once the photos are mounted and cut to the proper size, the box needs to be constructed. The mounted photos are joined using a colored tape with ¾- or 1½-inch width, depending on the size of the cube you are making. The tape should be wide enough to cover any borders on the print.

Once the cube is constructed, you may want to give it extra strength by gluing the inside of the box where the mounting boards meet. A water-soluble white glue will work.

If you make a rectangular box using vertical photographs, the top photo will be smaller than the four sides.

Instead of constructing your own cube or box, you might be able to find a ready-made box that is the correct size. All you'll have to do is trim your photos and attach them directly to the sides and top of the box, using a mounting adhesive.

A five-sided box can be made with square mounted photos, adhesive, and tape.

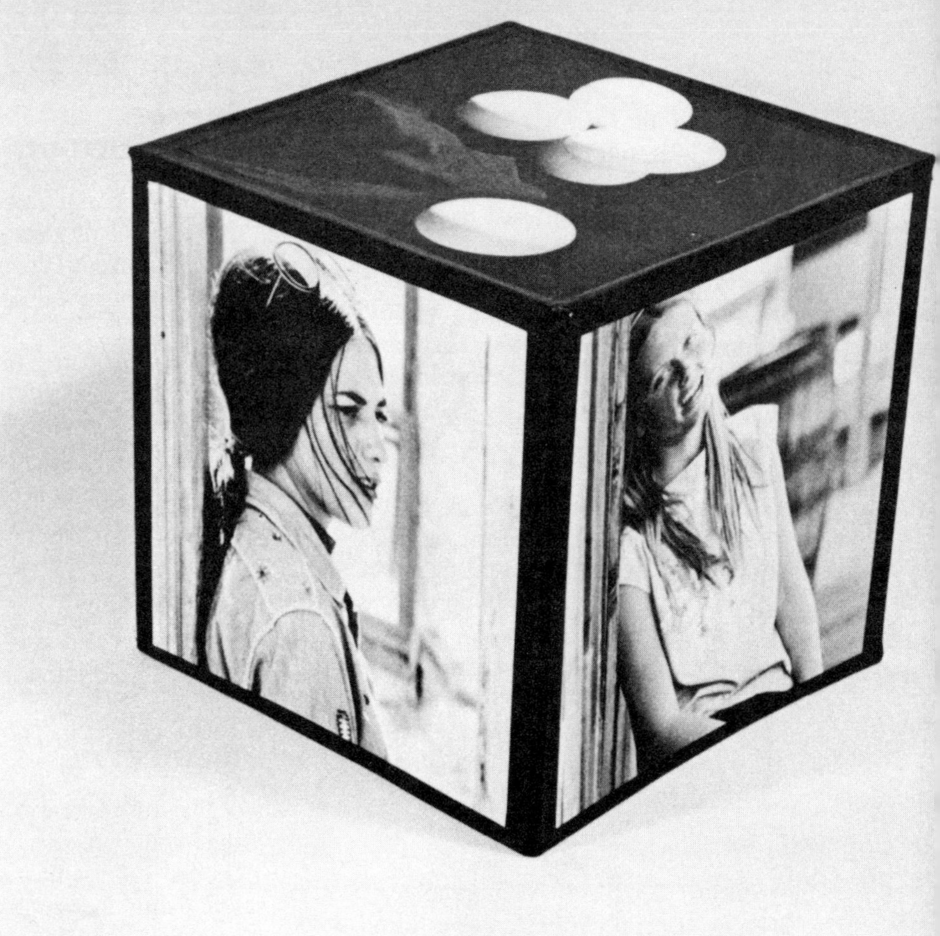

PHOTO PUZZLE

One way to display a single photo that will get plenty of viewing, especially while it's being constructed, is a photo jigsaw puzzle. A picture of the youngsters in the family will encourage them to put the puzzle together. Grandparents might like the picture puzzle if it's of their grandchildren.

Both color and black-and-white prints can be converted into puzzles. Depending on the manufacturer, either slides, negatives, or prints can be converted into a puzzle.

Two mail-order catalog companies that have offered the picture-printing and puzzle-cutting service are listed below.

Miles Kimball
41 West Eighth Avenue
Oshkosh, Wisconsin 54906

Horchow Collection
P. O. Box 34257
Dallas, Texas 75234

If there has been little demand for the service, it's possible the companies no longer offer it. Write for their catalogs to see if the picture puzzle making is still offered. If not, you might want to try making your own picture puzzle from an 8×10 color or black-and-white print.

One handcrafted puzzle I've seen illustrated was made from small square blocks of wood. Equal pieces from six different photographs were attached to each of the six sides of wooden blocks. Scramble all the blocks and you can spend hours searching for the correct pieces to the picture puzzles.

PHOTO MURALS

Large photographs, some capable of covering an entire wall, are called murals. The pictures are usually scenic landscapes that have the effect of bringing the outdoors into one's home decor.

Some manufacturers are selling ready-made murals that are attached to a wall, like wallpaper.

For those with their own quality photographs, some custom labs will produce the murals.

Photographic murals are printed in sections when they are going to be used to cover a wall. The sections can be glued right to the wall's surface or they can be mounted on separate panels. The panels are then attached to the wall.

Installing the murals is not an easy task. Care must be taken to join each section of the mural carefully. This will give the impression of a single photo instead of appearing as the joining of several sections.

Murals are expensive. Their installation can also be costly. Murals attached to panels for later wall attachment are even more expensive. Shipping costs from a lab may be prohibitive for most.

For the individual with the money and the appropriate photograph, a mural is well worth the investment for the enjoyment one will obtain from the environment the mural enhances.

POSTERS

Inexpensive 2×3-foot photographic posters can liven up a child's room or give the guest of honor a warm welcome at a reception.

Many companies advertise in the back of magazines for poster printing. The cost is small, but the results are often far from perfect. Both color and black-and-white can be reproduced.

Mounting a large poster might be a problem. Some frame shops have a special process that wraps the mounted poster in a plastic. When the plastic is subjected to heat, it will shrink, fitting tightly over the poster and the mount.

Lightweight mounting materials need to be used—such as Fome-Cor or cardboard. For large prints, such as the 2×3-foot poster, one should let a qualified framing shop supply the service. The results will be well worth the cost.

Two companies that have offered poster conversion are listed below.

Walter Drake
4201 Drake Building
Colorado Springs, Colorado 80940

Wallet Photo Company
Department 1015
P. O. Box 1758
Clifton, New Jersey 07015

PASSE-PARTOUT

Using a mounted and matted print, plus a protective piece of glass or plexiglass, you can create a passe-partout.

The protective glass or plastic needs to be exactly the same size as the mount and mat. Everything is held together using black or colored tape with a width of one to one and a half inches. The tape will act as a frame, supplying a border around the print.

Large prints treated in the passe-partout method are difficult to hang. Small photos, up to ten inches, can be attached to a flat surface using a two-sided tape such as the 3M Company's mounting squares. Another way to display the passe-partout is by using one of the many decorator tabletop easels.

BRAQUETTE

Matted prints can be hung from walls by using the commercially available Braquette picture frame. It is adjustable for pictures ranging in size from five to forty inches. Both clear and black are available, and they are reusable.

Braquette can be used with glass or plexiglass and a mounting material. The Braquette is placed on the top and on the bottom of a photograph sandwiched between two pieces of glass or a piece of glass and pegboard. A small lever is snapped closed and the picture is ready to be hung on a wall, using a small nail.

Look for Braquette in photo supply and frame shops. It is manufactured by:

F. Weber
Visual Art Industries, Inc.
Wayne and Windrim
Philadelphia, Pennsylvania 19144

PHOTO-GALLERY WALL BRACKETS

For the photographer who likes to change the photos he has on display regularly, the Falcon Photo-Gallery wall bracket might be the answer.

The small plastic bracket can be attached to a wall or other flat surface using screws or the included self-stick adhesive pads. Any mounted print can then be slid into place. Nylon friction

A very inexpensive framing technique is passe-partout. A print is sandwiched between mount and glass (or plexiglass), then a border is made of plastic or cloth tape.

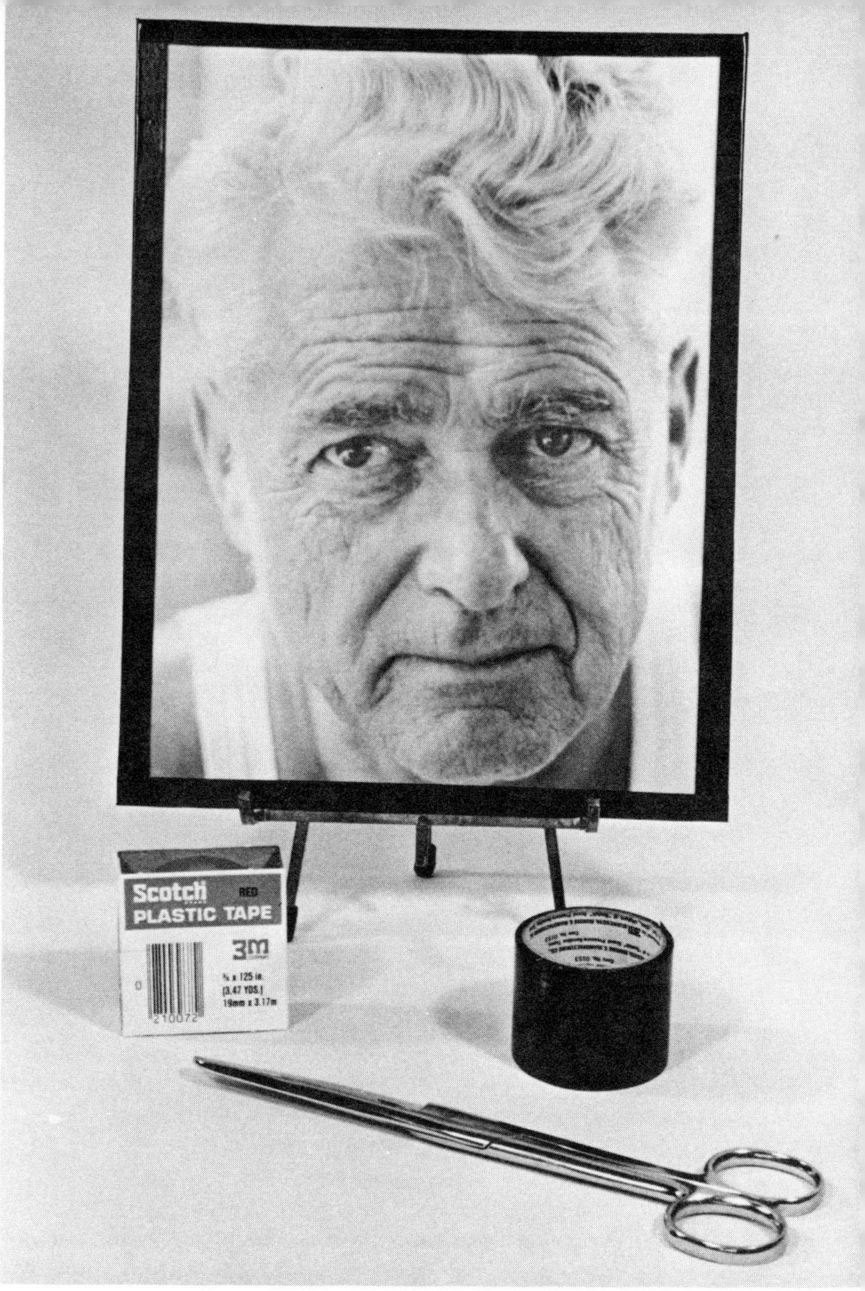

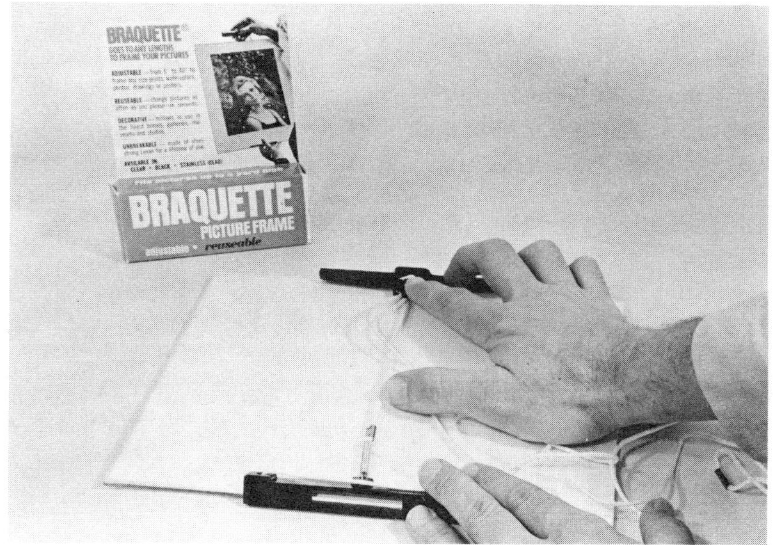

Adjustable Braquette will hold a protective covering of glass and mounted print for a frameless look.

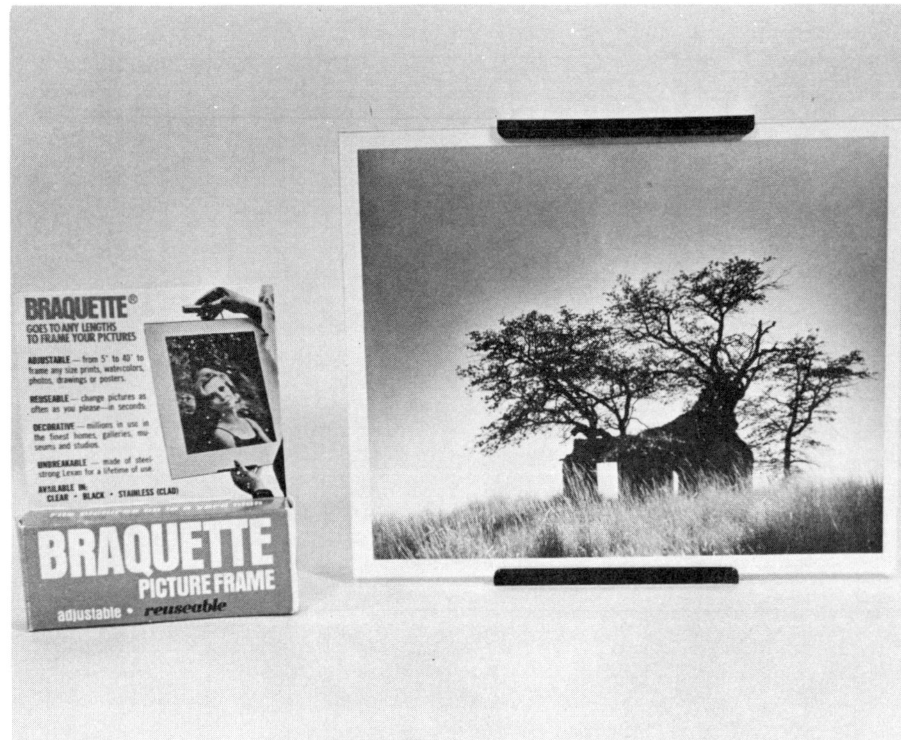

Two small strips are all that show when displaying photographs with Braquette.

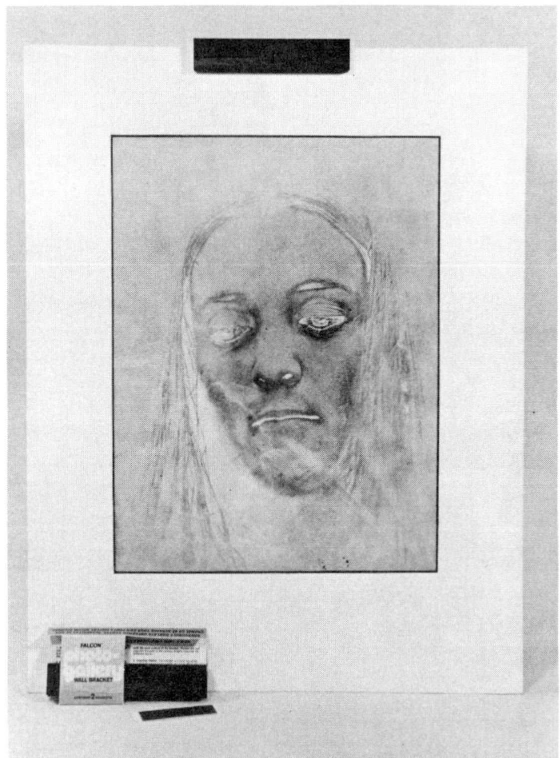

Photo-Gallery wall brackets, by Falcon Safety Products, make photo changing quick and easy.

rollers suspend the photo. A photo can be added or removed with the same ease.

The brackets come in black with a wood accent or white with a brushed aluminum strip to blend with most decors.

Photo-Gallery is manufactured by:

Falcon Safety Products, Inc.
1065 Bristol Road
Mountainside, New Jersey 07092

Check with your photo supply dealer or a local frame shop for the wall brackets.

SWISS CLIPS

Next time you are in an art supply store, ask for small metal Swiss clips. They can be used to mount glass and prints to Masonite or other ⅛-inch-thick materials.

Any matted print can be sandwiched between a piece of glass or plastic and Masonite. A small hole will have to be drilled in the Masonite for each Swiss clip used. From the front of the photo, all that will be visible are small portions of the Swiss clips that hold the glass in place.

The Swiss-clipped photos can be displayed on

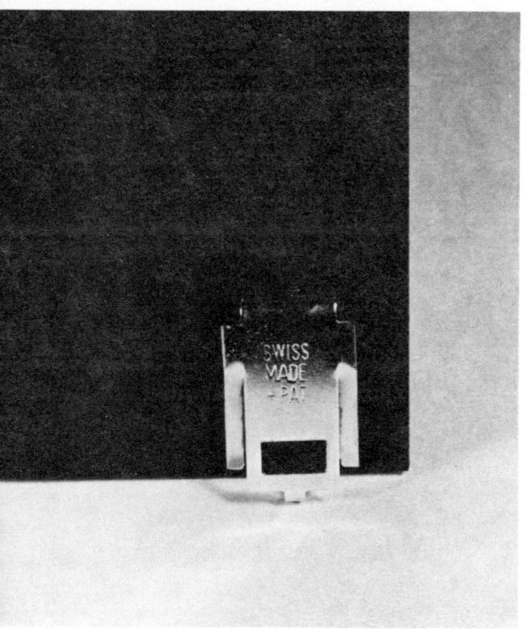

The Swiss clips hold a piece of glass or plexiglass over the matted or mounted photograph.

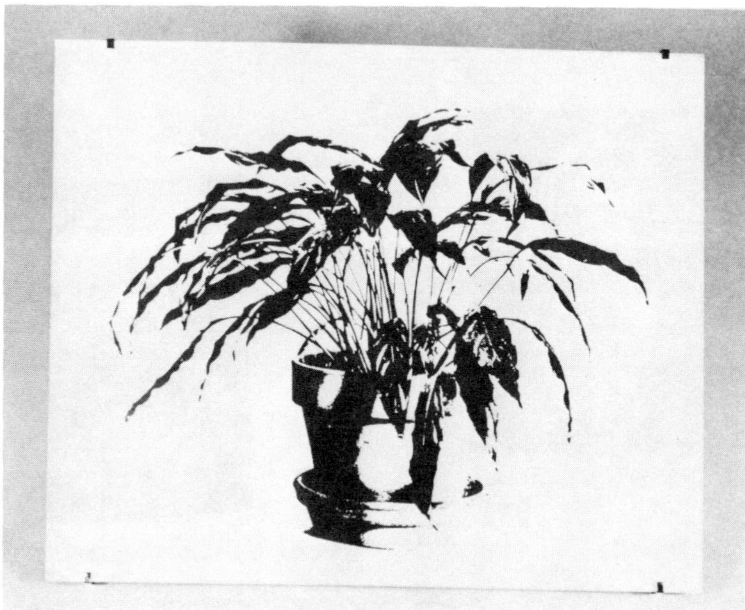

The four points of metal at the corners of the print are all that show when using Swiss clips.

a picture easel or hung from a wall using screw eyes and wire or any of the other picture-hanging devices mentioned in Chapter 4.

WOOD PICTURE STANDS

Using a little imagination and a few woodworking tools, you can design and construct your own, unique picture stands for displaying pictures on desks and tabletops. A single block of wood can be used, or you can use two separate pieces of wood as illustrated on page 78. The secret is to cut a groove using a table or jigsaw so that the mounted picture will fit snugly in the groove.

The small block stands are also useful for displaying photographs that use Swiss clips or passe-partout.

Make sure the wood picture stands are heavy enough to support the photo they are supposed to hold.

CREATE A DIORAMA

If you have an old aquarium that no longer provides a home for fish, you can convert it to a diorama using living plants.

You will need a scenic photo large enough to fit inside the aquarium and cover an entire side of one of the glass walls. The photo should be laminated to protect it from moisture when you water your plants.

If you plant tropical houseplants in the aquarium, you'll need a scenic photograph suitable for that type of vegetation. If you plan to use cacti, you will need a photo illustrating desert landscape or climate.

Add pieces of driftwood and, if desired, small ceramic animals to add interest to the scene. This type of photographic use makes a good project for the children in the family who have to prepare something for their science class.

If you don't wish to use an aquarium and living plants, you can use appropriate baskets, cardboard boxes, and dried vegetation available from variety stores.

PHOTOGRAPHY MOBILE

If you have a collection of small photographs you would like to see constantly and also use decoratively, you can turn them into a mobile. The photo mobile is easy to make and can add sparkle to a child's room.

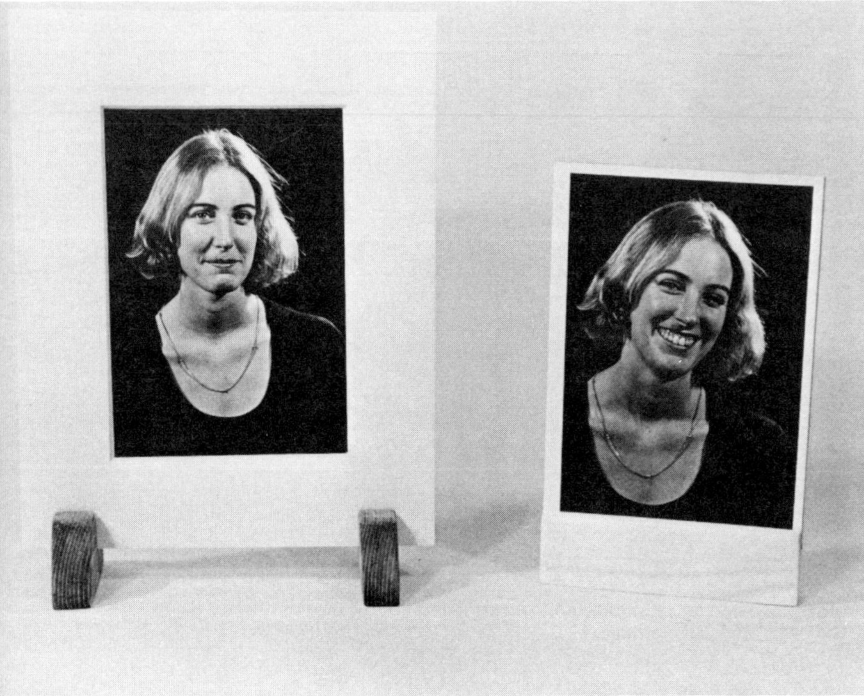

Scrap pieces of wood can be used to make unique picture stands.

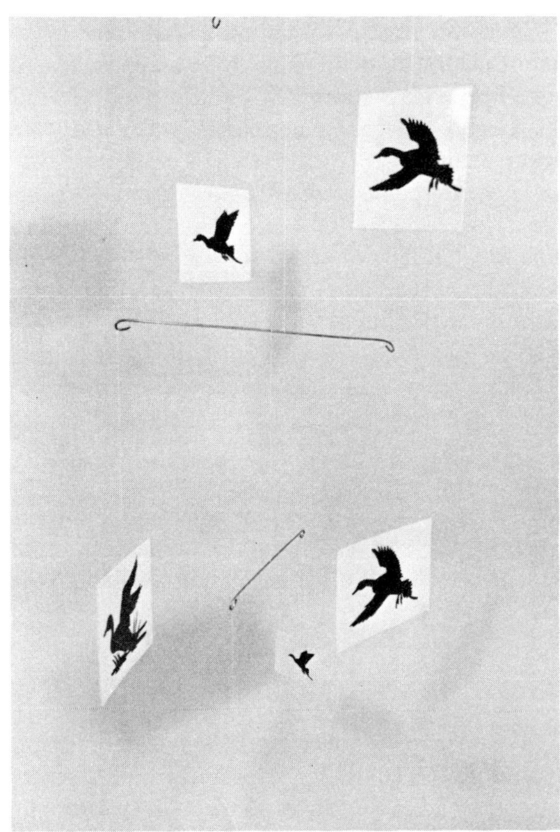

A photo mobile.

All that are needed are several photos, mounting adhesive (two-sided cold mount), string or thread, and some straight wire. The wire that makes a clothes hanger will work, but it's a bit obtrusive because of its size.

The first step is to mount the photographs back to back so there is an image on each side. When you are mounting the photos back to back, you'll have to insert a piece of thread or string between the photos and the mounting adhesive. The string should be placed so it is near a center point of the photograph.

Once the photos are attached to one another, you may want to cut interesting designs, such as squares, triangles, hexagons, circles, or anything else you can think of. In a sense, you are cropping the photos.

The next step is to bend small loops in the ends of the wire. The strings are then tied to the loops. The secret of a good mobile is balance. You'll have to make sure you have two fairly equal-weighted photos opposite one another on the supporting wires.

It is easiest to manipulate the strings and photos as the mobile hangs. Proper balance can be achieved, and the mobile is ready to be hung from the ceiling.

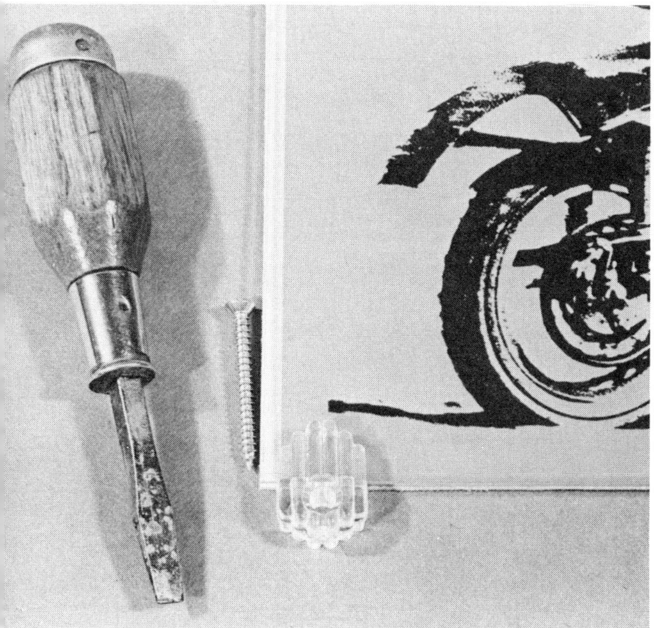

Mirror clips can be used to attach prints directly to a flat surface or to hold prints to the backs of frames.

MIRROR CLIPS

Small plastic mirror clips you can purchase in a hardware store can be used to help support and display mounted photographs.

Frames can be made of straight pieces of lumber. Instead of cutting or attaching a rabbet or lip for the photo to rest on the mirror, clips can be used to hold the photo in place behind the frame.

Four clips can be used for small prints. Larger prints may need more than four of the mirror clips to keep the photograph from warping.

Mirror clips can also be used to attach borderless or frameless prints to paneled or wood-covered walls.

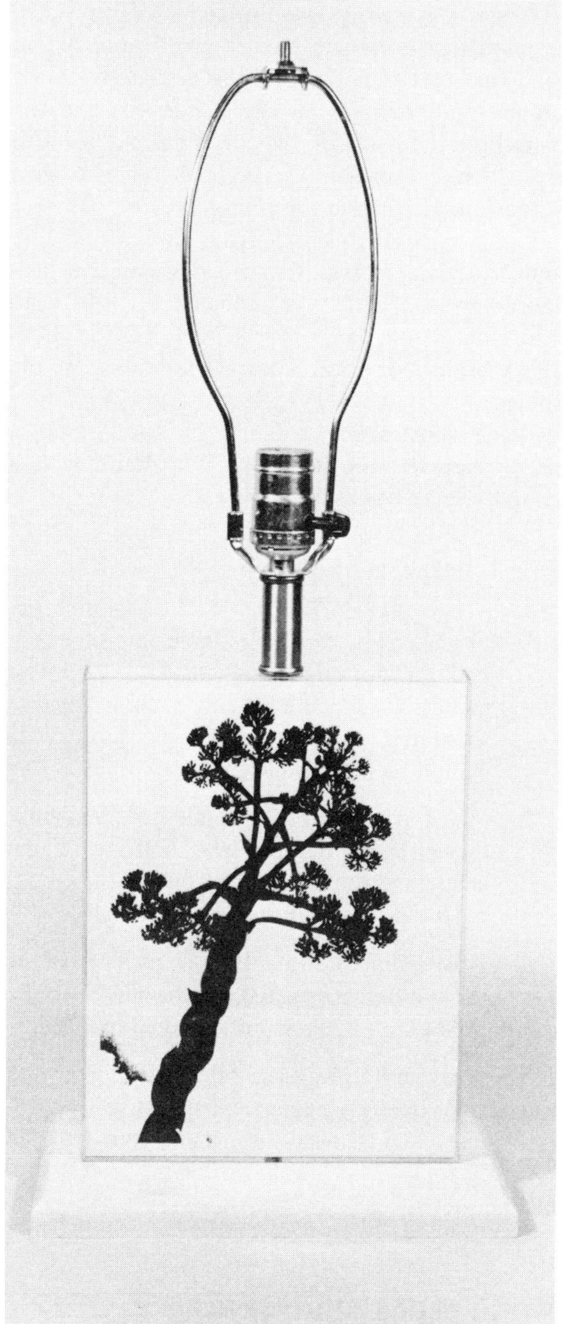

The plastic-box frame was converted into a lamp. The variations depend on the individual's creativity.

PHOTO-DISPLAY LAMP

Framed pictures generally hang on a wall, but with a little lamp-making knowledge and a few tools, you can convert a framed picture into a decorative and functional lamp. The lamp's picture has its own source of illumination for excellent viewing.

Illustrated here is a simple 8×10-inch plastic-box frame. Two holes were drilled, and a stability-giving wood base was added. This particular lamp uses only one photo, but variations of this can be constructed so you can use as many as four or more photographs.

When making picture-displaying lamps, keep in mind that a vertical picture gives more height than one that is horizontal. An alternative is to group small pictures within a mat to give the lamp base the necessary height. You may want to try attaching four identical vertical frames to give you a four-sided base for a lamp.

Lamp parts are available from electrical supply and hardware stores. Lampshades can be purchased from a variety of retailers. (If you need information on lamp parts and construction, check with your local library for books on the subject.)

When constructing a lamp, be sure it has a heavy base to keep it stable. You don't want a lamp that can be easily tipped over.

To help in your lamp construction, I've listed general rules you might want to consider:

1. When placed on a table, the distance between the bottom of a table lamp's shade and the floor is about forty to forty-two inches. If someone sits in a chair next to thc lamp, the bottom of the lampshade should be near eye level.

2. When constructing a small bedside lamp, the distance between the bottom of the shade and the mattress of one's bed should be about twenty inches.

3. Any lamp you make that uses a shade should be constructed so the glare of the bulb does not show outside the lampshade.

These are just a few basic rules you might want to consider before you start constructing a photo-displaying lamp. If necessary, make your own set of rules to fit your photo-displaying and lamp-making needs.

WOOD-BLOCK MOUNTING

Mounted, borderless prints can be attached to walls, using blocks or strips of wood. The photos will stand out from the walls as if they were floating.

Blocks of wood can be glued directly to the back of the mounted photograph. The blocks can then be attached to the wall using two-sided adhesive, or a small hole can be drilled in the wood and then slipped over a nail.

WOOD-BLOCK MOUNTING

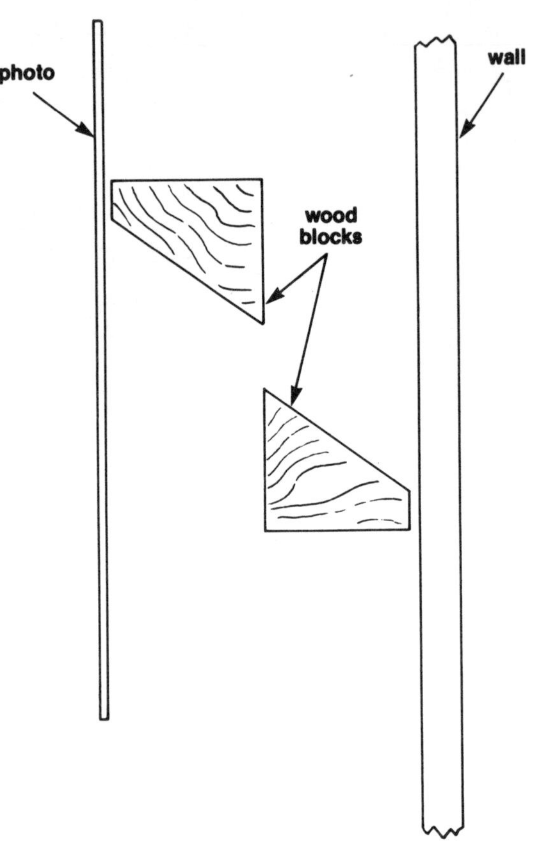

If you're skilled with woodworking tools, you might want to cut the wood block or strips so they have a diagonal cut. You can then mount half the block to the wall and the other half to the back of the print. The photo is then slipped into place.

Large prints may need the addition of a spacer block to keep the photo parallel to the surface of the wall.

PHOTO CLOCK

A visit to a large department store or a specialty shop will give you ideas on how to convert a favorite negative or slide into an attractive clock. A large print with a portion presenting time information isn't difficult to construct.

You will have to have your favorite photo lab make a fairly large print, of 11×14 inches or

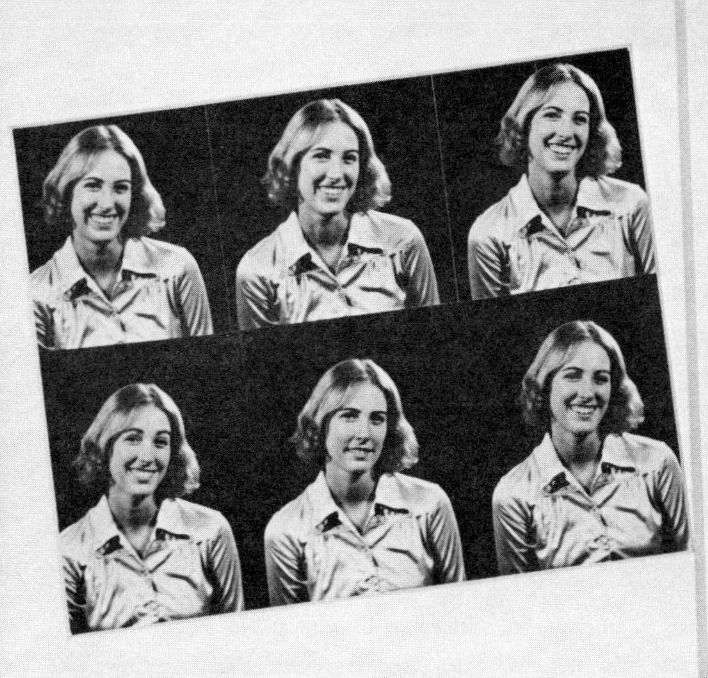

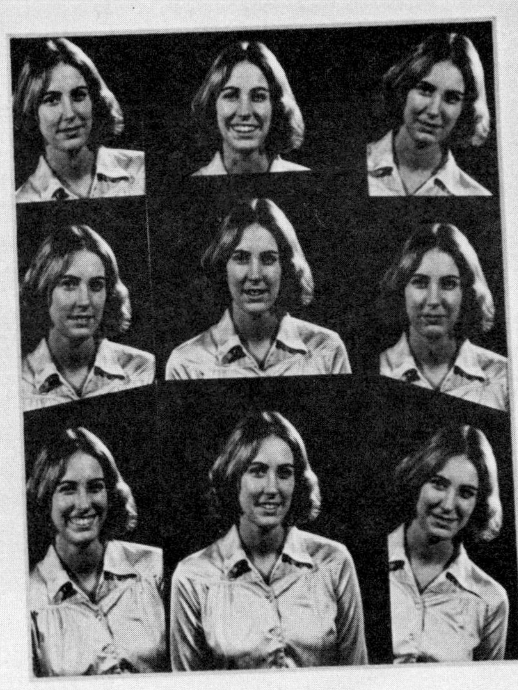

Several photos can be mounted together to give a montage display.

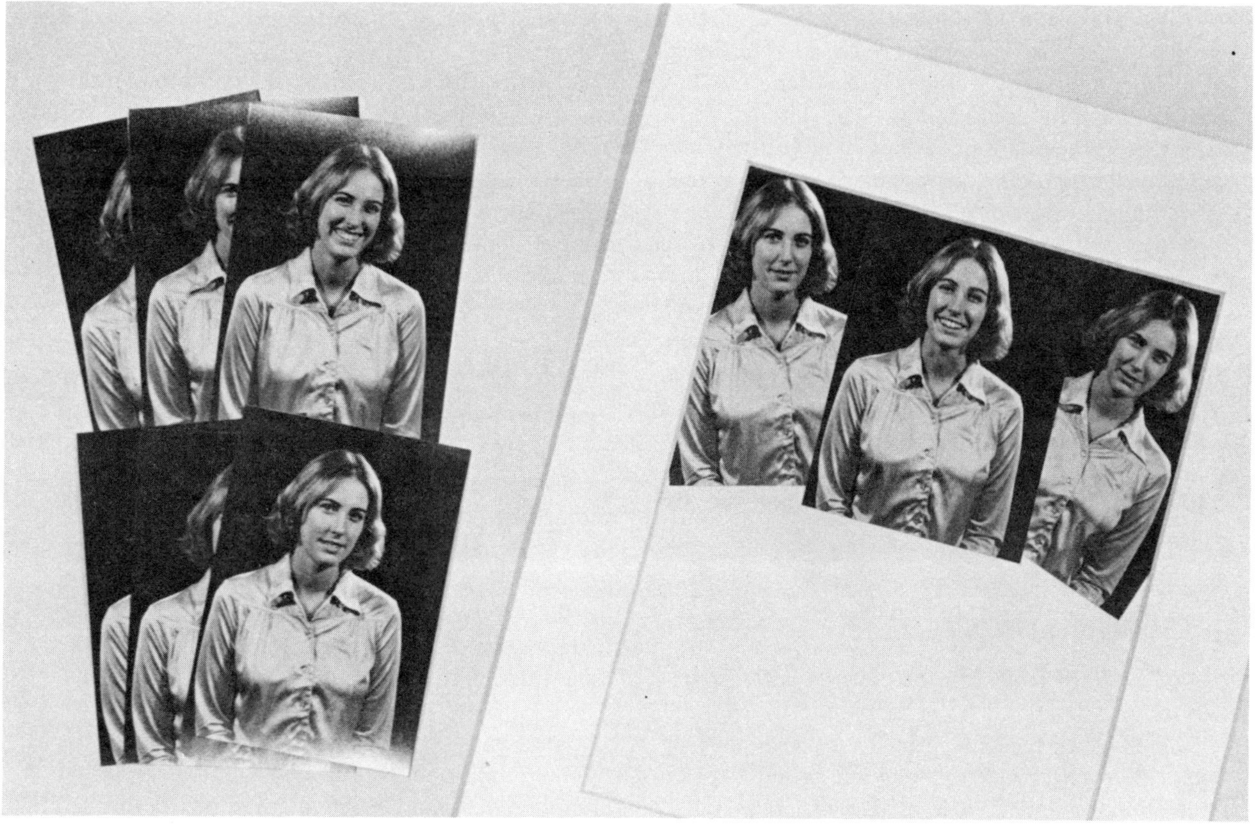

Arrange your photos before you mount to see which display is the most appealing.

larger. Scenic photographs are the most popular images used for the commercially produced clocks.

The print needs to be trimmed and mounted to a heavy mount such as Masonite. With a little shopping around at clock shops, you will have to purchase a clock mechanism, preferably one that is battery operated so you won't have a distracting electrical cord showing on the wall behind the finished product.

The clock mechanism is attached to the back of the mounted print. You'll have to construct a frame for the back of the mounted print so that it will sit parallel to the wall. Furring strips of 2×2-inch pine will work adequately.

A small hole is drilled through the print for the clock arm drive. Attach the hands and then the appropriate numbers, using self-sticking numbers or transfer type. Add a battery to the clock and you're ready to hang the print for creative display and have a pleasant way to keep track of the time.

MONTAGE

A combination of similar or related photographs under one mat can create an interesting display requiring careful examination by the viewer for full appreciation. The photos in a montage can be just about anything you capture on film. Perhaps the most popular montage is one of family members or a family tree.

There are any number of ways to create a visually pleasing montage. Illustrated here are 3×5 snapshots attached to a mounting board and covered with an 11×14 mat with an 8×10-inch window. A 16×20-inch mat with a horizontal 8×10-inch window was also used.

There are no limits to the number or size of photographs you can use in a montage photo display. Black-and-white and color prints can be mixed in the display.

TABLETOP DISPLAY

All types of tables can be covered with a variety of photographs. The pictures used to decorate a tabletop are held in place by a piece of clear glass. The glass not only holds the prints in place but also protects them from damage. If possible, photos should be matted to prevent them from sticking to the glass cover.

Once you know the dimensions of your table, any glass and mirror supplier will cut a ¼-inch piece of glass to the size you need.

Try not to clutter a tabletop with too many prints, and be careful to blend the colors of the prints so they match the home or office decor.

Abstract photos showing close-ups of plant foliage, rock texture and unusual patterns may be more appealing than a child's smiling face. One large photo covering the table may be better than a collection of four or five small ones.

PRINT DIVISION

Very large prints can be cut in pieces of various sizes and each section individually framed. The framed but divided prints can then be hung. The first glance will show several prints hung on the wall. With close scrutiny, the grouping will reveal an individual theme or print.

There are unlimited ways to divide the print. The print can be divided into thirds, fourths, or any combination of sizes. The secret to displaying a divided print is to use identically constructed frames.

Print division can also be done without framing the photos. Depending on the size of the print, a one-inch or larger space can be left between the prints when they are attached to the wall. The viewer will still get the impression there is more than one photo on the wall, until the images are closely studied and pieced together.

SUSPENDED PHOTOGRAPHS

Not all pictures need to be attached to a wall or other flat surface. Large prints can be suspended in air, using fine wire or translucent fishing line.

A whole wall of suspended photographs can be produced, acting as a room divider. Passe-partout for the photos would work best. That way, a photograph could be attached to each side of the mounting board and covered with glass. The suspended photos would then provide images for study on both sides of the divider.

The lines used to suspend the passe-partout photographs would have to be attached through

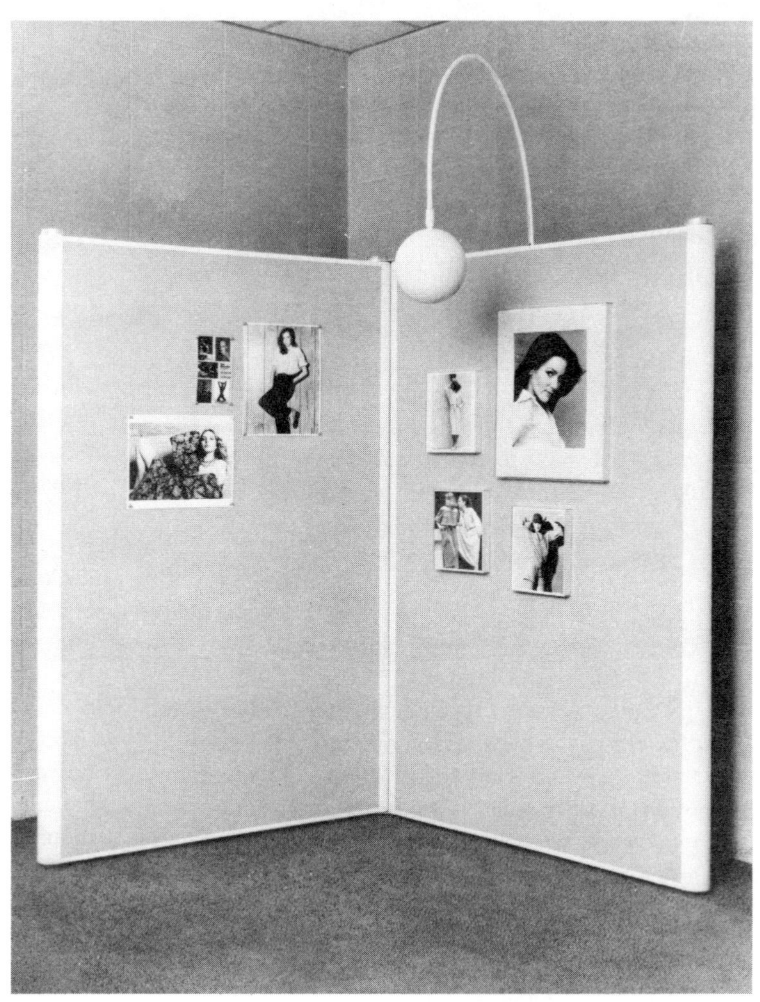

You can design your own changeable wall mount or purchase a system such as this. Photo courtesy The Brewster Corporation.

the tape and held in place using a strong adhesive.

If only one side of a suspended print is to be viewed, frames of wood, metal, or plastic could be used. Screw eyes can be attached to the tops of wood frames. Small holes can be drilled in the plastic or metal framing devices. The wire or fishing line can then be inserted through the holes and tied in a knot so it can't be pulled back through the holes.

Suspended photographs should be fairly heavy so they will remain stationary instead of blowing in any air currents produced by heating or cooling units.

Various-size photos can be mixed and matched for hanging to enhance the visual appeal of floating photographs.

Plant-hanging hooks or large screw eyes can be used in the ceiling. If the prints and frames are very heavy, make sure you attach the hanging hooks to a wood beam in the ceiling to give the display as much strength as possible.

CHANGEABLE WALL MOUNTS

Photographers, especially the home darkroom enthusiast with a new favorite print showing up every trip to the darkroom, may want to make a permanent but changeable wall-mounted print display.

Before designing a changeable wall mount, you'll have to decide what is the most common print size you'll be using—5×7, 8×10, or

11×14—and what size mount and mat will be used. You should also consider whether you wish to display one print or several.

L-SHAPED MOLDING

A simple wall mount can be created using two strips of L-shaped molding attached directly to the wall. The molding can be stained or painted before it is attached to the wall using finishing nails. Mounted photographs are then slipped into place from the ends of the molding strips. The length of the strips of molding will determine how many prints can be displayed.

CHANGEABLE FRAME

A frame that has an open end on top can be constructed so that photographs can be slipped in and out from the open side.

Decide what size prints are to be displayed. Make two identical frames, using hardwood or pine. Using lattice strips or narrow molding, make a three-sided support that is sandwiched between the two identical frames you have constructed. Small finishing nails and glue will hold the frame together.

Your mounted prints are then slid into place between the frames and guided by the spacer of lattice or molding.

USING CORK

A visit to a home improvement center will give you an idea of all the types of cork and corklike materials that are available. What you develop as a means of creative photo display is up to you.

Cork comes in one-foot squares or can be purchased in rolls with a width of three feet or more. Thickness of the cork material varies also.

What can be done with the cork? All types of things. Entire walls can be covered, bulletin boards made, or even picture mats can be cut from some of the thinner cork. Don't try for a beveled edge on a cork mat. A straight cut will have to suffice, to prevent the cork from chipping.

Cork not only makes an attractive background but also makes it easy to change mounted and unmounted prints you would like to display. Pushpins can be used to hold the photographs in place. These small pins have a large plastic head that comes in colors or clear plastic. The head of the pushpin will hold the print in place without having to make a hole in the actual picture or mounting board. One pin used at each corner of a print will be adequate for holding small and medium-size prints in place.

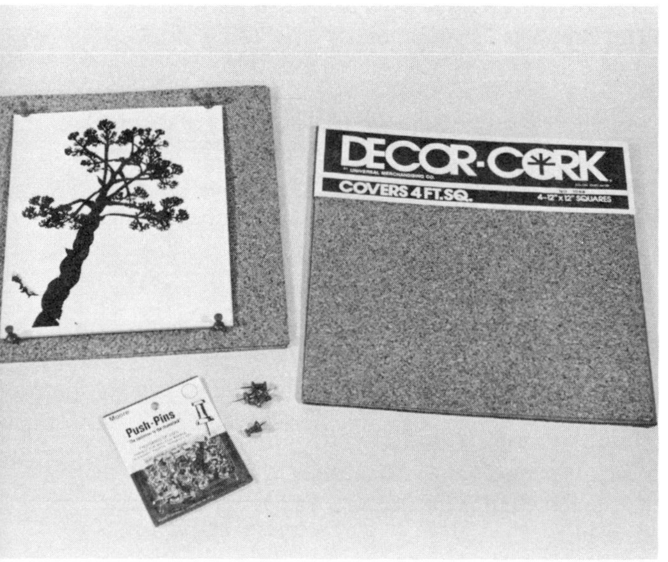

Sheets of cork can be useful for designing changeable wall displays for photographs.

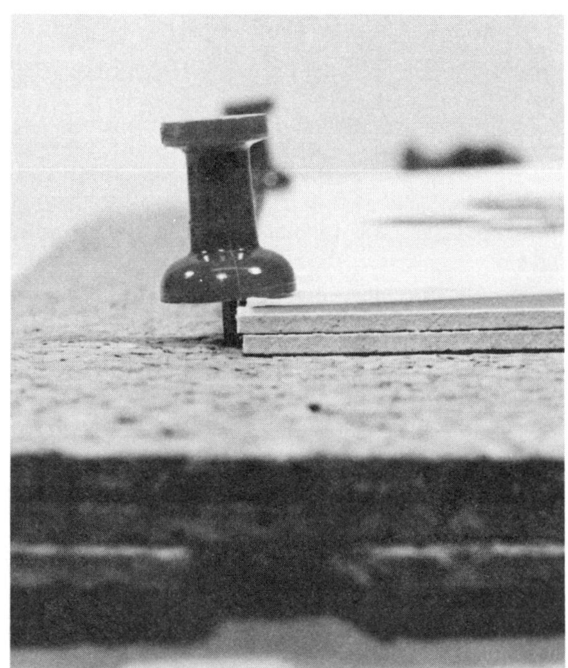

Plastic pushpins hold photos in place without damaging the print, mount, or mat.

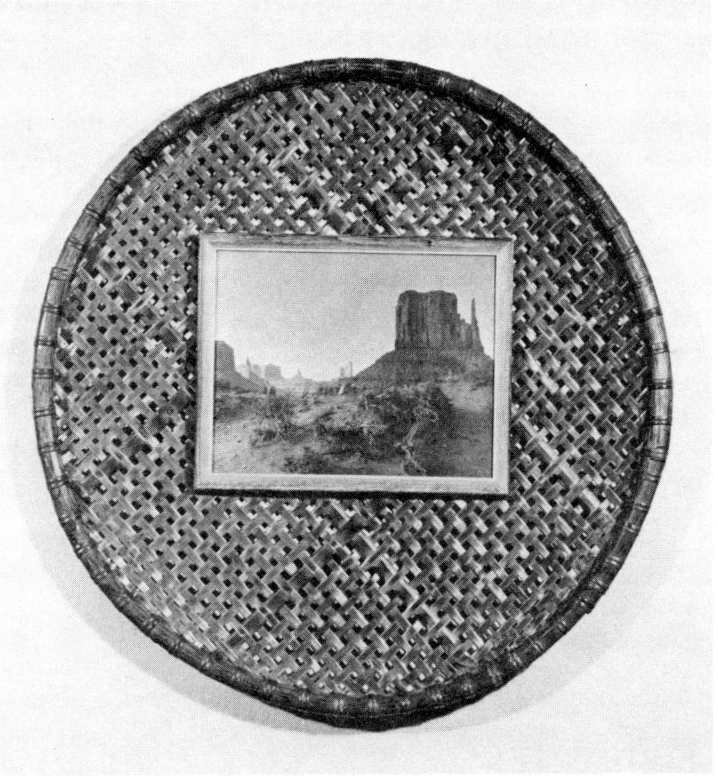

Background material such as the basket and the fan can add interest to your hanging photographic displays.

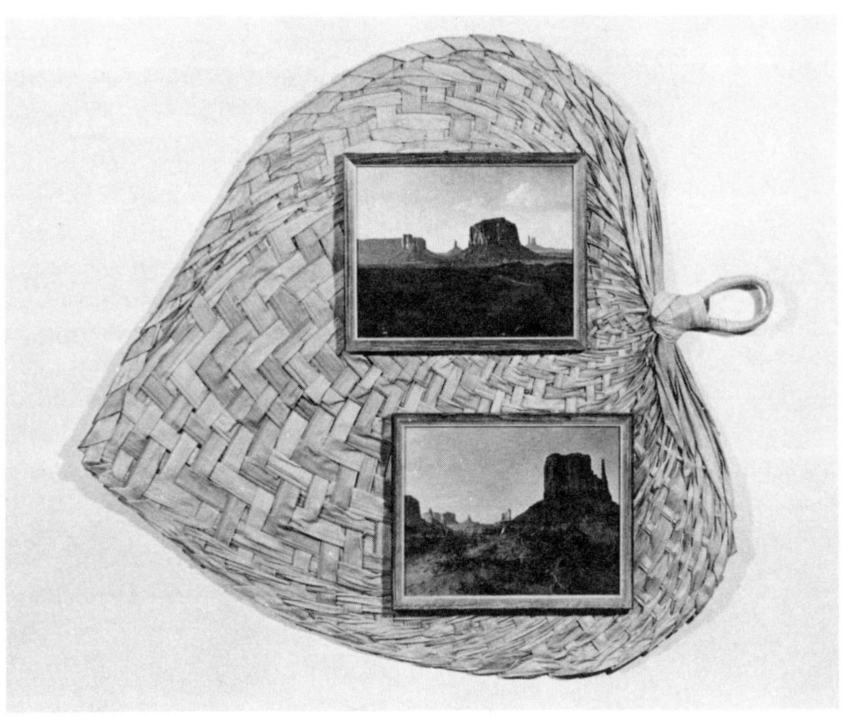

DECORATIVE BACKGROUND DISPLAY

You can enhance the appearance of photographs hanging on a wall by adding some sort of decorative background. What you use for a background will be influenced by the content of the photographs you plan to display.

A series of photographs showing boats, seabirds, and seascapes might be enhanced if the background material is a fishing net. Photographs of a ghost town may be enhanced in their display if the background is old or weathered wood.

Planning and selective purchasing will help you to match the right background to the photographs. Illustrated on page 85 are a three-foot-diameter basket and a large woven fan.

Display judgment is left to the individual's taste. Which background works better with the photos shown—the basket or the fan? Then again, you might not like either arrangement.

CREATIVE DISPLAY IS JUST BEGINNING

Seldom is a book of nonfiction complete. New ideas are always being introduced or at least tried somewhere. This chapter on "Creative Display" is not complete; it is just a guide to help you to develop your own ideas for showing your favorite photographs.

How one can display photographs is, in my opinion, unlimited. Whether you decide to decorate a planter, lampshade, or the kitchen cabinets, it's all creative photographic display.

Every negative or slide is somewhat different from every other. What that image conveys to each individual viewer varies. No two people are exactly alike, nor is the way we see, feel, and think like anyone else's.

Depending on your individual makeup, some photographic images can make you feel as happy or confused as the first time you fell in love. Photography can communicate happiness, loneliness, desolation, fear, triumph, excitement, beauty, death, bewilderment, humor, life, and just about anything else you might want. If you have the right image to fit your feelings or mode of life, by all means find a creative means of display.

CAMERA CLUBS

With a little planning and promotion, you can start a camera club or even join one of the many established clubs throughout the country. A camera club will give you a chance to show your best work and give you new and interesting photographic ideas by viewing the work of others.

Starting a camera club will require a little work to get enough members to make the organization worthwhile. With as few as ten members, you can have a club that offers educational entertainment and fellowship.

Your organizational meeting will be the most difficult task. You'll have to establish a club constitution and bylaws. To help in your organization of a new club, there are a few basic topics that will have to be discussed and voted on.

1. Club name. What do you want to call your club?
2. Officers. A list of club officers and their specific duties. A president, vice-president, secretary, and treasurer will get you started. The number of officers varies according to the membership in your club.
3. Membership requirements and dues, if any.
4. A meeting place. Many banks, libraries, and parks will have facilities that are free to various clubs and organizations.
5. How many meetings per month, and when. One or two meetings a month should be adequate.
6. Competition requirements. What categories are there for competition of prints? Is there a slide competition? Is there going to be both black-and-white and color print competition?
7. Judging. Who'll do the judging? Club members or qualified professional photographers in the community?
8. Points for judging. A 1-through-15 scale should be adequate.
9. Do you want to become affiliated with the Photographic Society of America (PSA)?

The society sponsors competition among clubs, presents awards, and has a selection of photographic educational aids. For further information, write:

PSA
2005 Walnut Street
Philadelphia, Pennsylvania 19103

10. Type of programs for the club members. You'll need qualified speakers on all types of photographic topics. Topics can range from cleaning equipment to using filters correctly.

These are just a few topics that will have to be covered in your organizational meeting. It will give you a base from which to start. Once your club has been organized and is under way, a newsletter can be started, banquets held, and just about any other activity your membership wants.

I have belonged to a camera club and have participated in competition. Two major problems that occurred and should be avoided if possible are listed below.

1. Start your meetings on time. If the meeting is supposed to start at seven-thirty, start it at seven-thirty. People become restless and it's not fair to keep your guest speakers, judges, or members waiting.
2. Another problem is lack of membership participation. Unfortunately, there are only a few members who like responsibility, and it seems they are elected to office over and over again. Get everyone involved in the club's operation at one time or another.

6

SLIDE PRESENTATIONS

Of all the pictures photographers take, those that are taken with slide film are the most difficult to exhibit. The size of the slide is the same as the film you use in your camera. These small, positive images are effective only when they are projected onto a large screen or converted into color prints.

Even though it is somewhat difficult to view without the proper equipment, many picture takers rely on slide film. Their reasoning is economics: Slides are less expensive than prints.

Negative, or print, film has to be changed into a picture by using photographic paper and special equipment that projects and enlarges the negative image onto the paper. Basically there are two steps. First, the film has to be developed. Then the developed film, which is a negative, is projected onto a piece of photographic paper and the paper has to be developed to produce the finished positive print.

For slide film, the process involves developing the film, cutting the film, and then attaching each individual picture to some type of slide mount. The slide mounts are far less expensive than sheets of photographic paper.

Professional photographers who do work for book and magazine publishers use slide film. Economics may be involved, but the actual quality of the printed matter can be reduced if slides are not used to produce the color illustrations. There is an apparent loss of detail and color tones when prints are used as the basis for the reproduction or printing process.

If slides are difficult to exhibit, why shoot them? Slides are not difficult to exhibit if you have the proper equipment. Plus, as with negatives, prints can be made from slides. It's not necessary to have a whole roll of slides converted into prints. Through selective editing, only slides offering a subject that appeals to the owner will be enlarged into prints. The finished prints can then be added to photo albums or displayed in a number of other ways.

You may even find some of your favorite prints from negatives suitable for slides. With the help of your local or favorite photo-processing dealer, you can take prints and have them converted into mounted slides. There's not much a good lab can't do. Slides can become prints, and prints can be transformed into slides.

In a sense, you have a chance to edit the slides before any prints are made. With negative film, you don't get to edit until the prints are returned from the processing lab.

If one is going to use slide film almost exclusively, he will have to invest in equipment that makes slide viewing possible. The basic equipment might be a light box or a hand viewer. This will enable individual inspection of each slide but does not allow for projection. A slide projector and screen enables the pictures to be enlarged so that viewing is simplified.

Unfortunately, even the finest equipment cannot improve a slide presentation that is not edited and organized. Without the proper preparation, a slide show is nothing more than a way for viewers to catch up on their sleep while the lights are off.

A slide presentation does not have to be boring. With a little creativity, selective editing, and organization, slides can be one of the most dramatic and effective ways to show photographic images.

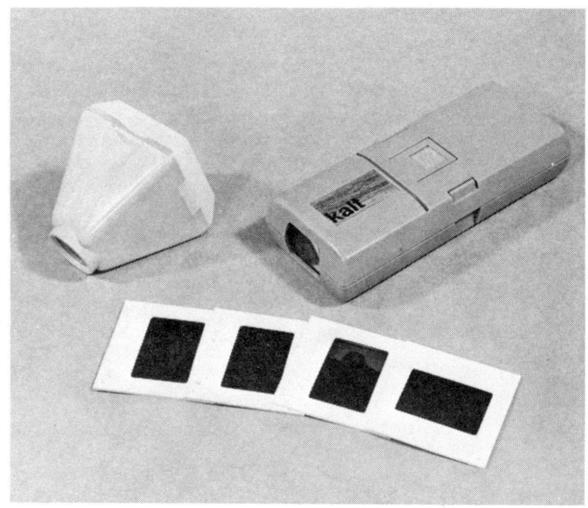

Hand-held slide viewers.

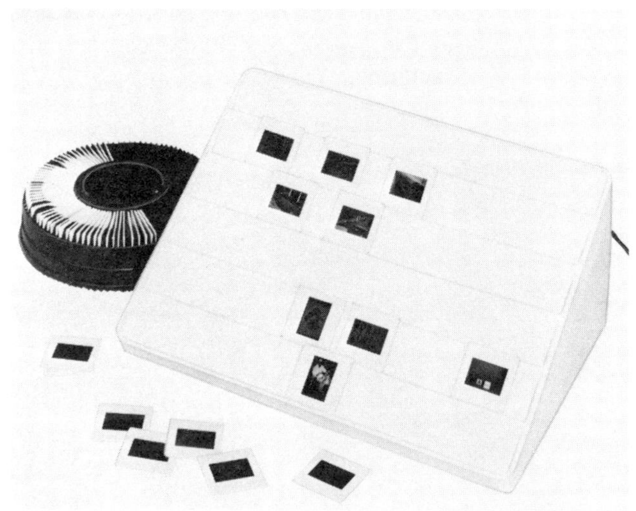

Slide sorters enable quick slide editing and sorting. Photo courtesy KustoMold.

EDITING AND CROPPING SLIDES

As with all photographic images, slides need to be edited to remove those that are far from excellent. There are a number of ways to view the slides for sorting and editing.

Simple, hand-held viewers give you a chance to look at individual slides. Some hand-held viewers have their own light source. Others need a nearby window or light bulb to work. This process for editing is slow, but it will work.

Many manufacturers make small portable light boxes or slide sorters. These are nothing more than a translucent screen that holds the slides, with a light source beneath the screen. Some slide sorters may hold only one roll of film, while others may hold as many as two or three rolls of film.

Generally, a sorter's illumination is fairly uniform. You can lay down several slides and compare exposure. The slides with poor exposure can be quickly eliminated.

To check the focus of a slide, you need either very good eyes or some type of magnifying glass. If you're unsure about the focus, hold the slide until it can be viewed on a projection screen or a hand-held viewer. Any slide that is not as sharp as it could be should be discarded.

When the remaining slides are in focus and possess the proper exposure, you need to study composition. For the slides that have minor composition problems, you can crop to improve appearance. As with prints, the cropping is limited to the edges of the slide. There are two ways to crop slides.

1. Cover up the area to be cropped with thin, opaque tape.

2. Vary the slide mount.

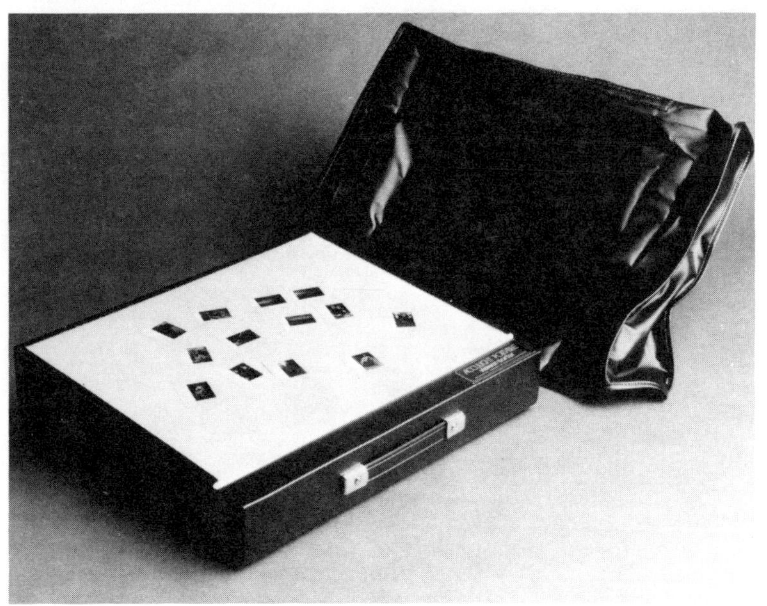

Portable light box for sorting and viewing slides and transparencies. Photo courtesy Knox Manufacturing.

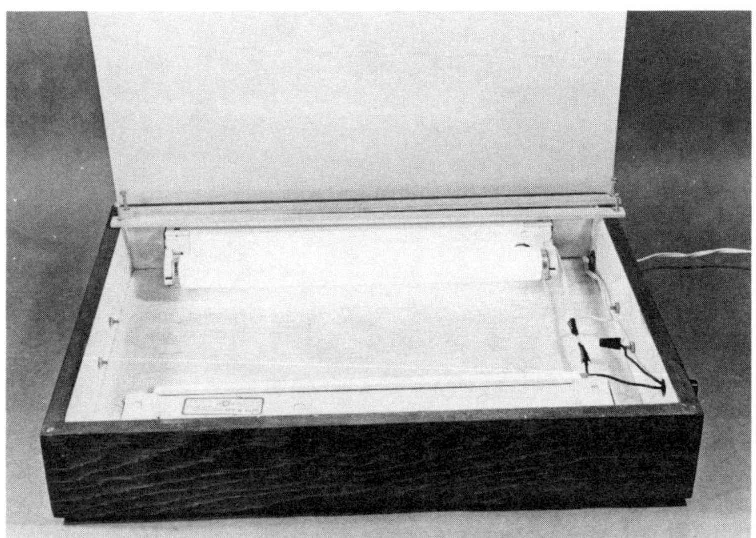

If you're skilled with a few tools, you can construct your own light box.

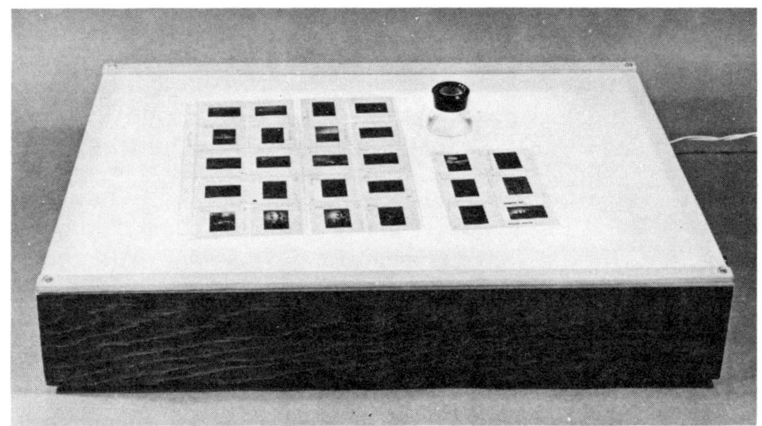

If a print is to be made from the slide, limited cropping can be done by the photo-processing lab.

CROPPING WITH TAPE

Special, slide-binding tape can be used as a cover-up or cropping tool for a slide. The use of the tape is restricted to the outer edges of the image. The tape can also be used to alter the shape of the projected image. Squares, long horizontals, and verticals can be made, using the tape. They'll add diversity to your slide presentations and crop out unwanted or distracting background.

Black vinyl tape can also be used, depending on the projector. If the taped slide hangs up when inserted in the projector, the tape is too thick, and slide-binding tape will have to be used.

Caution must be taken when using tape. It must be placed on the slide mount and cover the slide image so all lines are straight and parallel. Otherwise, the cropping will be noticed when the image is projected.

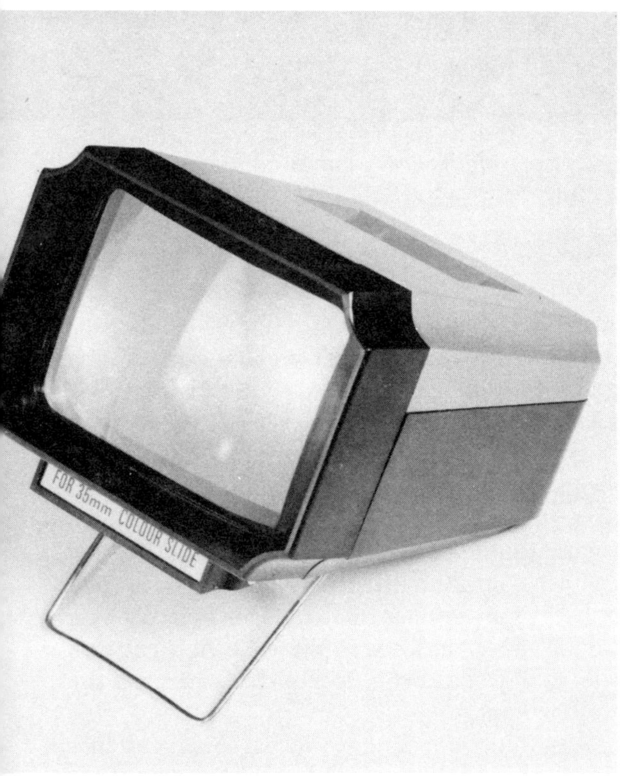

Photo courtesy Ehrenreich Photo-Optical Industries.

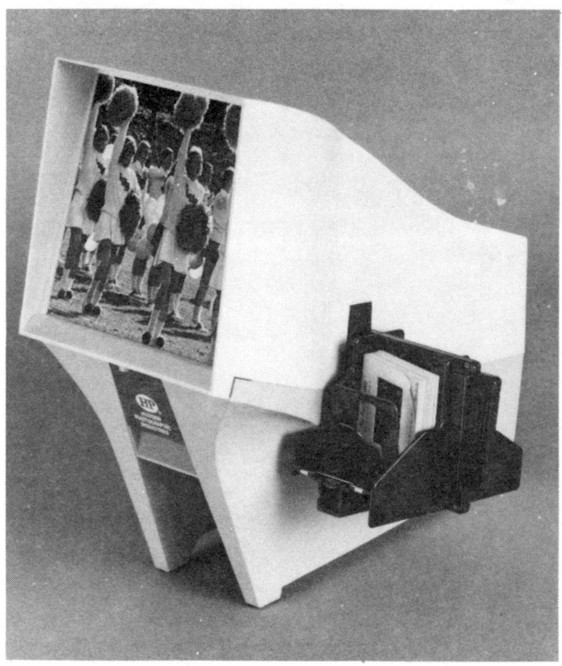

A slide viewer with enlargement screen. Photo courtesy Hudson Photographic Industries.

Some slide mounts have rounded corners on the cutout portion. If you crop the top portion of a slide, you should crop the bottom portion just enough to eliminate the rounded corners. This will make the projected image have four equal corners instead of two that are a sharp 90 degrees and two that are slightly rounded. Most viewers wouldn't notice the slight discrepancy in corners, but, then, there are always one or two avid photographers that might. It's better to eliminate any chance for criticism before the slide is projected.

SLIDE-MOUNT CROPPING

Another way to crop your slides is to vary the cardboard or plastic mount that holds the slide in place. A variety of cutouts are available at photo supply dealers and through mail-order catalogs.

Rectangular, oval, circular, square, star, keyhole, diamond, and even heart-shaped slide mounts are available. Once again, the cropping is limited to the outer edges of the slide. Care must be taken not to damage the transparency when it's moved from one mount to another.

Slide mounts can be separated using a sharp knife or a single-edge razor blade. To prevent any unnecessary contamination to the slide, clean

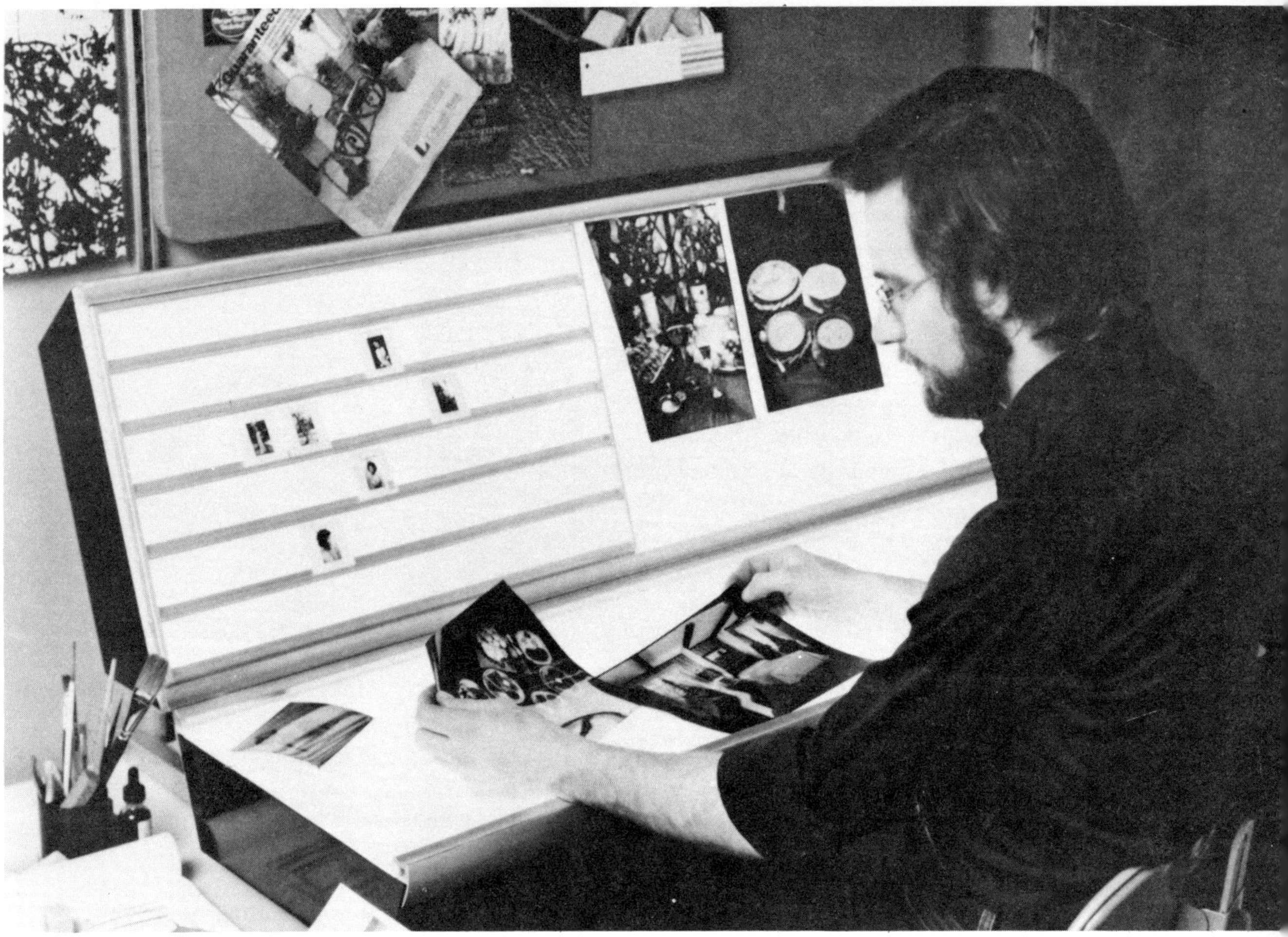

The Acculight modular transparency editing and sorting system. Photo courtesy Knox Manufacturing.

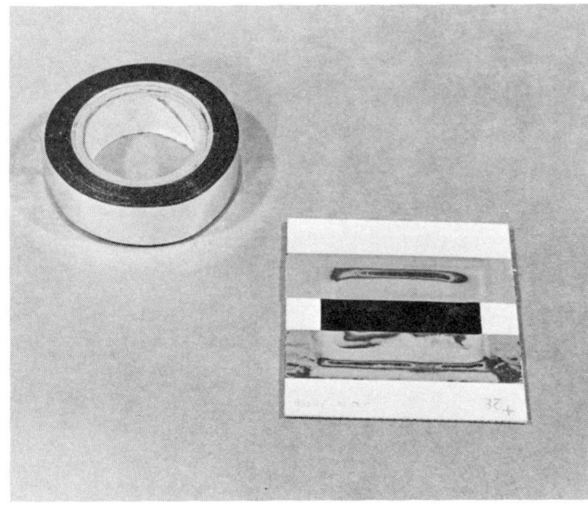

Slide-binding tape can be used to crop the perimeter of mounted slides.

cotton gloves should be worn and the slide handled only on the edges. Tweezers can also be used for handling unmounted slides.

Many cardboard mounts are held together with an adhesive that softens under heat. The slide is aligned in the mount. The two sides are then brought together, and the slide is placed beneath a warm iron until the two sides adhere.

Other cardboard mounts have slots and grooves for holding the slide in place. You should always make sure the slide film lies flat, without any waves or ridges, which can affect the projected image.

Glass slide mounts have to be bound together with tape, as do some of the plastic mounts. Taping mounts together can be a time-consuming process, but the tape does add dust protection to the slides. Other alternatives are pressure-sensi-

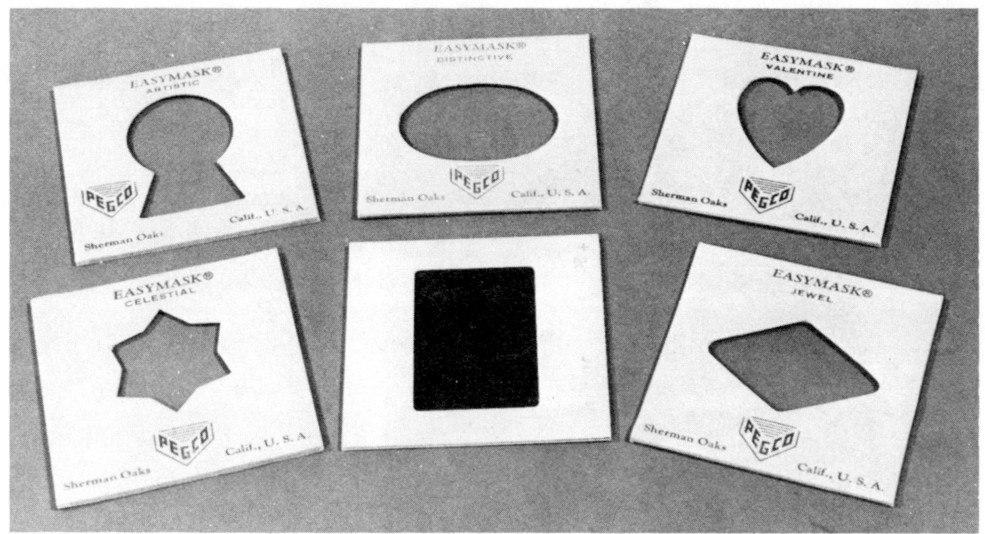

Various shapes and sizes of mounts can be used to crop or add interest to slides.

tive and snap-together slide mounts of plastic and cardboard.

If you plan on mounting a great number of slides, you should do it with consistency. If there is any type of writing on the slide mount, use it as a guide. For example, all slides mounted by the Eastman Kodak Company have the emulsion side of the film facing the Kodak name. The emulsion side of the film is dull as compared to the opposite, shiny, antihalation backing.

Mount your slides all the same way, and if necessary, put a small mark on the upper right-hand corner of the mount so you know which way is the top of the slide and which is the front. Then you'll be able to tell the slide's position by looking at the mount and not by having to hold the slide to the light. This will make projector loading simpler.

Slides that are mounted variously not only make cropping possible but can enhance a slide presentation by reducing the routine of strictly vertical and horizontal images. Subtle changes in slide mounting are far less noticeable by the viewer than sudden unusual shapes such as hearts, stars, and keyholes.

Before one gets carried away by unusual slide mounts, consider that anything overdone can become monotonous and give the impression of photographer infatuation or even gimmickry. Slides of good composition, exposure, and subject, in standard mounts, will be impressive without having to rely on methods out of the ordinary.

By this time, you should be ready to prepare your slide show, but before we discuss slide presentations, we need to look at types of projection equipment and screens. Each has its own, unique characteristics. Whether they are beneficial to your needs or wants can only be decided by you.

If you already own a projector and screen, you may want to consider the options that are discussed. Whatever the case, you can't have a slide show without the proper equipment, just as you can't have slides without the camera and film.

SLIDE PROJECTORS

Quality slide projectors can be as expensive as good cameras. There are a number of options available, which may or may not be needed.

Basically, a slide projector has a light source, a slide holder, and a lens that can magnify the image on a flat surface. Originally, most projectors required individual hand-fed slide loading. The process was slow and reduced the chances of a well-timed slide presentation. Needless to say, "things have changed."

What you as an individual are looking for in a projector may not be the same as your picture-taking neighbor or even a relative. Your best way to discover what exactly is available is to visit a photo dealer and see what he has to offer.

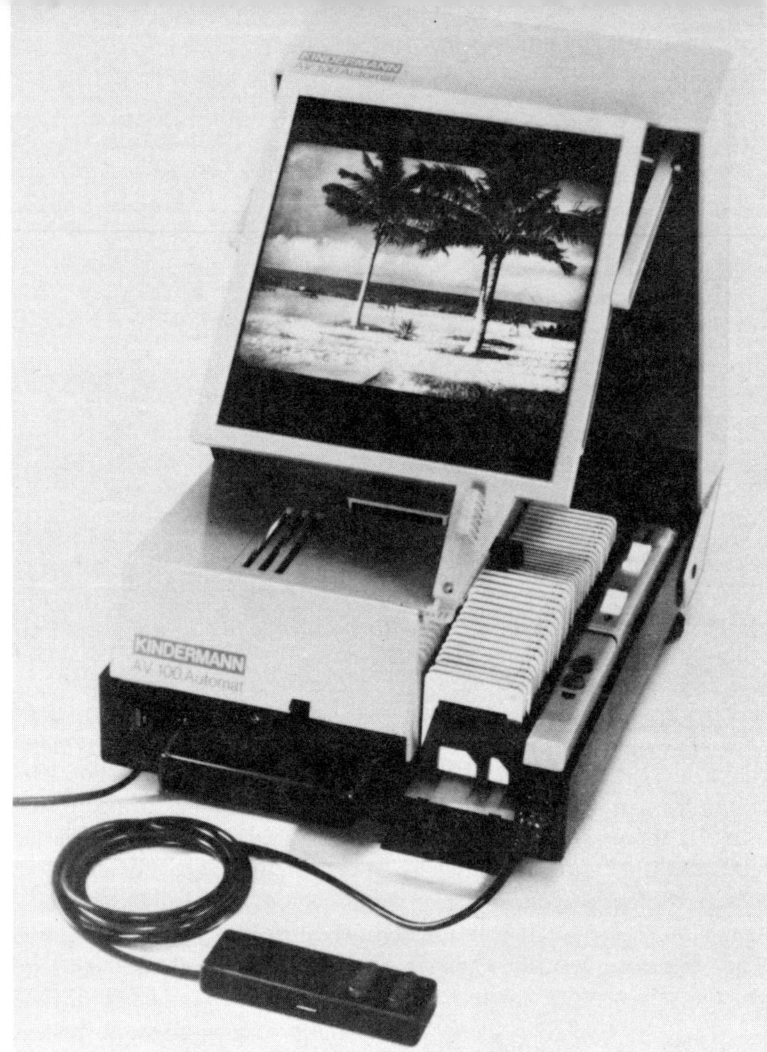

A Kindermann slide projector that has its own built-in screen besides the capability of projecting on a large screen. Photo courtesy Ehrenreich Photo-Optical Industries.

A popular Kodak Carousel projector. Photo courtesy the Eastman Kodak Company.

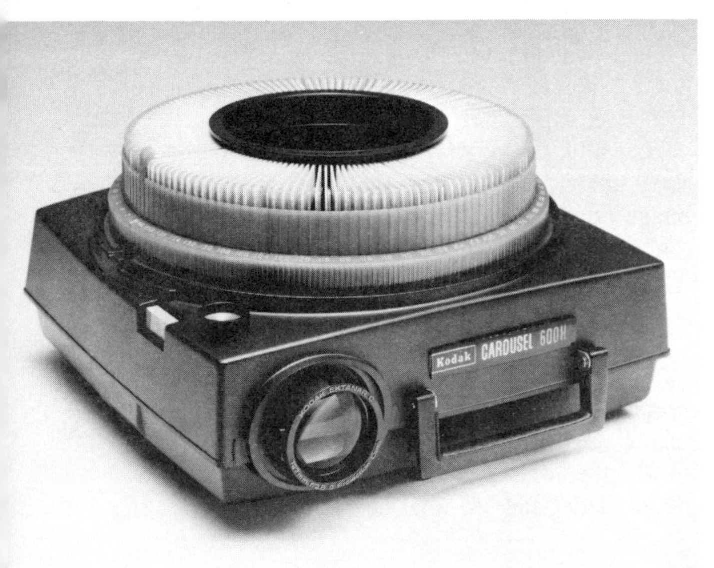

An inexpensive projector for limited viewing.

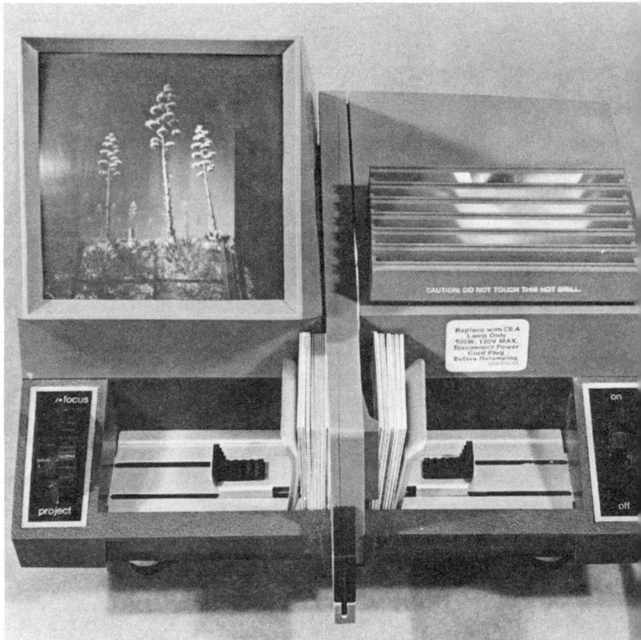

SLIDE-HOLDING MECHANISMS

Usually, the first thing considered by those interested in purchasing a slide projector is the slide-holding and changing mechanism, even though it's not the most important aspect of a good projector.

The push-pull mechanisms are still available, but most people are turning to Slide Cubes and straight or circular trays. Stack loaders, which can be quickly loaded and unloaded, are also popular.

The benefits of trays and cubes are the one-time loading and slide-storage capabilities. When the slides are to be shown, the tray or cube is attached to the projector, and with a push of a button, you're off and running. Each slide is fed into the projector, shown, and removed, and the next slide is projected. Both forward and reverse movement is possible.

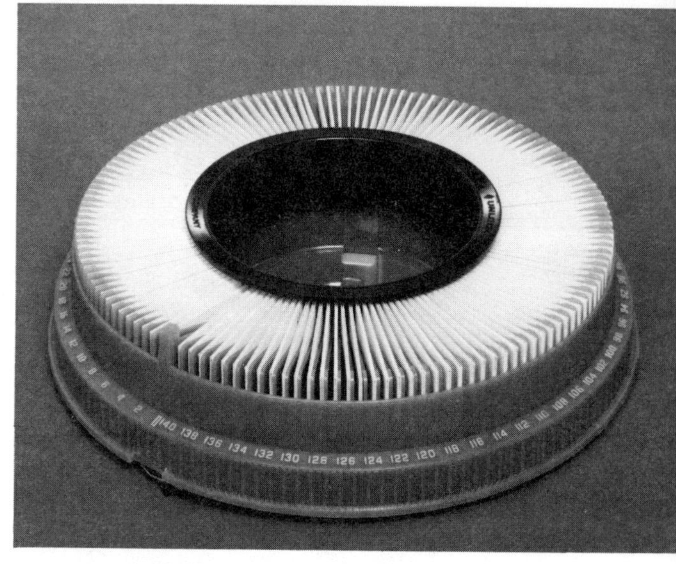

A circular slide tray. Photo courtesy the Eastman Kodak Company.

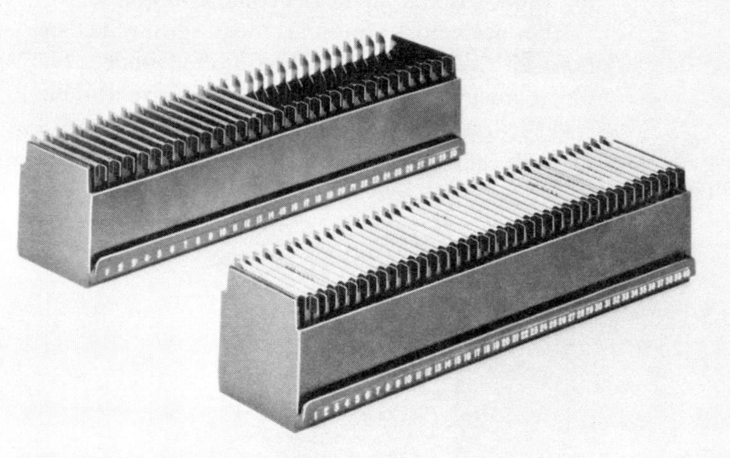

Straight trays used on some projectors. Photo courtesy the Eastman Kodak Company.

The number of slides a tray or cube holds varies. A circular slide tray can hold up to 140 two-by-two-inch mounts. Eighty-capacity trays are also available. Straight trays may hold forty slides.

The plastic cubes also hold forty slides. The Slide Cube system doesn't hold as many images, but according to Bell & Howell Manufacturing, 640 slides can be stored in the same space occupied by a 140-capacity circular slide tray.

The stack loader, which fits some of the tray-using projectors, holds up to forty slides. It can be used only for forward projection, but it is useful for editing and organizing slides, due to easy loading and unloading.

THE PROJECTION LENS

Once the slide-holding mechanism is decided upon, the quality and type of projection lens should be considered. If your slides are sharp and clear, you want them to retain that clarity during projection.

Lenses vary in length and in the size of the image they project at a given distance from the screen. There are two types of lenses: the curved-field and the flat-field.

The curved-field lens is supposed to compensate for any bowing of the slide during projection. When slides are projected and focused, you'll find that the center of the image may be

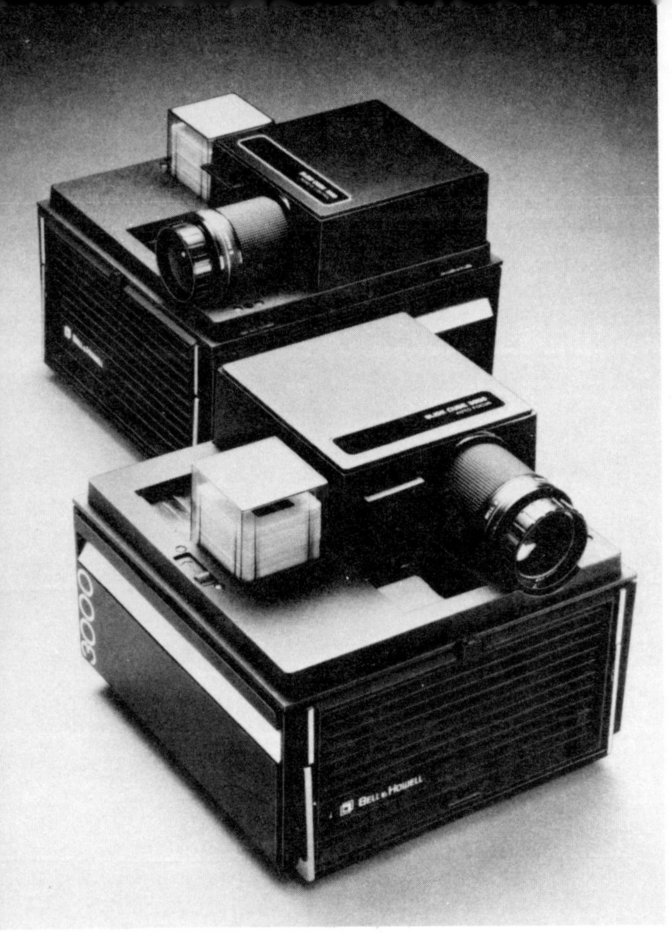

The Bell & Howell Slide Cube projectors. Photo courtesy the Bell & Howell/Mamiya Company.

very sharp while the edges are slightly out of focus. If you then focus for the edges, you'll find the edges very sharp and the center of the image slightly out of focus. Preferably, you want the total projected image sharp from edge to edge.

Have your photo supply dealer project one of your own personal slides using both a flat- and a curved-field lens. Then you decide which is the sharper.

Zoom lenses are also available for most slide projectors. The advantage to a zoom lens is the capability of varying the projected image size on the screen without having to relocate the projector.

AUTO OR REMOTE FOCUSING

The lens-focusing mechanism should be considered carefully. The most advantageous for uninterrupted slide presentations is automatic focus. Once the first slide is focused, the following slides will automatically come into focus.

The projector's internal focusing mechanism does all the work for each projected image. On rare occasions, the mechanism will have trouble focusing on a particular slide due to the nature of the subject. Photographs of mirrors and reflec-

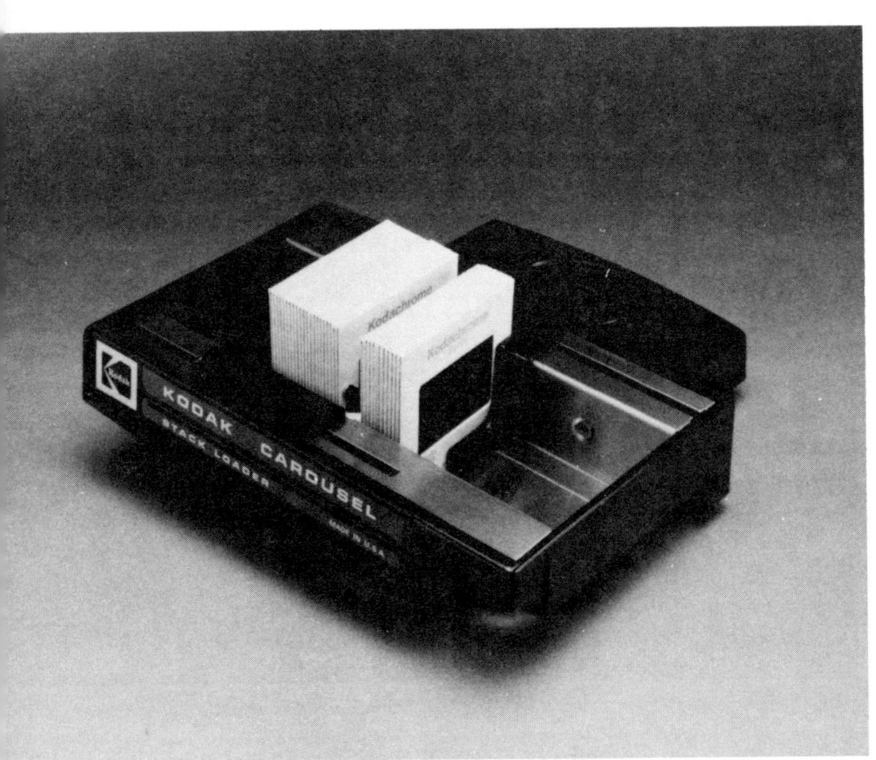

The easy-to-use Stack Loader. Photo courtesy the Eastman Kodak Company.

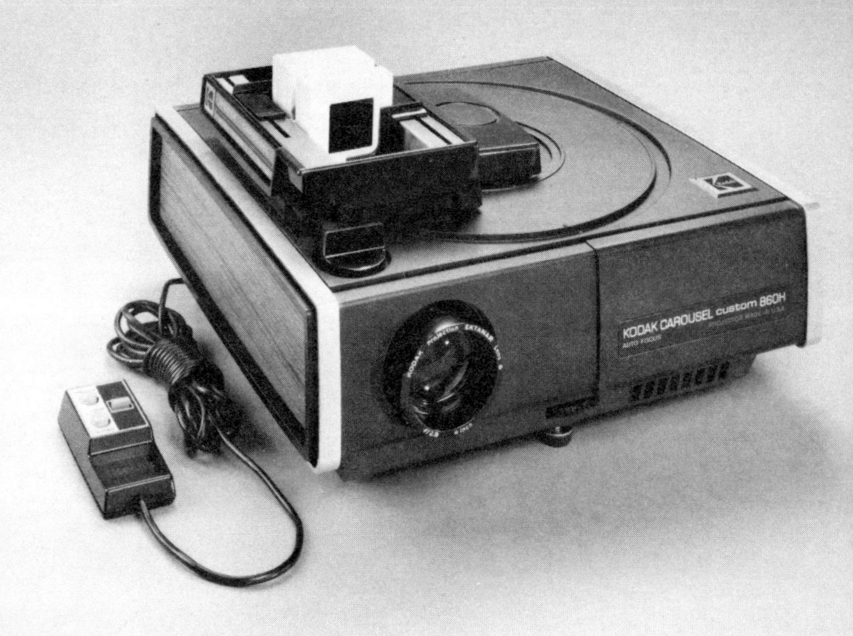

A Kodak projector with remote focus and forward-and-reverse control. Photo courtesy the Eastman Kodak Company.

tions can confuse the auto focusing, and you may have to readjust the focus manually.

Another type of focusing is through a remote-control unit held in your hand. By pushing a button, you control the focus without having to stand over the projector. Forward and reverse buttons are also on the remote control.

LIGHT SOURCE

When purchasing a projector, you may want to consider the slide illumination. Does it offer a high-and-low setting? The benefits of a high-and-low setting are improved projection for both underexposed and overexposed slides.

The majority of your slides will be presented at the low setting and switched to high when you wish to bring out the detail in slightly underexposed slides, which are darker than those of normal exposure.

PROJECTOR NOISE

There's nothing more distracting during a slide presentation than the noise of a poorly constructed projector. (The only thing worse is the snoring of someone in the audience.)

Projection noise can come from the fan or its motor. The actual slide changing can also be bothersome if the mechanism is of inadequate design.

Never purchase a projector until you've checked out its noise level during operation. Distractions of any sort can ruin a well-planned slide presentation.

PROJECTOR OPTIONS

There are several options available for projectors, which may be included on the more expensive models. Some projectors offer automatic timing, which changes the slide at preset intervals, usually in seconds. Preview windows that show the slide before it is projected are also available. This gives the projectionist a chance to see the next slide and organize his thoughts for narration.

There may be special accessory plugs for sound synchronization, or the projector may have its own built-in sound transmitting system. (Sound synchronization will be discussed in more detail later in this chapter.)

Carrying and storage cases are made for all types of projectors, Slide Cubes, and trays.

PROJECTION SCREENS

If you plan on showing slides to an audience, you'll need an appropriate projection screen. Bare walls will work, but the imperfections in the plaster and possibly the color of the wall will distract attention from the projected image.

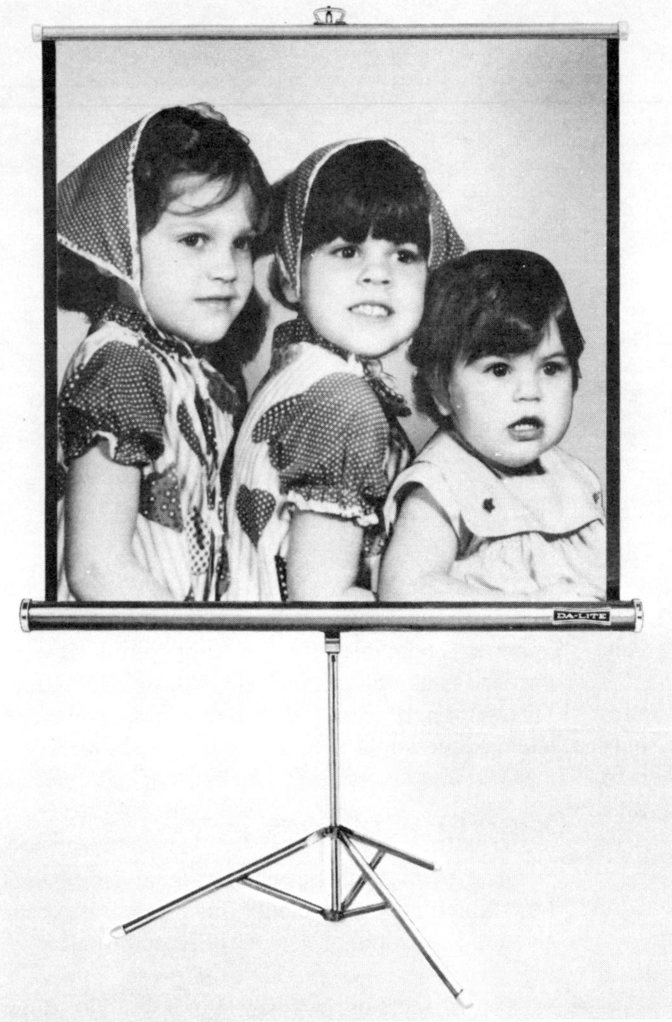

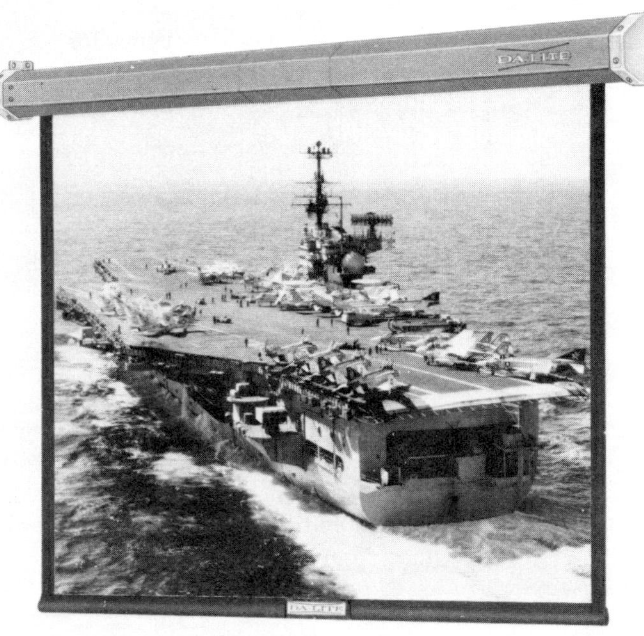

A free-standing tripod screen and a wall-or-ceiling-mounted projection screen. Photos courtesy Da-Lite Screen Company.

Very few homes have totally bare walls. Usually there are pictures of some sort covering a portion of the wall. When the pictures are removed for a slide presentation, the nails or nail holes are still there. Then, sometime during the slide show, the nail or hole will show up on the end of someone's nose or, even more distracting, penetrate an eye.

To avoid the problem, a screen is needed. Projection screens vary not only in size but in the covering as well. Some are portable, having their own tripod stand; others are mounted directly on the wall.

The first thing to consider before purchasing a screen is the size needed. It shouldn't be so small that the projected image fills the whole screen, nor should it be so large that only half the screen is filled.

Consider where the screen is to be used the majority of the time. Set up the projector and show a slide on a hanging sheet or wall. Then measure the dimensions. Be sure to project both a vertical and a horizontal slide.

Another consideration is your potential audience. They shouldn't have to sit three feet from the screen, nor should they have to sit a half mile away. Make your audience as comfortable as possible, to make it easier for them to concentrate on the presentation. If your slide presentations are dull, which they shouldn't be after reading this chapter, you might as well make it easy for the viewers to catch a nap.

Finally, the covering of the screen should be evaluated. Your local photo dealer can help you decide what type of projection screen you need. You should have an idea of what is available and know your own screen requirements before making a purchase.

There are three basic screen surfaces to choose from. Each has its advantages and disadvantages.

MATTE-WHITE

This type of screen surface offers a plain white covering that is perfectly flat. The simple construction produces the sharpest picture, capable of being viewed from fairly diverse angles. The matte-white projection screen can be cleaned with a damp cloth to remove dirt and dust that might have accumulated.

Matte-white screens are not the brightest. Light is absorbed as well as reflected. For optimum viewing, a very dark projection room is needed.

GLASS-BEADED

The screen's surface is covered with thousands of very small, optical-quality glass beads that reflect the majority of light striking them. The screen offers the viewer a bright image but narrows the audience's angle of view. A relatively dark room is needed for best projection and viewing.

Depending on the use and quality of a glass-beaded screen, there will be a certain amount of bead loss as they fall from the surface. Cleaning should be restricted to a light dusting with a soft brush and only when absolutely needed.

LENTICULAR

The screen's surface possesses a definite pattern of ribs or rectangles that reflect the light. Depending on the manufacturer, the screen may reflect the projector's light over a wide area, or the light can be reduced to a narrow beam, at the same time increasing the intensity of the reflected light. The type of lenticular construction should be considered carefully to match the viewing room most often used.

A lenticular screen should not be used if your audience has to sit so close that the screen's pattern is noticed through the projected image. To make the best use of the screen's design, projection should be perpendicular to the lenticular surface. The projection room should be dark, but it does not have to be as dark as a room needed for a matte-white or a glass-beaded screen.

MISCELLANEOUS

There are two other types of screen available. Their use is limited, and for most photographers, especially the amateur, their application makes them somewhat impractical.

One is the high-gain, which can produce as much as six times the brightness of a lenticular screen. The specially treated aluminum surface is bulky and made for permanent installation. The size is for small audiences, and specific construction helps reflect ambient or unwanted light away from the viewing area and, at the same time, concentrates the projected image. The screens are costly and are used when a dark room is unavailable.

Another type of screen is for rear projection. The image is shown through a translucent screen viewed from the front but projected from the

Projection Distance Tables (Courtesy Eastman Kodak Company)

for KODAK CAROUSEL and Pocket CAROUSEL Slide Projectors

Projection Distances Are Approximate and Are Measured (in Feet) from Slide to Screen

Nominal Aperture Dimensions* of 2 x 2-inch Slide Mounts (Shown Full Size)	Screen-Image Width	Lens Focal Length (in inches)				
		3	4 (102 mm)	5 (127 mm)	7	4 to 6 Zoom (102 mm to 152 mm)
		Projection Distances (in feet)				
22.9 mm; 34.2 mm	20 in.	4	5½	7	10	5½ to 8½
	30 in.	6	8	10	14	8 to 12
	40 in.	8	10½	13	18½	10½ to 16
	50 in.	10	13	16½	23	13 to 19½
	5 ft.	11½	15½	19½	27	15½ to 23½
	6 ft.	14	18½	23	32½	18½ to 28
	8 ft.	18½	24½	30½	43	24½ to 36½
	10 ft.	23	30½	38	53	30½ to 45½
	12 ft.	27	36½	45½	63½	36½ to 54½
135—35 mm						
26.5 mm; 26.5 mm	20 in.	5½	7	9	12½	7 to 10½
	30 in.	7½	10½	13	18	10½ to 15½
	40 in.	10	13½	17	23½	13½ to 20
	50 in.	12½	16½	21	29	16½ to 25
	5 ft.	15	20	25	34½	20 to 30
	6 ft.	18	23½	29½	41½	23½ to 35½
	8 ft.	23½	31½	39	55	31½ to 47
	10 ft.	29½	39	49	68½	39 to 58½
	12 ft.	35	46½	58½	81½	46½ to 70
126						
15.9 mm; 22.9 mm	20 in.	6	8	10	14	8 to 12
	30 in.	9	12	14½	20½	12 to 17½
	40 in.	11½	15½	19½	27	15½ to 23
	50 in.	14½	19	24	33½	19 to 28½
	5 ft.	17	23	28½	40	23 to 34½
	6 ft.	20½	27½	34	47½	27½ to 41
	8 ft.	27	36	45	63½	36 to 54
	10 ft.	34	45	56½	79	45 to 67½
	12 ft.	40½	54	67½	94½	54 to 81
135—Half Frame						

NOTE: Kodak supplies a 2½-inch EKTANAR Projection Lens (not shown). It is designed especially for use in study carrels and in small rear-projection cabinets. With a standard 35-mm slide, the lens produces an 8-inch-wide image in a 26-inch distance (back of projector to the front of the screen). Image sizes over 12 inches wide are *not* recommended.

*Dimension tolerances may vary with mounts of different sizes and manufacture.

(Courtesy Eastman Kodak Company)

Nominal Aperture Dimensions* of 2 x 2-inch Slide Mounts (Shown Full Size)	Screen-Image Width	Lens Focal Length (in inches)								
		1.4	2	3	4 (102 mm)	5 (127 mm)	7	9	11	4 to 6 Zoom (102 mm to 152 mm)
		Projection Distance (in feet)								
127—Super-Slide (38 x 38 mm) 828—(26.2 x 38 mm)	20 in.	2	2½	4	5	6½	9	11½	14	5 to 7½
	30 in.	2½	3½	5½	7½	9	13	16½	20½	7½ to 11
	40 in.	3½	5	7	9½	12	17	21½	26½	9½ to 14½
	50 in.	4	6	9	12	15	20½	26½	32½	12 to 17½
	5 ft.	5	7	10½	14	17½	24½	31½	38½	14 to 21
	6 ft.	6	8½	12½	16½	21	29½	37½	46	16½ to 25
	8 ft.	7½	11	16½	22	27½	38½	49½	60½	22 to 33
	10 ft.	9½	13½	20½	27½	34½	48	61½	75½	27½ to 41
	12 ft.	11½	16½	24½	33	41	57½	73½	90	33 to 49
KODACHROME Duplicate or KODACOLOR Slide from 1⅝ x 1⅝-inch or 2¼ x 2¼-inch slide or negative, respectively	20 in.	2	3	4½	6	8	11	14	17	6 to 9½
	30 in.	3	4½	6½	9	11	15½	20	24½	9 to 13½
	40 in.	4	6	9	11½	14½	20½	26½	32	11½ to 17½
	50 in.	5	7	11	14½	18	25½	32½	40	14½ to 21½
	5 ft.	6	8½	13	17	21½	30	38½	47½	17 to 26
	6 ft.	7	10½	15½	20½	25½	36	46	56½	20½ to 31
	8 ft.	9½	13½	20½	27	34	47½	61	74½	27 to 40½
	10 ft.	12	17	25½	34	42	59	76	93	34 to 50½
	12 ft.	14	20	30½	40½	50½	70½	91	111	40½ to 60½

Nominal Aperture Dimensions* of 30 x 30-mm Slide Mounts (Shown Full Size)	Screen-Image Width	Lens Focal Length (in inches)		
		2½	2 to 3 (Zoom)	4†
		Projection Distances (in feet)		
110	20 in.	7	5½ to 8½	11½
	30 in.	10½	8½ to 12½	17
	40 in.	14	11 to 16½	22
	50 in.	17	13½ to 20½	27½
	60 in.	20½	16½ to 24½	33
	70 in.	24	19 to 28½	38

* Dimension tolerances may vary with mounts of different sizes and manufacture.

†In a KODAK CAROUSEL Projector with 110 slides in KODAK 2x2 Adapters for 110 slides or 2x2-in. mounts. Dimensions for 3-in., 5-in., 7-in., and 4- to 6-in. zoom lenses vary proportionately. For best results, however, we recommend projecting 110 slides in 110 slide projectors.

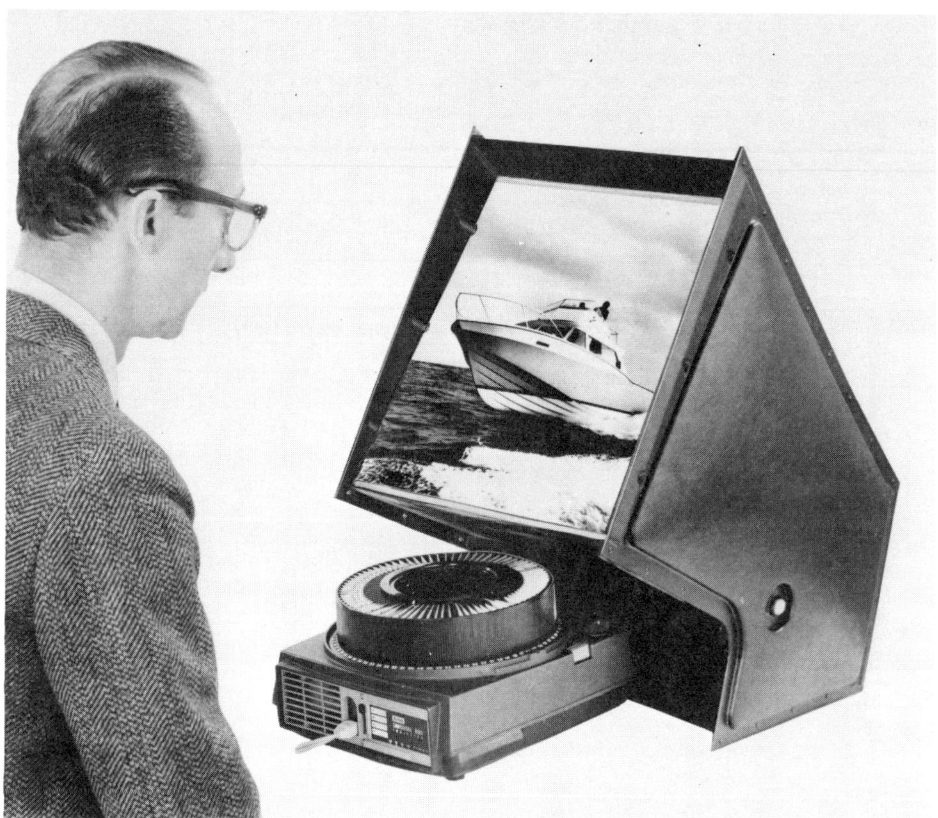

Small and portable screens with rear projection for limited viewing. Photos courtesy Hudson Photographic Industries.

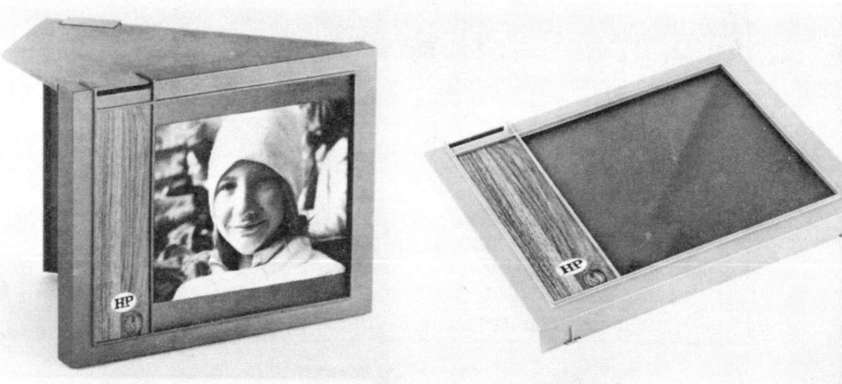

rear. The screen is small and is generally used for elaborate multimedia slide presentations at conventions, product shows, and sales meetings.

The projection screen is one of the most important pieces of equipment, in addition to the projector and slides, in presenting a good show. Give careful consideration to what you need in a projection screen before you make your investment. Be sure to consider the following:

1. Screen size. The projection lens, the distance between the screen and the projector, and the projector's light intensity are all factors that can influence your choice of screen.

2. Portable or permanent. Projection screens are available in portable units with their own tripod, or as permanent well-mounted units. A portable unit should be easy to set up, and when it's up, make sure the screen's surface is wrinkle-free. Wall units are for those that have a den or viewing room specifically designed for photographic display.

3. Screen surface. Matte-white, glass-beaded, or lenticular surface should match the viewing room. Can the room be darkened sufficiently? Where will the audience be sitting? How large is the audience? These are some of the questions you need to ask yourself before you decide on the screen surface you need.
4. Cost. Undoubtedly you will purchase what you feel you can afford. As with all photographic equipment, consider your purchase as an investment that can be enjoyed today, tomorrow, and the years ahead.

DO YOU NEED A PROJECTION TABLE?

A projector and a screen are the basic equipment you need for a successful slide presentation. Usually, at the last minute before the show is to begin, one starts reaching for the nearest table on which to place the projector. Generally, any available table will be too low, and books will be used to raise the projector to the right height.

To make projection easier, you may want to invest in a small projection table. There are many to choose from, and some are quite portable, with folding and/or removable legs.

Projection tables are designed for slide showing. They are taller than an ordinary card table or whatever you might have on hand. The height makes it possible to project on a screen without having to raise the front of the projector with books, ashtrays, or whatever. This reduces the amount of distortion to the projected image. If the projector has to be aimed upward, the image on the screen will be wider at the top than at the bottom. It's better to raise the whole projector than just its front, to control projection distortion.

A projection table is an extra expense that adds expertise to your projection know-how.

PREPARING THE SLIDE SHOW

Since you are reading these words, you must have some interest in slides and their showing. The reason might be strictly economical, since slides are less expensive to produce than color prints. However, there are other reasons you might show slides. First, there is home entertainment, which might include showing family portraits and activities. You may wish to show slides to a church group, club, or other organization. At one time or another, you may be called upon to give a lecture and slide presentation dealing with material you are considered to be an authority on.

Now, before you decide not to prepare slide shows, you might want to remember that showing slides while narrating in the dark is a lot easier than having to stand up in front of an audience with nothing to do but talk. If you feel a little uneasy about public speaking, make it less painful by including a slide presentation.

Mobile tables that can be used for slide projectors. Photo courtesy Bretford Manufacturing.

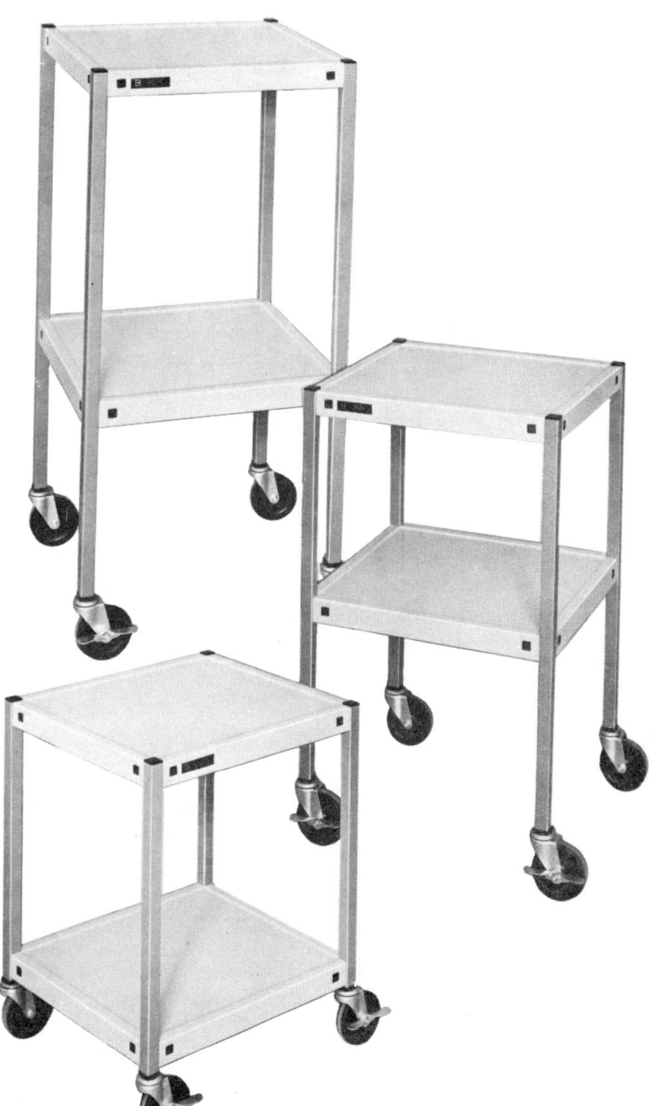

You know what type of equipment is needed for the basic slide presentation. Now you need to decide if you have the right type of slides for an interesting show.

GOOD SLIDE-SHOW MATERIAL

You probably have a large collection of family-related pictures. Save those for showing to family members only! No one likes to spend time looking at someone else's family. Frankly, it's boring.

Travel photography, on the other hand, has always been popular slide-show material. There are a great number of people who do "arm-chair traveling." They sit at home and read *National Geographic, Arizona Highways, Holiday,* and other publications that offer stories and pictures of exotic places. To many, it's as much fun as being there, and a lot less expensive.

If you and your family have visited an interesting place and have taken good photographs, you can share the sights with friends and church or club members.

Educational materials such as birds, animals, insects, and even sporting events, can be organized to produce an interesting presentation.

A collection of unrelated pictures might prove interesting if they are of excellent quality and offer the viewers something unusual. Photo essays of related, but unusual, material can also be organized to make a slide show. Unusual views of shadows, rocks, rivers, etc., are just a few ideas.

The topics that can be chosen for slide shows are unlimited. It all depends on where you've been, what you've done, and how well you've captured the events, places, and things on film. If you feel you have enough slides on a particular topic to produce a show, the next step is one of the most significant: slide organization.

SLIDE-SHOW ORGANIZATION

As mentioned early in this chapter and in the first chapter of this book, you need to edit and crop your slides. I can't elaborate too much on editing. Few people do it correctly.

I learned my lesson early in life, when an editor of a prestigious magazine asked me why I hadn't edited my submissions for publication. I sincerely thought I had. I've learned from my mistake and edit photographs quite carefully.

Just because you have five excellent pictures of a particular subject doesn't mean you need to show them all. Once in a while, two pictures may be better than one. But most of the time, one good picture of a subject is enough. Pick out the very best image of any particular subject and include that one in the slide show you are preparing. The other images can be filed or discarded.

Once your slides are edited correctly, you'll have to place them in some sort of order for projection. But before you do that, count your slides. If you have more than one trayful, it's probably too many.

It's not easy to keep the attention of an audience for much longer than fifteen to twenty minutes. People get fidgety, thirsty, and anxious to use the bathroom. Try to please your audience by being a gracious host and use only as much time as is truly needed to make an interesting and entertaining show. Such audience remarks as "Short but sweet" and "It wasn't long enough" are far better than yawns, closed eyes, and looks of boredom on the viewers' faces.

Not too surprisingly, slides are put in order so the images appear in the same sequence as they happened. Slide shows are organized this way because it's the quickest way to do it, not necessarily the best.

Try putting yourself in the audience as you organize. Imagine what you will remember after the slide show is over. What you'll remember is the last slide, just before the lights go on. Since that is the slide best remembered, it should be your most outstanding—a slide worth remembering.

The first slide should be of superior quality also. It should be an image with visual impact to wake up your audience. Visually speaking, the very first slide should have "Hey, watch me!" written all over it.

In between the first and last slides are a mixture of very good and good slides that make the presentation informative, educational, and, by all means, entertaining.

Try not to project all horizontal or vertical slides. There needs to be a little geometric variety. Show a series of horizontals, and then show a series of verticals.

Hopefully, you've organized your slides into some sort of presentable order. You will soon know. It is time for a test run.

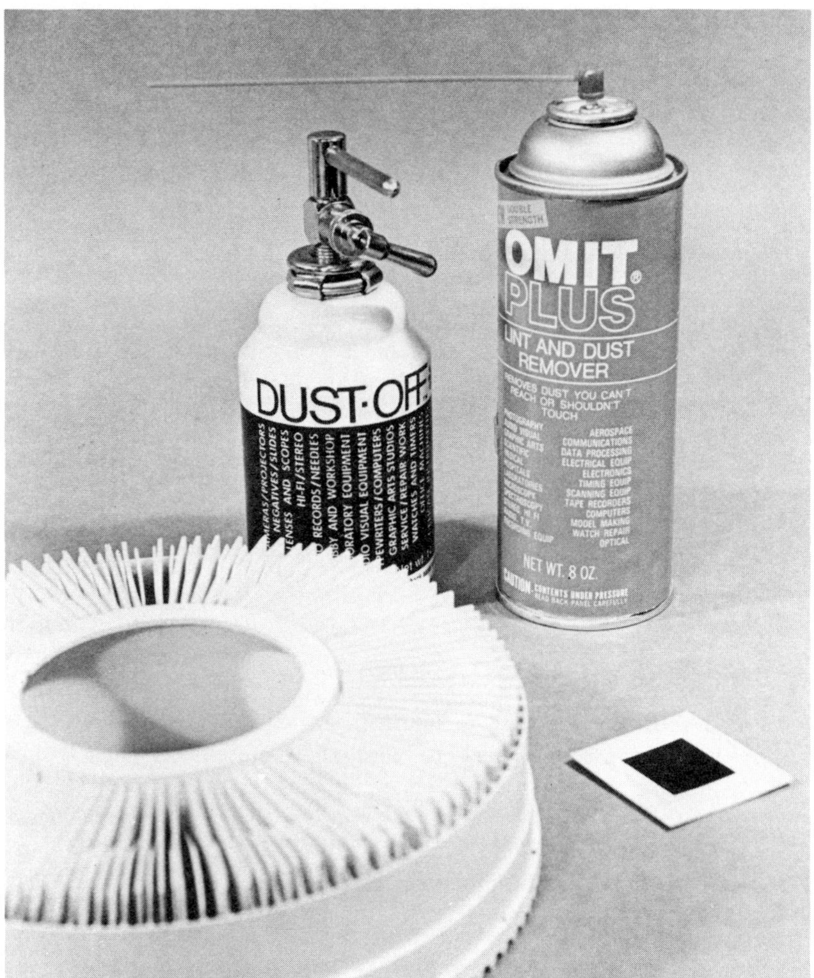

Canned compressed air will efficiently remove dust from slides before you place them in a slide-carrying mechanism.

THE TEST RUN

Once the slides are placed in the necessary tray or cube, run them through your projector to see how your organization looks. If further editing or organization is needed, do it. Run another test, but, this time, watch for dirty slides and possible fingerprints, along with organization.

By now, you should have the slides in the desired place. You may want to lift each slide from the carrying device and clean it with a soft brush to remove dust. Cans of compressed air make dust removal even easier. They can be purchased from your local photo supply dealer.

The slides are clean and loaded, but you're not done yet. You're now ready to see how long your presentation will be. The pacing of the slides can be as important as the organization. If you have an automatic projector to which a timer can be set, each image will be projected for three, four, five, or however many seconds you designate. The automation is convenient, but the consistent pace of the slides can be far from stimulating.

Some slides deserve to be viewed longer than others. Their content can't be fully appreciated in just a few seconds. Other images can be flashed on the screen, because there are fewer elements in the composition and less to be studied with the eyes. It's important to experiment with pacing your slides to increase their visual effectiveness.

SIGHT AND SOUND

To give your slide presentation a touch of professionalism, you might wish to add sound. It can be as simple as an appropriate record playing in the background or just your own brief but informative narration. Or you might want to add both narration and music on a prerecorded tape.

TAPE RECORDERS

All types of tape recorders are available. The type of equipment—reel-to-reel, eight-track, or cassette—is not important. The quality of the sound reproduction is. When recording the narration, it should be done at a time and place where outside noises such as airplanes, trains, and cars are not picked up in the background. Your audience might wonder what is going on as they look at a landscape on the screen and the narration discusses desolation and loneliness while freeway noises hum in the background.

Late at night or early in the morning is a good time to record your sound track. Try recording after your neighbors go to bed and before they get up.

SOUND SYNCHRONIZATION

If you have the right equipment, you can synchronize the sound track to your slide presentation and have automatic slide-changing at the same time.

With complete sound synchronization, all you have to do is start the projector. Once the show is in progress, you can sit back and listen for the audience's reaction to your work.

The synchronizing unit records narration and music on one channel of a stereo tape, and a special slide-changing signal is recorded on the other. During projection, the slide-changing signal is inaudible.

DUAL PROJECTION

The ultimate in slide presenting is with the use of two projectors and a dissolve unit. This setup enables various fade rates from one picture to the next without the blackness between slides that comes from single-projector use. A dissolve unit is an expensive piece of equipment but well worth the investment if you plan on producing a great number of slide presentations. Two projectors are needed, which also adds to your production costs.

Loading slide trays can be a little tricky, because you have to alternate the slides between projectors. After a little practice, it becomes as easy as loading a single tray.

If sound synchronization is added, you can produce a show that spells professionalism. But

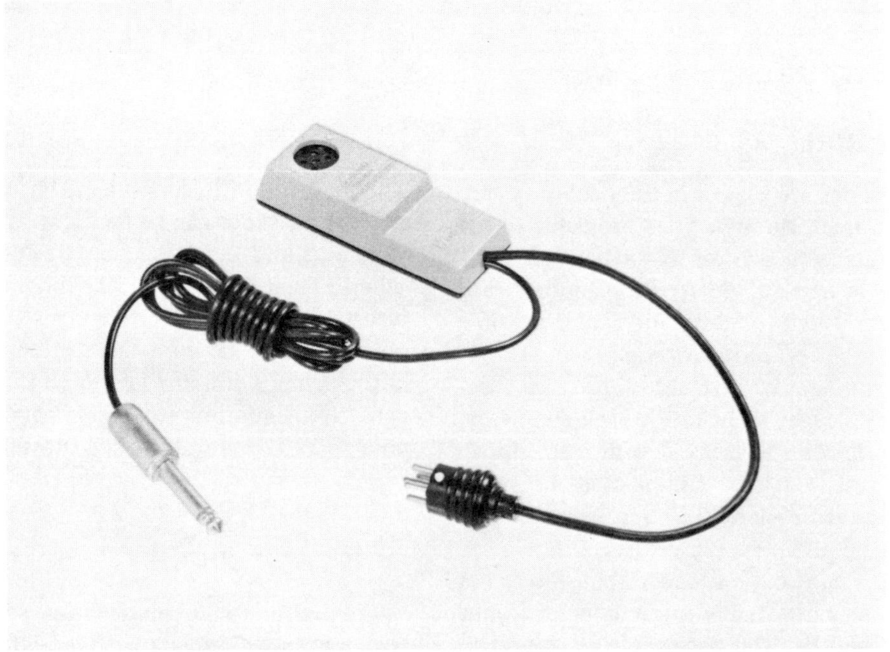

Kodak Sound Synchronizer enables preparation of automated and synchronized slide presentations. Photo courtesy the Eastman Kodak Company.

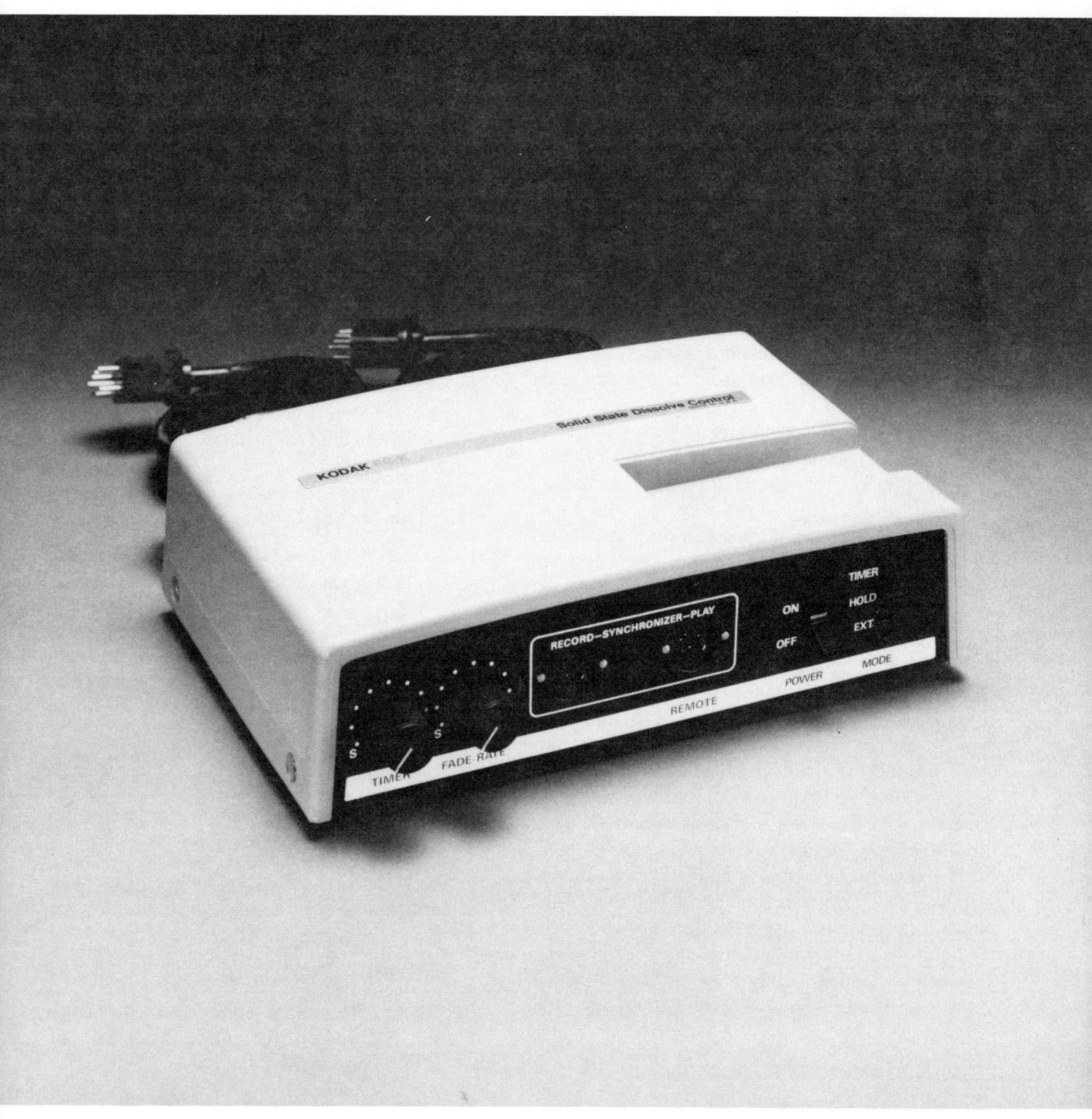

Dissolve Control for use with two projectors. Photo courtesy the Eastman Kodak Company.

don't get caught up in the equipment trap. No matter how elaborate your projection and sound system, if your pictures are not the very best you can produce, they will still be bad and you will have trouble holding an audience's attention.

OPENING AND CLOSING

One last thing you can do to enhance your slide presentation is to add title and closing slides. Transfer type, stencils, or just plain printing with marking pens can be used. Then all you have to do is take a picture of the title you've made. The same can be done for "The End" or "Finis."

End your slide shows with a blank, opaque slide. Again, this is professional courtesy to your audience. The bright light from a projector can be quite a shock to the viewer's eyes after sitting in a dark room for several minutes.

At times, your audience may not realize the presentation is over. Either they are hoping for more, or your ending wasn't what it could have been. If this happens, all you can do is tell them it's over. If possible, turn on just one light to give your eyes and your audience's eyes a chance to adjust. Gradually turn on more light until the desired intensity is reached.

Good slide shows do not happen overnight. They take time to be planned, photographed, and organized. Practice is the only way to improve your slide presentations. Your audience can tell you whether you are producing good or bad slides. Don't be afraid of criticism. No one likes to be told he is not doing his very best work. But that's how we learn.

If you truly enjoy photography, there is no better way to combine learning and fun than with preparing and presenting a good slide show.

Learn or memorize the basic steps for producing and presenting a slide show and you'll be on your way to an enjoyable life of photography.

BASIC STEPS FOR PRODUCING A SLIDE SHOW

1. Choose a topic that will appeal to everyone in your audience.
2. Edit your slides so there is little, if any, picture repetition. Forty quality slides are better than eighty slides of mixed quality.
3. If necessary, crop your slides with tape or vary the slide mount.
4. Organize the slides in some order for projection. The first slide should be an attention-getter; the last slide should be one worth remembering.
5. Test-run to check organization and length of the slide show: twenty-minute maximum, even when the slides are truly outstanding.
6. Plan your narration, whether written, impromptu, or recorded.
7. Additional sound can be added by mixing music and narration.
8. Begin and end the presentation with an opening and closing slide or opaque blank. Don't shock the audience with the bright light of a projector.

   Optional:

9. Slide titles and closing.
10. Dual projection with dissolve unit and sound synchronization.

STEPS FOR SHOWING YOUR PRESENTATION SUCCESSFULLY

1. Have all the necessary equipment set up ahead of time.
2. Check equipment operation.
3. Have a spare projection bulb in case it is needed.
4. Check the room for unwanted reflections and for proper darkness.
5. Check the seating arrangement to make sure everyone in the audience can see the screen comfortably.
6. Have the slides loaded and by all means correctly inserted in the slide-carrying mechanism, so they are projected right side up.
7. Preset the focus for the first slide.
8. Happy viewing.

GLOSSARY

ADHESIVE MOUNTING any sticky substance used to attach prints to various types of rigid backings.

ALBUM any book form that holds a collection of photographs. Some have bound pages, others are loose-leaf so pages can be added or removed.

ANTIHALATION a light-absorbing substance incorporated into film.

APERTURE opening within the camera lens. Referred to as the f/stop. Varies in size to help control the amount of light striking the film.

ARCHIVAL relates to photographic images processed, displayed, and stored in such a way that they will not deteriorate.

AVAILABLE LIGHT the existing lighting condition. Generally relates to indoor and nighttime picture taking.

AWL small pointed tool useful for marking wood and starting holes for small wood screws. Can be used in picture-frame construction.

BACKSAW used with a miter box for making fine, angled cuts in wood.

BEVEL the slanted edge of a mat or frame molding.

BLEED a mounted photograph without a border; same as a borderless print.

BOUNCE LIGHT indirect lighting; light that has been reflected off a surface such as a ceiling or wall.

BRACKET the act of taking several pictures of the same subject using various exposures, with hopes of getting the best possible negative or slide for picture quality.

CLAMPS come in various sizes and shapes; used to hold picture-framing materials together while glue is drying or nails are being set.

COMPOSITION the specific arrangement of the elements found in a photograph or slide.

COUNTER MOUNT a piece of paper or mounting material attached to the back of an already mounted print.

COUNTERSINKING the act of driving nails below the surface of the frame molding, using a nail set. The nail hole is then hidden with filler material.

CROP the act of trimming or covering the edges of a photo to improve the appearance or composition of the picture. Cropping can also be done, to a limited extent, by a photo-processing lab.

DISSOLVE UNIT a mechanical device used with two slide projectors to control the timing of a slide's projection on a screen.

DRY MOUNTING the attachment of a print to a mat or other backing, using heat, pressure, and a special adhesive.

DRY-MOUNTING PRESS used in dry mounting, the press supplies the heat and pressure to melt the adhesive between the print and mounting material.

DRY-MOUNTING TISSUE a thin, paperlike material that becomes an adhesive when subjected to heat.

DULLING SPRAY substance sprayed on the completed print to reduce the amount of shine or gloss.

EDIT to revise and prepare visual material; also, to eliminate any photographic errors, for example in composition, exposure, focus, etc.

FADE produced by a dissolve unit: one projected slide slowly vanishes while another slide gradually takes its place.

FLEX TAPE used for measuring lengths of both molding and mat materials. Should be capable of locking in place; can be purchased in various lengths.

FOLDER MAT a hinged mat held together with a paper or fabric tape.

GLASS CUTTER small tool used to score glass so that it will break evenly.

GLASSINE special transparent material used for negative storage.

GLOSSY any print that has a shiny surface or finish.

GRAIN the visible grain texture of the film's silver particles. Generally, grain becomes more apparent as the picture's size increases.

GUILLOTINE specifically designed tool for cutting miter edges on frame and carpentry molding. Fast and accurate.

HAND DRILL small tool used for drilling holes in frame construction and for hanging pictures.

HANGERS small loops or rings of steel that attach to frame molding for attaching picture-hanging wires.

KRAFT PAPER a brown paper used for covering the back side of framed pictures to prevent dust and other debris from entering the frame. A finishing touch to framing.

LIGHT BOX a plastic- or glass-covered box filled with lights; used for viewing and sorting slides.

LINER a frame within another frame, usually of cardboard with a fabric cover.

MAT the border area between the picture and the frame; can vary in color and texture, but generally of cardboard or fabric-covered cardboard. Mats help isolate the photograph for visual appeal.

MAT CUTTER can be a knife or a precision tool for cutting the window in a mat. Some can cut a beveled edge facing toward the mounted photograph.

MITER BOX handy tool for accurately cutting the 45-degree angles needed in frame construction.

MOLDING either building or frame. Builder's molding is purchased from lumber supply dealers, the other from frame shops. Both are used in the construction of picture frames.

MOUNTING BOARD a variety of materials used to keep prints flat. Generally of cardboard, but Masonite, sheet aluminum, plywood, and Fome-Cor are used.

NAIL SET a pointed tool used for driving finishing nails beneath the surface of wood. Used in frame construction.

NEGATIVE a photographic image in which the subject tones have been reversed.

OVEREXPOSED designating a photographic image that has received too much light.

PASSE-PARTOUT a simple method of framing: print, protective glass, and mat are held together with tape attached to the edges.

PEBBLE BOARD mat board with a textured finish of small bumps and indentation.

PICTURE-FRAME CLAMP a special clamp designed to hold the mitered ends of frames together while glue is drying and finishing nails are being set.

PICTURE GLASS thin glass used in framing. Some glasses are clear; others are designed to cut down on reflections.

PRINT any positive photo image printed on paper. Generally derived from either a negative or a positive transparency.

PRINT QUALITY the technical aspect of a photographic print. Print quality is unrelated to the actual subject matter.

PROCESSING the producing of prints or the development of film into negatives or slides.

PROJECTOR any machine capable of enlarging an image onto a viewing screen.

RABBET the small groove on the side of a frame that the picture, mount, mat, and glass rest on.

SANDPAPER Various grades of surface from coarse to extra fine are used in smoothing and finishing wood frames.

SELECTIVE FOCUS by varying the size of the aperture one can control the foreground or background so that it is in sharp focus or out of focus. Selective focus is controlled by the photographer using the lens aperture and actual focusing point.

SHARPNESS relates to clarity and crispness of the image found in photographic negatives, prints, and transparencies.

SLEEVE protective envelope of vinyl, polyethylene, or glassine for negatives, transparencies, and prints.

SLIDE transparency, or positive image, usually mounted in glass, plastic, or cardboard for projection on a screen.

SOFT describes any photographic image that is diffused or slightly out of focus, lacking sharpness.

STEEL SQUARE an L-shaped instrument used to determine mat, frame, and corner squareness.

TACK HAMMER a small hammer used in attaching small nails to the back of frames for securing mount, mat, picture, and glass.

TACKING IRON a small electrically heated tool used to attach dry-mounting tissue to the back of prints and prints to mounting boards before placement in a dry-mounting press.

TRACK LIGHTING special light fixtures that are attached to an electrically charged track. The lights can be moved anywhere along the track.

TRANSPARENCY any photographic image viewed by transmitted light. A positive image on film, generally in color. Same as a slide.

UNDEREXPOSED designating a photographic image that has not received enough light for proper exposure.

SLIDE VIEWER small, often battery-operated viewer for looking at individual slides.

WET MOUNTING a method of attaching prints to mounting boards using liquid adhesives, or the mounting of a wet print.

DIRECTORY OF MANUFACTURERS AND DISTRIBUTORS

The following list supplies the names and addresses of manufacturers and distributors who have supplied information and/or photographs of their products for use in this book.

Many of the items mentioned or illustrated should be available from frame, art, photography, and hardware stores. If a product cannot be found locally, write the manufacturer or distributor for information and the name of the dealer nearest you.

Ace Art Company
24 Gould Street
Reading, Massachusetts 01867
MOUNTING CORNERS, LAMINATING SHEETS, PICTURE HANGERS, AND MOUNTING STRIPS

After Image
P. O. Box 315
Schenectady, New York 12301
OFF-THE-WALL PHOTO DISPLAY SYSTEM

American Printing and Envelope Company
900 Broadway
New York, New York 10003
ALL TYPES OF PHOTOGRAPHY-RELATED ENVELOPES, NEGATIVE PRESERVERS, AND RELATED PRINTED MATERIALS

Bedford Creations, Ltd.
375 Executive Boulevard
Elmsford, New York 10523
THE PHOTO BOX, FOR 3½×5-INCH PHOTOS; STORAGE AND SHOW SYSTEM

Bell and Howell/Mamiya Company
7100 McCormick Road
Chicago, Illinois 60645
PHOTOGRAPHY EQUIPMENT AND SLIDE CUBE PROJECTORS

Beseler Photo Marketing Company
8 Fernwood Road
Florham Park, New Jersey 07932

PHOTOGRAPHY PROCESSING EQUIPMENT, ROTATRIM PAPER CUTTER, ROTAMATTE OVAL AND CIRCULAR MAT CUTTER

Bogen Photo Corporation
100 South Van Brunt Street
P. O. Box 448
Englewood, New Jersey 07631
DRY-MOUNTING PRESS AND OTHER PHOTO EQUIPMENT

Bretford Manufacturing Inc.
9715 Soreng Avenue
Schiller Park, Illinois 60176
STORAGE CABINETS AND PROJECTION TABLES

The Brewster Corporation
48 River Street
Old Saybrook, Connecticut 06475
PORTABLE PANELS FOR EXHIBITING PHOTOGRAPHY

Brookstone Company
Vose Farm Road
Peterborough, New Hampshire 03458
MAIL ORDER; FINE TOOLS CATALOG. SPECIAL SECTION ON FRAMING TOOLS

Callen Photo Mount Corporation
P. O. Box 5085
Jersey City, New Jersey 07305
PHOTOGRAPHY MATS, CUTOUTS, ETC.

Coda Inc.
196 Greenwood Avenue
Midland Park, New Jersey 07432
COLD MOUNT, GALERIE PHOTO EXHIBIT, ETC.

Da-Lite Screen Company
State Road 15 North
Warsaw, Indiana 46580
ALL TYPES OF SLIDE PROJECTION SCREENS

Dax Manufacturers, Inc.
955 Midland Avenue
Yonkers, New York 10704
DAX FRAMES

Eastman Kodak Company
343 State Street
Rochester, New York 14650
FILM PROCESSING, PHOTOGRAPHY EQUIPMENT, PHOTO BOOKS, SLIDE PROJECTORS, SCREENS, DISSOLVE UNITS, ETC.

Eberhard Faber, Inc.
Crestwood
Wilkes-Barre, Pennsylvania 18703
CUSTOM PROJECTION SCREENS, HOLDIT PLASTIC ADHESIVE

Ehrenreich Photo-Optical Industries
101 Crossways Park West
Woodbury, New York 11797
SLIDE PROJECTORS, MOUNTING TISSUE, MOUNTING PRESSES, TACKING IRONS, AND SLIDE VIEWERS

Elden Enterprises, Inc.
Box 3201
Charleston, West Virginia 25332
ABODIA SLIDE-STORAGE SYSTEMS

Falcon Safety Products
1065 Bristol Road
Mountainside, New Jersey 07092
PRINT TRIMMER, PERMA MOUNT, PHOTO SHOWCASE, PHOTO-GALLERY

Flecto Company
Oakland, California 94604
DECOPOUR LIQUID PLASTIC

Holes-Webway Company
Webway Park
St. Cloud, Minnesota 56301
PHOTO ALBUMS

Hollinger Corporation
3810 South Four Mile Run Drive
Arlington, Virginia 22206
ACID-FREE PRINT BOXES, ENVELOPES, NEGATIVE HOLDERS, ETC.

Hudson Photographic Industries, Inc.
Irvington-on-Hudson, New York 10533
REAR-PROJECTION SCREENS, SLIDE VIEWERS, ETC.

Kalt Corporation
2036 Broadway
Santa Monica, California 90406
DISTRIBUTOR OF A WIDE SELECTION OF ACCESSORIES FOR PHOTOGRAPHIC DISPLAY

Karmel Plastics
10 Island Brook Avenue
Bridgeport, Connecticut 06606
A VARIETY OF ACRYLIC FRAMES

Knox Manufacturing
111 Spruce Street
Wood Dale, Illinois 60191
SLIDE-PROJECTION SCREENS, LIGHT BOXES, AND SORTERS

Kulicke
Contract Products Corporation
636 Broadway
New York, New York 10012
METAL AND ACRYLIC FRAMES

KustoMold
14924 South Downey Avenue
Paramount, California 90723
KUSTOM FORTY-CAPACITY SLIDE SORTER

E. Leitz, Inc.
Rockleigh, New Jersey 07647
SLIDE PROJECTOR AND DISSOLVE UNIT

Light Impressions Corporation
Box 3012
Rochester, New York 14614
ARCHIVAL FRAMING PRODUCTS AND SERVICES, PUBLICATIONS, MAT AND PAPER CUTTERS, STORAGE ENVELOPES AND BOXES, FRAMING TOOLS

Luxor Corporation
2245 Delany Road
Waukegan, Illinois 60085
MEDIA STORAGE AND RETRIEVAL SYSTEMS

3M Company
3M Center
St. Paul, Minnesota 55101
A VARIETY OF ADHESIVES FOR MOUNTING AND DISPLAYING PHOTOS

Michel Company
4664 N. Pulaski Road
Chicago, Illinois 60630
ALBUMS, FRAMES, MOUNTS, AND OTHER PHOTOGRAPHIC SUPPLIES

Milton Bradley Company
Springfield, Massachusetts 01101
PAPER CUTTERS

Multiplex Display Fixture Company
1555 Larkin Williams Road
Fenton, Missouri 63026
MULTIPLEX SLIDE STORAGE AND MANAGEMENT SYSTEMS

Permabond International Corporation
Englewood, New Jersey 07631
FUN-TAK REUSABLE ADHESIVE

Photo Art Frames, Inc.
P. O. Box 40160
Santa Barbara, California 93103
FRAMES, FRAMING KITS, AND GLASS

Print File, Inc.
Box 100
Schenectady, New York 12304
NEGATIVE PRESERVERS, BINDERS, FILE CABINETS, AND FOLDERS

Roto-Photo Company
2835 North Western Avenue
Chicago, Illinois 60618
A VARIETY OF HORIZONTAL AND VERTICAL PHOTO-DISPLAY SYSTEMS

Seal Inc.
550 Spring Street
Naugatuck, Connecticut 06770
DRY-MOUNTING AND LAMINATING PRESSES, DRY-MOUNTING TISSUES, EXHIBITEX PHOTO TEXTURIZING PROCESS

Smith Victor Corporation
Lake & Colfax Streets
Griffith, Indiana 46319
SLIDE SORTERS AND FILES

The Stanley Works
New Britain, Connecticut 06050
FINE TOOLS FOR FRAME MAKING

Taprell Loomis
2160 Superior Avenue
Cleveland, Ohio 44114
ALBUMS AND ALL TYPES OF PHOTO-HOLDING MOUNTS

Twentieth Century Plastics, Inc.
3628 Crenshaw Boulevard
Los Angeles, California 90016
VINYL PAGES FOR SLIDES, PRINTS, AND NEGATIVES

Walker System
520 South 21st Avenue East
Duluth, Minnesota 55812
PICTURE-HANGING DEVICES

F. Weber
Visual Art Industries, Inc.
Wayne and Windrim
Philadelphia, Pennyslvania 19144
BRAQUETTE PICTURE FRAME

Wood Moulding and Millwork Producers
P. O. Box 25278
Portland, Oregon 97225
INEXPENSIVE BROCHURE: *Fun to Make Picture Frames*

Zip-Seal Protectors
11 Rankin Avenue
P. O. Box 72
Basking Ridge, New Jersey 07920
PLASTIC ZIP-SEAL PHOTO PROTECTORS

A GUIDE TO PROCESSING TERMINOLOGY AND A DIRECTORY OF PHOTOGRAPHIC PROCESSING LABORATORIES

Photographers of every stature often have difficulty turning their slides and negatives into the product they want. Services vary from lab to lab, and unless you can see the finished product you may not be sure what you are getting.

Custom labs deal with camera films that are usually 35 mm and larger. Other films, such as subminiature and 110, used with Pocket cameras, are generally too small for quality results when making bigger-than-average enlargements. These films are geared for the mass market and the popularity of the "snapshot."

Prints from instant films that develop themselves also have their limitations for custom work. They are usually restricted to duplication and limited enlargement.

Each lab should have a price list and some sort of directory of services available. The terminology for labs is standardized. The following list includes terms used for photo processing. Familiarize yourself with their meaning so you can fully understand what you want from your processing lab.

PROCESSING TERMINOLOGY:

AIR BRUSH a special device and technique used to paint out undesirable elements in a photographic print such as blemishes and scratch marks.

BORDERLESS PRINT color or black-and-white print made without a border. Actually increases the size of the print slightly.

BRUSH TEXTURE A thick, transparent substance is spread over a color print to give brushstroke-like texture, producing a print similar in appearance to an oil painting.

BURNING IN the process of darkening specific areas of a print.

CANVAS MOUNT A special artist canvas is mounted to the print and then attached to a stretcher board or other mounting material.

CIBACHROME a process for prints made from color slides. The prints are generally longer-lasting than those from other printing methods.

COLOR CORRECTION the process of color manipulation of a print or transparency that is not true in color.

CONTACTS small prints made exactly the same size as the film used.

CUSTOM PRINT print made by an enlarger with various printing methods for correction used in the making.

DECORATOR PRINTS large prints or murals with color modification to match specific decors.

DIRECT PRINT made from a transparency without an internegative. Also called a type "R" print.

DISPLAY TRANSPARENCIES large transparencies made from negatives or original slides for viewing methods other than projection.

DODGING a process that reduces the intensity in a specific area of a print; makes it lighter; opposite to burning in.

DUPE a copy of a slide.

DYE-TRANSFER PRINT special print made using color separations of blue, red, and yellow.

INTERNEGATIVE a negative made from a slide or transparency; used to produce a quality print.

LACQUER a clear, luster, or matte finishing spray applied to the face of the print.

MACHINE PRINT a print made on a fixed-focus printer.

MATTE dull finish.

MURAL PRINT a large color photograph often made in sections; generally a landscape.

PANALURE PRINT a black-and-white print made from a color negative.

PROOFS small prints made to help in the selection of negatives for the best possible print. Often called "contacts."

RETOUCHING the process of improving a negative or print by removing blemishes, scratches, and dust marks.

"R" PRINT a color print made directly from a positive slide.

SPOTTING Similar to retouching but usually relates to removal of minor blemishes and spots on the print.

TEXTURE SCREEN special patterns added to the print at time of processing.

Film development, print making, slide duplication, and other routine photographic services are readily available. The "yellow pages" of your phone book will offer a complete list of laboratory services in your area under the PHOTO FINISHING heading.

Most photographic supply retailers offer photo-processing services. They deal directly with an Eastman Kodak Processing Lab or other local commercial photo finishing dealer. The retailer's employees should have a thorough knowledge of what can and cannot be done with your negatives, slides, and prints.

Not all the photo labs are the same. The services offered, cost, and quality of work vary. It is necessary to find a photographic lab that produces consistently good work suitable to your needs. You should keep in mind that the processing quality can be only as good as the negatives, slides, or prints supplied by the photographer.

Listed on the following pages are processing laboratories taken from the membership roster (1979) of the Association of Professional Color Laboratories (APCL). Only those members that list themselves as "full service" or "commercial" labs are included in the directory. The companies marked with an asterisk (*) offer mail-order photofinishing.

The list is by no means complete. There are many quality photo labs throughout the country.

The Eastman Kodak Company operates ten photo-processing labs for development of film delivered to them in the Kodak prepaid mailers purchased from photo supply retailers. Eastman Kodak Processing Laboratories are situated at:

1065 Kapiolani Boulevard
Honolulu, Hawaii 96814

925 Page Mill Road
Palo Alto, California 94304

1017 N. Las Palmas Avenue
Los Angeles, California 90038

3131 Manor Way
Dallas, Texas 75235

1712 South Prairie Avenue
Chicago, Illinois 60616

1100 East Main Cross Street
Findlay, Ohio 45840

Kodak Park
Rochester, New York 14650

16-31 Route 208
Fair Lawn, New Jersey 07410

1 Choke Cherry Road
Rockville, Maryland 20850

4729 Miller Drive
Atlanta, Georgia 30341

ASSOCIATION OF PROFESSIONAL COLOR LABORATORIES MEMBERS:

Alaska

*Castleton Enterprises
3340 Mountain View Drive
Anchorage, Alaska 99505

Arizona

*Colormark Laboratories
2212 E. McDowell Road
Phoenix, Arizona 85006

California

Photomation Color
2551 W. La Palma Avenue
Anaheim, California 92801

Olson Photo Associates, Inc.
527 S. Harbor Boulevard
Anaheim, California 92805

Action Photo Service
1741 Clayton Road
Concord, California 94520

Alfa Color Lab
535 W. 135th Street
Gardena, California 90248

*Rapid Color Inc.
1236 S. Central Avenue
Glendale, California 91204

*M S Color Labs
740 N. Cahuenga Boulevard
Hollywood, California 90038

Personal Color Lab
1552 N. Gower Street
Hollywood, California 90028

*Laursen Color Lab
1641 Reynolds Avenue
Irvine, California 92714

G P Color Inc.
215 South Oxford Avenue
Los Angeles, California 90004

Gibbons Color Lab
606 N. Almont Drive
Los Angeles, California 90069

*Newell Color Lab Inc.
221 N. Westmoreland Avenue
Los Angeles, California 90004

Tom's Chroma-Lab
5818 W. 3rd Street
Los Angeles, California 90036

Custom Color Laboratories
947 Industrial Avenue
Palo Alto, California 94303

Keith Cole Photography
604 Price Avenue
Redwood City, California 94063

Camellia Color Corporation
P. O. Box 160207
Sacramento, California 95816

Colorich Color Lab
1925 Euclid Avenue
San Diego, California 92105

Photic San Diego Inc.
P. O. Box 80487
San Diego, California 92138

Faulkner Color Lab
1208 Howard Street
San Francisco, California 94103

Ramell Corporation
650 Howard Street
San Francisco, California 94105

*Spectra Color Lab Inc.
11037 Penrose Street
Sun Valley, California 91352

Colorado

The Pro Lab Inc.
1200 W. Mississippi Place
Denver, Colorado 80223

Connecticut

Century Color Lab Inc.
234 Prestige Park Road
East Hartford, Connecticut 06108

Arthur Brown Photo Services
25 Hurlbut Street
Elmwood, Connecticut 06110

District of Columbia

Dunlop Photographic
2321 4th Street
Washington, D.C. 20002

Delaware

Tricolor Inc.
118 Valley Road
Wilmington, Delaware 19805

Florida

D & S Color Inc.
P. O. Box 2330
Bradenton, Florida 33506

*Thomson Photo Lab Inc.
4210 Ponce De Leon Boulevard
Coral Gables, Florida 33146

*Kraft Color Lab Inc.
6432 Fifth Avenue South
St. Petersburg, Florida 33707

*S & S Pro Color Inc.
2801 S. MacDill Avenue
Tampa, Florida 33609

*Pec Laser Color Labs
Fairfield Drive
West Palm Beach, Florida 33407

Georgia

Meisel Photochrome
Box 4002
Atlanta, Georgia 30302

Color Image
478 Armour Circle
Atlanta, Georgia 30324

Garrett & Lane Color Lab
Box 5608
Columbus, Georgia 31906

Hawaii

Light Inc.
765 Amana Street
Honolulu, Hawaii 96814

Idaho

Bach Photographs Inc.
1516 Grove Street
Boise, Idaho 83706

Illinois

Astra Photo Service
6 Lake Street East
Chicago, Illinois 60601

*Cameo Color/La Salle
1700 W. Diversey Park
Chicago, Illinois 60614

The Foto Lab Inc.
160 E. Illinois Street
Chicago, Illinois 60611

*Gamma Photo Labs Inc.
314 W. Superior Street
Chicago, Illinois 60610

K & S Photo Labs
180 N. Wabash Avenue
Chicago, Illinois, 60601

U C Color Lab, Inc.
3936 N. Pulaski Road
Chicago, Illinois 60641

Photon Color Labs Inc.
5611 Dempster Street
Morton Grove, Illinois 60053

*Champagne Color
214 N. Church Street
Rockford, Illinois 61105

Indiana

Burrell Colour Inc.
1311 Merrillville Road
Crown Point, Indiana 46307

Photo Pro Color Lab
P. O. Box 1234
Fort Wayne, Indiana 46801

The Firehouse Color Lab
1030 E. Washington Street
Indianapolis, Indiana 46202

Iowa

American Professional Color
P. O. Box 625
713 E. 18th Street
Cedar Falls, Iowa 50613

Kansas

*Chromatech Corp.
339 Indiana Street
Wichita, Kansas 67214

Louisiana

Color Pix, Inc.
P. O. Box 15286
New Orleans, Louisiana 70175

Primary Color Lab Inc.
P. O. Box 50502/11
New Orleans, Louisiana 70150

Maryland

B/L Labs, Inc.
916 N. Charles Street
Baltimore, Maryland 21201

Gordon Professional Color Lab
2021 Maryland Avenue
Baltimore, Maryland 21218

*Photographic Processing Inc.
7 N. Annapolis Road
Linthicum, Maryland 21090

Color Photo Service
3310 Perry Street
Mount Rainier, Maryland 20822

Massachusetts

Boris Color Labs
37 Lands Downs Street
Boston, Massachusetts 02215

Subtractive Technology
335 Newbury Street
Boston, Massachusetts 02115

Teck Corp. Color Lab
716 Columbus Avenue
Boston, Massachusetts 02120

*Lustre Color Corp.
540 Turnpike Street
Canton, Massachusetts 02021

Industrial Color Lab
9 Proctor Street Box 563
Framingham, Massachusetts 01701

New England Color Lab
86 Sanderson Avenue
Lynn, Massachusetts 01902

Northeast Color
40 Cameron Avenue
Somerville, Massachusetts 02144

Michigan

Color Detroit Inc.
533 W. Congress Street
Detroit, Michigan 48226

*Color Perfect Inc.
24 Custer Street
Detroit, Michigan 48202

Copy Craft, Inc.
33 Eliot Street
Detroit, Michigan 48201

Grossman Knowling Company
5715 Woodward Street
Detroit, Michigan 48202

*Allied Photo
517 32nd Street S.E.
Grand Rapids, Michigan 49508

Tri-Color
4850 Delemere Avenue
Royal Oak, Michigan 48073

Color by Spencer Inc.
249 Park Street
Troy, Michigan 48084

Meteor Photographic
2741 John Road
Troy, Michigan 48084

Minnesota

Camera Art
Box 100
Lewiston, Minnesota 55952

*Brown Photo Company
3842 N. Washington Avenue
Minneapolis, Minnesota 55412

Professional Color Service
605 4th Avenue South
Minneapolis, Minnesota 55415

*Supra Color Inc.
7125 Ohms Lane
Minneapolis, Minnesota 55435

Mississippi

The Camera House
1615 Main Street
Columbus, Mississippi 39701

Missouri

Custom Color Corporation
300 W. 19th Terrace
Kansas City, Missouri 64108

Allied Photocolor
3218 Olive Street
St. Louis, Missouri 63103

Lisle Ramsey, Inc.
7808 Maplewood Industrial Center
St. Louis, Missouri 63143

Dameron Color Labs
1514 S. Enterprise Avenue
Springfield, Missouri 65806

Nebraska

Midwest Photo Company
2514 Farnum Street
Omaha, Nebraska 68131

Nevada

Allen Professional Processing
3141 Industrial Road
Las Vegas, Nevada 89109

New Jersey

*Vi-Tech Corporation
196 Newton Avenue
Camden, New Jersey 08103

Alfie Custom Color
155 N. Dean Street
Englewood, New Jersey 07631

Linden Color Labs
1622 S. Wood Avenue
Linden, New Jersey 07036

New Mexico

Photech Inc.
114 Water Street
Las Cruces, New Mexico 88001

New York

Don Graham Color Lab
3815 Barnes Avenue
Bronx, New York 10467

*Allied Color Labs Inc.
6605 20th Avenue
Brooklyn, New York 11204

*Professional True Color Photo
1708 McDonald Avenue
Brooklyn, New York 11230

*Berkey Professional Processing
130 Front Street
Hempstead, New York 11550

ASAP Photolab, Inc.
40 E. 49th Street, 3rd Floor
New York, New York 10017

Berkey K & L Custom Service
222 E. 44th Street
New York, New York 10017

*Fine Art Color Lab
221 Park Avenue South
New York, New York 10003

Kurt Mayer Color Lab
1170 Broadway
New York, New York 10001

Langen & Wind Color
265 Madison Avenue
New York, New York 10016

Modernage Color Inc.
319 E. 44th Street
New York, New York 10017

P I C Color Corp.
25 W. 45th Street
New York, New York 10036

Photorama
239 W. 39th Street
New York, New York 10018

Quality Color Lab
305 E. 46th Street
New York, New York 10017

Sharma Photochrome
13 W. 36th Street
New York, New York 10018

Wometco Photo Service
209 W. 40th Street
New York, New York 10018

Epd Color Services Inc.
5 Nassau Street
Rockville Center, New York 11570

Silver Image
3102 Vestal Parkway East
Vestal, New York 13850

Pro Color, Inc.
955 Yonkers Avenue
Yonkers, New York 10704

North Carolina

*Personal Color Prints
P. O. Box 12369
Winston-Salem, North Carolina 27107

North Dakota

Northwest Professional Color
Box 517
Fargo, North Dakota 58078

Ohio

*Osborne of Cincinnati
910 Dalton Avenue
Cincinnati, Ohio 45201

*A C Color Lab Inc.
P. O. Box 6716
Cleveland, Ohio 44101

Precision Photo Labs
5758 Webster Street
Dayton, Ohio 45414

Oregon

Wy East Color
4321 S.W. Corbett Avenue
Portland, Oregon 97201

Pennsylvania

Shiflet Enterprises
459 Franklin Avenue
Aliquippa, Pennsylvania 15001

*Acculor Labs
206–12 N. 22nd Street
Philadelphia, Pennsylvania 19103

*Berry & Homer Inc.
1210 Race Street, Box 1319
Philadelphia, Pennsylvania 19105

Professional Color Processing Labs
7th and Ranstead Streets
Philadelphia, Pennsylvania 19106

The Darkroom Inc.
100 Wood Street
Pittsburgh, Pennsylvania 15222

Filmet Color Lab
7436 Washington Street
Pittsburgh, Pennsylvania 15218

Rhode Island

Crest Photo Labs, Inc.
334 East Avenue
Pawtucket, Rhode Island 02860

Abar Color Labs
367 Eddy Street
Providence, Rhode Island 02903

Colorlab
23 Peck Street
Providence, Rhode Island 02903

Tennessee

Coppinger Color Lab
2400 Georgetown Road
Cleveland, Tennessee 37311

Mid-South Color Lab
496 Emmett Street
Jackson, Tennessee 38301

Texas

Collins Color Photo Lab
2714 McKinney Avenue
Dallas, Texas 75204

The Color Lab Inc.
3130 N. Harwood Street
Dallas, Texas 75201

*The Color Place Inc.
135 Parkhouse Street
Dallas, Texas 75207

*Meisel Photochrome Company
Box 22149
Dallas, Texas 75281

Zintgraff Color-Craft
2507 Manor Way
Dallas, Texas 75235

*The Color Place Inc.
2901 W. 6th Street
Fort Worth, Texas 76107

*The Color Place
4201 San Felipe Street
Houston, Texas 77027

*Five-P Photo Processing
2122 E. Governors Circle
Houston, Texas 77092

*Photocolor Houston
P. O. Box 1405
Houston, Texas 77001

Photographic Labs
1926 W. Gray Street
Houston, Texas 77019

Photomurals, Inc.
P. O. Box 8391
Houston, Texas 77004

Wallace Laboratories
617 W. 29th Street
San Angelo, Texas 76902

*Texcolor Inc.
2900 E. Central Freeway
Wichita Falls, Texas 76307

Utah

Martin Photo Service
753 Columbia Lane
Provo, Utah 84601

Creative Color Service
340 W. 500 South
Salt Lake City, Utah 84101

*Replicolor Lab Inc.
P. O. Box 11889
Salt Lake City, Utah 84147

Virginia

Allen Photo Service
3808 Wilson Boulevard
Arlington, Virginia 22203

*Kelly & Green Inc.
514 Cumberland Street
Bristol, Virginia 24201

Washington

C-K Color Laboratories
P. O. Box 221
Edmonds, Washington 98020

Sound Color Corp.
P. O. Box 746
Edmonds, Washington 98020

Pacific Color Inc.
7107 Woodlawn Avenue
Seattle, Washington 98115

West Virginia

*Nashua Photo Products
120 Park Center
Parkersburg, West Virginia 26101

Wisconsin

F. J. Pechman Inc.
P. O. Box 346
Kaukauna, Wisconsin 54130

E. Colour
334 South 5th Street
La Crosse, Wisconsin 54601

Risser Color Service
5330 W. Electric Avenue
Milwaukee, Wisconsin 53219

BIBLIOGRAPHY

Davis, Phil. *Photography*. Dubuque, Iowa: Wm. C. Brown Co., 1972

DeCristoforo, R. J. *Handtool Handbook for Woodworking*. Tucson, Arizona: H. P. Books, 1977.

Dossett, Royal J. *Book-X6: Photographic Print Display*. Mound, Minnesota: Brand-X Corporation, 1973.

Eastman Kodak Co. *Creative Darkroom Techniques*. Rochester, New York: Eastman Kodak Co., 1975.

Heydenryk, Henry. *The Right Frame*. New York: James H. Heineman, Inc., 1964.

Holland, John. *Photo Decor—A Guide to the Enjoyment of Photographic Art*. Rochester, New York: Eastman Kodak Co., 1978.

Hyder, Max. *Picture Framing*. New York: Bonanza Books, 1963.

Jacobs, Lou, Jr. *Petersen's Basic Guide to Photography*. Los Angeles: Petersen Publishing Co., 1973.

Lahue, Kalton C. *Petersen's Big Book of Photography*. Los Angeles: Petersen Publishing Co., 1977.

Newman, Thelma R.; Hartley, Jay; and Scott, Lee. *The Frame Book*. New York: Crown Publishers, Inc., 1974.

Nuttall, Prudence. *Picture Framing for Beginners*. New York: Watson-Guptill Publishers, 1968.

Rodgers, Hal; and Reinhardt, Ed. *How to Make Your Own Picture Frames*. New York: Watson-Guptill Publishers, 1966.

Spencer, D. A. *The Focal Dictionary of Photographic Technologies*. Englewood Cliffs, New Jersey: Prentice-Hall, 1973.

Stroebel, Leslie; and Todd, Hollis N. *Dictionary of Contemporary Photography*. Dobbs Ferry, New York: Morgan and Morgan, Inc., 1974.

Taubes, Frederic. *Better Frames for Your Pictures*. New York: Viking Press, 1965.

Time-Life. *Caring for Photographs*. New York: Time-Life Books, 1972.

Toscano, Eamon. *Step-by-Step Framing*. New York: Golden Press, 1971.

Turnbull, Arthur T.; and Baird, Russell N. *The Graphics of Communication*. New York: Holt, Rinehart and Winston, Inc., 1968.

Wallace, Sandra; and Harris, Hank. *Petersen's Photographing Children*. Los Angeles: Petersen Publishing Co., 1974.

Wolf, Jack; and Wolf, Barbara. *Professional Picture Framing for the Amateur*. Blue Ridge Summit, Pennsylvania: Tab Books, 1974.

Yob, Parry C. *Petersen's Guide to Photo Equipment You Can Make*. Los Angeles: Petersen Publishing Co., 1973.